The Feminine in Fairy Tales

C. G. JUNG FOUNDATION BOOKS

The C. G. Jung Foundation for Analytical Psychology is dedicated to helping men and women to grow in conscious awareness of the psychological realities in themselves and society, find healing and meaning in their lives and greater depth in their relationships, and to live in response to their discovered sense of purpose. It welcomes the public to attend its lectures, seminars, films, symposia, and workshops and offers a wide selection of books for sale through its bookstore. The Foundation also publishes *Quadrant*, a semiannual journal, and books on Analytical Psychology and related subjects. For information about Foundation programs or membership, please write to the C. G. Jung Foundation, 28 East 39th Street, New York, NY 10016.

The Feminine in Fairy Tales

Revised Edition

Marie-Louise von Franz

Shambhala
Boston & London
1993

Shambhala Publications, Inc.
Horticultural Hall
300 Massachusetts Avenue
Boston, Massachusetts 02115

9 8 7 6 5 4 3 2 1

First Shambhala Edition
Printed in the United States of America on acid-free paper
♾
Distributed in the United States by Random House, Inc.,
in Canada by Random House of Canada Ltd, and in the
United Kingdom by the Random Century Group

Library of Congress Cataloging-in-Publication Data

Franz, Marie-Louise von, 1915–
[Problems of the feminine in fairy tales]
The feminine in fairy tales / Marie-Louise von Franz.—
Rev. ed.   p.   cm.
Originally published as:
The problem of the feminine in fairy tales.
Based on a series of lectures given at the
C. G. Jung Institute in Zurich, 1958–1959.
"C. G. Jung Foundation book."
Includes bibliographical references and index.
ISBN 0-87773-567-0 (alk. paper)
1. Women—Folklore.   2. Fairy tales—Psychological
aspects.   3. Femininity (Psychology)
4. Psychoanalysis and folklore.
I. Title
GR470.F72   1993   92-50439
398'.352'082—dc20   CIP

Contents

Preface   vii

The Feminine in Fairy Tales   1

Notes   215

Index   219

Preface

This book is based on a series of lectures which I gave at the C. G. Jung Institute in Zurich in 1958–1959. I wish to express my warmest thanks to Una Thomas, who with the help of Andrea Dykes transcribed the lectures. Later, Patricia Berry shortened the text. For this edition I have revised the text, corrected mistakes, and made short additions. I want to express my greatest thanks to Dr. Vivienne MacKrell for all her help and support and also to Mrs. Alison Kappes for typing the revisions.

MARIE-LOUISE VON FRANZ

The Feminine in Fairy Tales

1

Women in the Western world nowadays seem to seek images which could define their identity. This search is motivated by a kind of disorientation and a deep uncertainty in modern women. In the West, this uncertainty is due to the fact, as Jung has pointed out, that women have no metaphysical representant in the Christian God-image. Protestantism must accept the blame of being a pure men's religion. Catholicism has at least the Virgin Mary as an archetypal representant of femininity, but this feminine archetypal image is incomplete because it encompasses only the sublime and light aspects of the divine feminine principle and therefore does not express the *whole* feminine principle. In studying fairy tales, I first came across feminine images which seem to me to complement this lack in the Christian religion. Fairy tales express the creative fantasies of the rural and less educated layers of the population. They have the great advantage of being naive (not "literary") and of having been worked out in collective groups, with the result that they contain purely archetypal material unobscured by personal problems. Until about the seventeenth century, it was the adult population that was interested in fairy tales. Their allocation to the nursery is a late development, which probably has to do with the rejection of the irrational, and development of the rational outlook, so that they came to be regarded as nonsense and old wives' tales and good enough for children. It is only today that we rediscover their immense psychological value.[1]

If we look for feminine archetypal models of behavior, we at once stumble over the problem that the feminine figures in fairy tales might have been formed by a man, and therefore do not represent a woman's idea of femininity but rather what Jung called the anima—that is, man's femininity. Recent studies which concentrated on the question of who the storyteller is have brought to light that popular storytellers are sometimes men and sometimes women. The originator of the tale can therefore be of either sex. A feminine figure in a fairy tale with the whole story circling around it does not necessarily prove that the tale has to do with a woman's psychology. Many long stories of the sufferings of a woman have been written by men and are the projection of their anima problem. This is particularly the case in the theme of the rejected woman, who has to go a long way in suffering in order to find the right bridegroom, as, for instance, in the story of Amor and Psyche within the *Golden Ass* by Apuleius.[2] Also in various antique gnostic teachings there appears the figure of Sophia, a feminine personification of the divine wisdom, about whom the most amazing stories are told: that she was the youngest daughter of the Godhead, that she wanted to know the unknown Father, called Abyss, and by this bold wish got herself into a lot of trouble and suffering, fell into matter, and begged for redemption. This motif of the Sophia lost in matter is not only a theme in late antiquity; it appears also as the idea of the lost Shekhinah in the Jewish kabbalistic tradition. The authors of these religious writings were men. Under such circumstances, we can say that the figure of Sophia represents certain aspects of the man's anima. At other times, however, we could just as well say that the figure represents feminine psychology. The whole problem becomes in one way more, in another less, complicated if we try to concentrate on how the psychology of the feminine and the psychology of the anima are intertwined.

The real woman has an effect upon the anima and the anima upon the real woman. A woman has an educative and transforming influence on the man's eros. A man, especially if very much engaged in mental activities, tends to be a little bit coarse or undifferentiated on the eros side. He comes home tired, reads his newspaper, and then goes to bed (particularly if he is a Swiss). He does not think it necessary to demonstrate any feeling for his wife. He does not see the feminine person and her needs. Here the woman can have a transforming effect. If she can stand for her human rights without animus, and if she has a good relationship with the man she loves, she can tell him things about feminine psychology which will help him to differentiate his feelings. Since the anima of the man will have many characteristics of his mother, his first experience of woman, women in general will have a strong influence in forming and building up the man's relationship with his eros function.

On the other hand, women are influenced by the man's anima projections. For instance, they behave in a certain way and then notice that the man reacts in a bewildered or a shocked manner, because their behavior does not fit in with his anima image. Even small girls find out that if they play the part of the father's anima, put their arms round his neck, etc., they can get a lot out of their father. Fathers' daughters push aside the mother who insists on clean fingernails and going to school. They say "Daddy" in a charming way and he falls for the trick; thus they learn to use the man's anima by adapting to it. Women who behave in this way we call "anima women." Such women simply play the role intimated to them by the man in whom they are at the moment interested. They are conscious of themselves only as mirrors of the man's reaction. Their lover will tell them they are wonderful, but if there is no man around, they feel as if they were nobody. It is only the man's reaction to them which makes them aware of their feminine personality.

Thus some women give in entirely to the anima projection. A woman I know had very small and rather weak feet, but her husband liked her to wear very high heels. She tortured herself by wearing these shoes, though doctors told her she should not. Such a woman is afraid of losing the man's affection. If he only likes her as an anima figure, she is forced to play the role of the anima. This interreaction can be positive or negative, but the woman is very much affected by the man's anima figure, which brings us to a very primitive and simple and collective level where we cannot separate the features of anima and real woman. Frequently they are mixed to some extent and react upon each other.

In our Christian civilization, as I mentioned, the image of the woman is incompletely represented. As Jung has said, she has no representative in the Upper Parliament. One could say that the anima is neglected and the real woman is uncertain as to her own essence, her own being, of what she is, or could be. So either she regresses to a primitive instinctive pattern and clings to that, which protects her from the projection that civilization exerts on her, or she falls into the animus and builds up a picture of herself to compensate the uncertainty within her. In a matriarchal structure, such as in South India, women have natural confidence in their own womanhood. They know their importance and that they are different from men in a special way, and that this does not imply any inferiority. Therefore they can assert their human existence and being in a natural way.

On a primitive level, the image of the real woman and the image of the anima of man is more or less the same thing and in our civilization underwent certain slow, secular processes of transformation which took about three to four hundred years. This slow movement of development is probably the sum of thousands of individual reactions, which in the course of centuries have surfaced and suddenly broken out as a movement in time. Possibly the bitterness resulting from being rejected and insufficiently appreciated, experienced by many thousands of women, brought forth the collective outburst of women's emancipation in the early 1900s. It slowly developed in many individuals, and then suddenly appeared on the surface so that people became aware of it. Previously reactions had taken place underground. Thus there are movements which have a psychological background and are the sum of many individual experiences.

We have thus to start with a paradox: feminine figures in fairy tales are neither the pattern of the anima nor of the real woman, but of both, because sometimes it is one, and sometimes another. But it is a fairly good guess to say that some fairy tales illustrate more the real woman and others more the man's anima, according to the sex of the last person who wrote down the story, thereby giving it a slightly different nuance. A friend of mine, a schoolteacher, taught drawing and painting and gave as a theme for painting a scene out of the fairy tale entitled "Faithful John." In

4

my view, the story mirrors masculine psychology; there is only one pale anima figure in it. The teacher gave it to a mixed class of boys and girls, who might choose any scene. All the children were enthusiastic, and the boys naturally chose heroic and dramatic scenes, while the girls picked on the one feminine figure in the tale, identifying with that as the boys identified with the male figures, so that the pictures gave quite different aspects of the story.

Thus obviously different characteristics are emphasized according to the sex of the person retelling the story. We therefore may make the hypothesis that in some fairy tales the feminine formative influence has been greater and in others the male, but one can never be sure whether the woman or the anima is represented. A good approach is to interpret the tale both ways. Then it can be seen that some, when interpreted from the feminine angle, give a lot of rich material, but from the man's angle seem not so revealing. Following these impressions, I have selected a few of Grimm's stories which can be interpreted from the feminine angle, but I do not assert that they have nothing to do with the anima problem.

As to the figures in the story, it has been said, wrongly I think, that the myth is the story of the gods and the fairy tale the story of ordinary people, that the heroes and participants in fairy tales are ordinary beings while in myths they are gods and semigods. A problem with this theory, however, is that in some fairy tales the names point to gods. For instance, I shall discuss "Sleeping Beauty," or "Briar Rose," in which, in many versions, the children are called Sun and Moon. Now, the mother of the Sun and the Moon is not an ordinary human being, so you could say it is a symbol. But if the children are called Sun and Moon, or Day and Dawn, as in other versions, you are away again in the realm of what we normally call the world of the gods. So you cannot build up a theory on the basis of this difference. From a psychological angle, we know that they are archetypal figures and have, in their essence, nothing to do with ordinary human beings and human personalities as we deal with them in human psychology. For this reason, I will assume that there is no difference between fairy tales and myth, but rather that they both deal with archetypal figures.

If we really want to get the feeling of what this concept means, we have to ask ourselves how it is possible that people tell each other stories in which, in one case, the figures have the names of gods whom they worship in their national religion, in their *représentations collectives* and, in other stories the figures do not refer to the *représentations collectives*. The difference lies in historical reasons which I cannot discuss here. Let us assume that, drawing upon their dreams and waking visions, people are able to project into empty space certain figures of their unconscious and can speak of these figures.

I have a case of a very simple woman. She is the daughter of a carpenter and grew up in a primitive country and is very poor. She is a very severe schizophrenic borderline case, if not an actual schizophrenic. She has the most amazing voices, visions, and dreams and archetypal material. Though she had learned to be a hairdresser, she could not carry on because of her many fantasies, so she is a charwoman, but so quarrelsome and crazy and difficult that she has to clean up empty factories and work when there is nobody else around. She has been thrown out to the borders of human society, but she is a really religious person who might be compared with the German mystic Theresa von Konnersreuth— except that she is so swallowed up by her visions that she cannot function outwardly. She wanted to get into contact with me, but was not able to function for the first sixty minutes of the analytical hour. Her ego complex is too weak. First she had to get the feeling of the place, and of me, and she said that one could not talk about such subjects as God right away. I think that is true, for the atmosphere needs intimacy and friendship to be able to share a tremendous secret. So, in this special case, I agreed that we would see each other less often and for that I would give her a whole afternoon. Also I do not see her in my consulting room. We go to an inn and drink something together, or go elsewhere. She either does not talk or only on foolish subjects for about an hour and a half, which is exhausting, and then generally I either begin nervously to look at my watch or remark that I have to be back at seven o'clock, to call her back to reality. Then she suddenly starts to talk about her inner experiences, usually with a jump, and very often tells me a dream as though it were real. To strengthen her consciousness and keep her out of the archetypal world, I say, "Yes, but it was a dream," and to this she always agrees; she is not too confused to realize that. But then I notice that she cannot go on, for she is disturbed like an artist when you intrude upon his or her work. If you are artistically inspired and in the full swing of a new inspiration, you can be lamed by such an interruption and lose the thread. The first welling up of a creative idea must not be disturbed. One should never talk about such ideas before they have taken definite shape, for they are as delicate as newborn babies.

Creative people are generally very easily disturbed, and I noticed the same thing in this woman, so that usually I kept my comments for the end, at which time I thought I ought to get her more into reality, thereby following the pattern of the fairy tale, where very often a remark that comes at the end kicks you right out of the story—but only at the end!

This woman told me the most amazing archetypal stories and treated them as real, and there you have, *in flagranti*, an example of the possible origin of the fairy tale. Here someone tells you a classic literary dramatic story, and at the end he remarks that it was a dream! In such a case there is complete identity, but in the process of retelling the stories get changed and personal motifs left out. The remark at the end is likely to run: *"Et le coq chanta ki-keri-ki, l'aube est venu et mon conte est fini"* (The cock crowed *ki-keri-ki*, the dawn has come, and my tale is ended)—so it is time to wake up! As the cock crows you must get out of bed! Or, it might be: "There was a wonderful wedding and a marvelous feast, and I," the fairy tale teller says, "I was in the kitchen, but I got nothing, because the cook gave me a kick in the bottom, and here I am telling you the story"; that is, he flies back into reality. The gypsies say: "They married and were happy ever after, but we, poor devils, are so hungry that we are sucking our teeth," and then they start begging for money.

So the listeners are reminded that the fairy tale is not about ordinary people. They are quite aware that the participants and events take place in another sphere, which we call the dimension of the unconscious; they feel it to be the other world and in strong contrast to their conscious reality. In this way, on a primitive level, there is a kind of shifting contact with the unconscious. The scene shifts without definite demarcations, but there is more emphasis on the feeling level. Fairy tales actually tell us about figures of the unconscious, of the other world. One could say that in myth the figures are confused with the gods of religion; they correspond to what Lucien Lévy-Bruhl calls *représentations collectives*. Fairy tales, on the contrary, migrate and cannot be linked up with a national collective consciousness. They rather contain a tremendous amount of compensatory material and usually contradict or compensate collective conscious ideas.

My schizophrenic charwoman sometimes brings dreams full of Christian traditions. God the Father appears and speaks to her, and then what appears corresponds with what she has learned in her Christian education. There is no difficulty in calling one figure the Father and the other the Holy Ghost. Once she had a vision of a beautiful male figure whose voice was heard and who stood beside her on a mountain and said: "You have to paint this green to redeem yourself and mankind." She said that she was not capable of that, and the voice said: "I will help you." She seemed then to have done it somehow and was therefore allowed to come down the mountain. Next she was at a hotel and waking up. I asked her whose voice it was, and she said that it was the Holy Ghost; the man fitted the *représentation collective* of the Holy Ghost, and she had no difficulty in identifying it, although the voice did not.

In another religious system, the figure would have received a different name. If a figure turns up which is not within the domain of the *représentations collectives,* if there is nothing which fits a figure, you have to say that something appears which seems like So-and-So; you cannot pin it onto a collective idea. Supposing there is an experience of a feminine goddess who has all the features of the Earth Mother, but is as sexually extravagant as Baubo was in Grecian times. If you were brought up as a Catholic, you cannot call this figure the Virgin Mary. But since that is the only representative you have of the feminine numinous figure, you must continue to call her the Mother or give her a fantastic name, say "Little Mother Evergreen." But that is not an official name, and we do not worship such a personage. In this way, fairy tales are to a great extent built up by inner experiences which do not quite fit the *représentations collectives*. Therefore, figures usually have no names, or odd names, but not the names of religious symbols or known systems. They give us more information about what is going on in the compensatory function of the unconscious than myths do.

What does the collective side want to express which is not expressed in the *représentations collectives*? We get valuable information on this point. Fairy tales also take official names and tell abominable stories about religious personages. In one country a number are told about the Lord Jesus, who behaves outrageously— going about with Saint Peter, whom he tricks into getting the beating from the innkeeper, for Saint Peter has always been naive and is naturally the fitting person to get the beating. In a Czecho-slovakian fairy tale there is a helpless old man sitting up in a tree who has to be helped down, and at the end of the story the jittery old man turns out to be God himself. Now, imagine God himself being a helpless old creature not able to climb down a tree! But that a nice girl has to help him down is a very useful compensation for our ideas of God.

My charwoman sometimes gets into a rage with God. She says he is awful—he runs after women, and sometimes she has to shut him out of her bedroom. She says, "God has gotten too close again." He is indecent and a trickster, and she has found out that sometimes she must trick him too. Then he leaves her alone for a while. But let her tell that to a parson! She used to tell parsons, and none of them wanted to listen! She is very uncomfortable when God gets too close; but that is the time when she has her visions. When he is not so close, she is more comfortable and normal and nearer reality. This case taught me how an uneducated, simple mind deals with the power images of the collective unconscious.

In a similar manner, in fairy tales the figures of the *représenta-tions collectives* either are not used or are misused. Christ in the previous story is just a trickster hero, and God is a boring old man, or an old man sitting in a tree, but the implication of the story shows that it was God. The figures are anonymous because it would be much too shocking if they were given their own names, which leads to the most amazing discoveries, and to restoring their real meaning.

This seeming distortion is not what it appears to be, but has to do with the law of compensation, which, according to Jung's discovery, characterizes the products of the unconscious. Dreams either compensate for the lopsidedness of our conscious view or complement its lacunae. Fairy tales, because they are also mostly unsophisticated products of the storyteller's unconscious, do the same. Like dreams, they help to keep our conscious attitude in a healthy balance, and have therefore a healing function.

As the conscious religious views of Western Europe in the past two thousand years have not given enough expression of the feminine principle, we can expect to find an especially rich crop of archetypal feminine figures in fairy tales giving expression to the neglected feminine principle. We can also expect to retrieve from them quite a few lost goddesses of pagan antiquity.

The Sleeping Beauty, or Briar Rose[3]

The fairy tale I want to discuss is called in the English translation either "Briar Rose" or, more generally, "The Sleeping Beauty." It is the translation of a German fairy tale collected by the Brothers Grimm. Taking fairy tales from a literary angle, as first done by the Brothers Grimm, became a kind of modern movement and many collections appeared. In the Anglo-Saxon world our story is known only through translation. It was not well known even in Germany until the Grimm Brothers unearthed it through a woman living in Cassel, who was one of their main sources. The story immediately had an enormous effect. Poets used it in their writings and it had a sort of literary revival. It was naturally well suited to carry the projection of the poet's anima.

It is amusing that the fairy tale underwent the same fate as the Sleeping Beauty herself, for the tale faded out of people's memories, then suddenly became alive again and very popular. There were two versions of it, an Italian and a French one, which are romances or novels of the fourteenth century. The story is the same, however, with only slight variations, so we can conclude that it is very old and was suddenly revived. In the French fourteenth-century novel, the hero who wakes the princess bears the name of Perceforet, thus linking the tale with Parsifal and the Holy Grail legend. In that cycle the story was told as one of the many adventures of the chevalier hero. In the Italian variation the hero is called the Brother of Joy, and the heroine, the Sister of Pleasure. Both are allegoric novels written at the time of the Renaissance. In the Perceforet version, three goddesses are called to the girl's birth: one who carries the name of Lucina, the old Roman birth goddess Juno; Themis (a Greek name); and a fairy godmother who bears the name of Venus—thus going back to antique mythology. This is an interesting fact which throws some light on the feminine figure of the mother archetype in the late Middle Ages.

In the Renaissance they made the discovery, or mistake, of giving these figures antique names. Unfortunately, they thereby gave the fairy tales a historically regressive character in an unreal way because actually in the Renaissance people were Christian in their outlook on love and sex, so this play with antique names was half unreal. The use of antique names had been practiced in the eleventh and twelfth centuries, but what they told of their heroes and gods was quite different from what was told of the original antique gods. In spite of this there has been a theory, about which there have been many quarrels in literary circles, that the Sleeping Beauty is an ancient theme from *Aetnae,* one of the last tragedies by the famous Greek poet Aeschylus, in which the following story was told: Talia, one of the goddesses of charm, a daughter of the smith god Hephaestus, was one of the many women whom Zeus loved and who was persecuted by the jealousy of Hera. Zeus hid Talia in the bowels of the earth until she gave birth to two boys, who were called Palikes.

It has been thought that this idea of a girl disappearing from the surface of reality and then reappearing at a certain time represented an earlier version of our "Sleeping Beauty." In the Italian version of "Sleeping Beauty," the heroine is actually called Talia, which gives evidence for the theory. I think this is far-fetched, however, and could also be explained by archetypal kinship.

From the psychological angle, we cannot add to this literary quarrel. In general, we are more skeptical in regard to fantastic theories of survival and migration, because we know there is also the possibility of re-creating from the unconscious. On the other hand, it is astonishing how fairy tales do survive for hundreds of years. These are true facts but should not be exaggerated. I have not made up my mind what to believe, and I do not know what is more probable, but we certainly have to do with a very archaic and very archetypal motif, and you naturally see the idea of a feminine figure remaining dormant and reappearing after a time. For instance, there is the Demeter myth, in which Persephone disappears in winter and in spring returns to her mother on the surface of the earth—that is, of a girl goddess who disappears into death, or sleep, and returns at a certain time. That, as you know from Karl Kerényi's comments on the Kore myth, is an international myth, and our story is a special variation of it.[4]

Synopsis of the Tale

In olden times there lived a king and queen who lamented day by day that they had no children, and yet never a one was born. One day as the queen was bathing and thinking of her wish, a frog skipped out of the water and said to her, "Your wish shall be fulfilled—before the year passes you shall have a daughter."

As the frog had said, so it happened, and a little girl was born who was so beautiful that the king almost lost his senses, but he ordered a great feast to be held, to which he invited relatives, friends, and acquaintances, and all the wise women who are kind and affectionate to children. But as there were thirteen wise women in his dominions, and he had only twelve golden plates for them, one had to stay home.

As soon as the fête was over, the wise women presented the infant with their wonderful gifts—virtue, beauty, riches, and so on—but just as eleven had given their presents, the thirteenth old lady stepped in suddenly. She was in a tremendous passion because she had not been invited, and without greeting or looking at anybody, she exclaimed loudly, "The princess shall prick herself with a spindle on her fifteenth birthday and die!"

All were terrified, but then the twelfth fairy stepped up. Because she could not take away the evil wish, but only soften it, she said, "She shall not die, but shall fall into a sleep of a hundred years' duration."

The king, who naturally wished to protect his child, commanded that every spindle in the kingdom should be burned. But it happened that on the day when the princess was just fifteen years old, the king and queen were not at home, and she was left alone in the castle.

The maiden looked about in every place as she pleased. She came to an old tower and tripped up the narrow winding staircase, arriving at a door, in the lock of which was a rusty key. She turned the key and the door sprang open. There sat an old woman with a spindle, spinning flax. "Good day, my good lady," said the princess. "What are you doing here?"

"I am spinning," said the old woman, nodding her head.

"What thing is that which twists round so merrily?" inquired the maiden, and she took the spindle to try her hand at spinning. Scarcely had she done so when the prophecy was fulfilled, for she pricked her finger; and at the very same moment she fell back upon a bed which stood near, in a deep sleep.

This sleep extended over the whole palace. The king and queen fell asleep in the hall and all their courtiers with them. The horses in the stables, the doves under the eaves, the flies upon the wall, and even the fire upon the hearth, all ceased to stir. The meat which was cooking ceased to frizzle, and the cook at the instant of pulling the hair of the kitchen boy lost his hold and began to snore too. Even the wind ceased to blow.

Now around the palace a thick hedge of briars began growing which every year grew higher and higher, until the castle was quite hidden from view. Then there went through the land a legend of the beautiful maiden Briar Rose, and from time to time princes came endeavoring to penetrate the hedge into the castle; but it was not possible, for the thorns held them as if by hands. The youths, unable to free themselves, perished miserably.

After a lapse of many years, there came another king's son

into the land who had heard the legend and of how many princes had tried to penetrate the hedge and had died. But the youth was not to be daunted, and however much people tried to dissuade him, he would not listen.

Just at that time came the last day of the hundred years, when Briar Rose was to awake again. As the young prince approached the hedge, the thorns turned to fine large flowers, which of their own accord made a way for him to pass through and again closed up behind him. He saw horses and dogs fast asleep and in the eaves the doves with their heads beneath their wings. The flies were asleep upon the wall, the cook still stood with his hand on the hair of the kitchen boy, the maid at the board with the unplucked fowl in her hand. The courtiers were asleep, and so were the king and queen. At last he came to the tower and opened the door of the little room where slept Briar Rose. He bent over and kissed her. Just as he did so, she opened her eyes and greeted him with a smile. They went downstairs together; the king and queen and the whole court awoke, and all stared at each other in wonder. The horses in the stables shook themselves, the dogs wagged their tails, the doves flew away, the flies began to crawl, the fire to burn brightly and cook the meat—the meat began to frizzle; the cook gave his lad a box upon the ear, which made him cry out; and the maid began to pluck the fowl furiously. The whole place was once more in motion.

By and by the wedding of the prince with Briar Rose was celebrated with great splendor, and to the end of their lives they lived happy and contented.

The parallel stories show certain variations.[5] The general motif always is that a certain number of fairy godmothers appear, and one is furious because there is no golden plate for her, but the number varies, sometimes between seven and eight, sometimes between two and three. According to Grimm, seven were invited and the eighth was left out. But also in Grimm it is said later that six were asked and the seventh omitted. There is uncertainty here, which should be noticed to prevent any hard and fast theories. A certain number appear, but one is left out, either because she has retired to a tower and has been forgotten, or because there were not enough golden plates or goblets; and, being female, she turns up infuriated and curses the child, usually with the death curse, which is then softened by a benevolent fairy godmother. In some versions those who attempt to penetrate the hedge of briar roses die miserable deaths, torn by the thorns; in other versions, they are caught in the hedge and fall asleep—it's a kind of infection of sleep. In another version a prince comes who has made up his mind to free the beautiful girl, and the hedge of thorns becomes a hedge of roses which opens before him and closes after him. According to a typical German version, he is merely the lucky one who comes on the day when the hundred years expire, so there is no question of merit. According to other versions, he heroically fights his way and then the charm is over, and everybody wakes up again—the cook gives the slap, and the whole court awakens and returns to life. The two marry and are happy ever after.

This is a rather quick solution for a fairy tale. Usually there are complications and difficulties afterward. A Russian, French, and Catalonian version is that the prince comes to the Sleeping Beauty and sleeps with her without waking her. She then gives birth to two children and has to find the father later. Another type of variation in the French story is that the prince has redeemed the Sleeping Beauty but does not tell the story in his kingdom, where they do not know that he is married and has a child. Only after the death of his father does he take his bride home, where his mother tries to kill her and the child. There is a typical fairy tale motif of the destructive mother-in-law who tries to destroy mother and child. Then the cook or the hunter saves them, and when the evil mother-in-law is punished, the couple reunite happily.

These variations are probably written with the feeling that the original tale was too simple, that things could not be as simple as all that. Just to go through a hedge of roses does not seem to be a heroic enough deed. This shows how fairy tales can be mixed up with different archetypal motifs. It is interesting to see how they are combined in different countries at different times. One may be a more redeeming variation than another. But if you examine them, all the variations are quite meaningful. There is always a definite and meaningful thread running through, for people's fancy runs along the right lines. If one follows one's spontaneous fantasies, one cannot go wrong unless there is conscious interference. These people are so unconscious that instinctively the right motifs are linked together.

The first motif is that of the miraculous birth, which often occurs in the case of the hero or heroine of the story. It is said that the central figure in the story has not come into reality in the ordinary way but that a mystery or miracle surrounds his birth.

That poses a very abstract and ticklish problem concerning how we should interpret the hero or heroine. What do they represent? The particular and obvious problem in interpreting mythological material, which even well-known Jungians stumble over, is whether the hero has to be treated as an ego or not. We tend to say the hero is the ego, the beautiful woman is his anima, and so on. This is not an interpretation but a pinning of Jungian concepts onto mythical images. However, there *is* a temptation to call the hero figure the ego. It is as if this figure would lure us into that idea. That has to do with the trickster nature of the unconscious. Dreams also sometimes have an insinuating tone which makes one feel that one knows what they mean, and then one is blinded. An analyst who has interpreted thousands of dreams of other people cannot interpret his own. I am not surprised when this happens, for I know that in my own dreams I cannot interpret the most simple facts. One has to say: "What would you say if that was a patient's dream?" In a patient's dream one would have seen it at once. There is a kind of intimate feeling reaction which prevents one from having enough distance. If you wake up and think you know what the dreams mean, you are usually barking up the wrong tree—the trickster god has caught you. The unconscious loves to do that, especially with awkward, shadowy things. We would not have that particular dream if we could know its meaning as easily as that.

For instance, a married woman had a fairly harmless flirtation with a married man. It led nowhere, but she had felt it could go further than just talk. As she valued the man's wife very much, she interrupted the contact and retired from it. She forgot it, and it went underground. Then a tremendous creative problem emerged. The dreams showed that she should do something creative. Everything circled around this, so she made a step toward fulfilling the task of writing something—which she should have undertaken long before—and was interested to see what the unconscious would say. She dreamed that this other couple was divorced and that she was now somehow going to marry the man with whom she had flirted. Now suddenly there came up the thing she had avoided in reality. She thought that the unconscious was obviously rubbing her nose into the fact that she had had a sexual interest in the man. She was very much disturbed and would not even tell the dream. She thought the meaning was clear. But it meant something quite different, namely the divorce of animus and shadow.

If a woman keeps herself unconscious, there is a negative couple in her unconscious for which neighbors offer a good hook for projection. The secret interplay of this shadow tendency and her mental operations has been stopped, and she is now going to marry the man; that is, she is going consciously to make contact with her spiritual and mental side. In alchemical symbolism the feminine figure is often first married to the wrong kind of man, and it is the heroic deed to separate the couple. The hero has to win his partner and separate her from the wrong man. That was the kind of dynamism underlying that awkward business. Why did the unconscious pick on that? It is very obvious that if creative energy in a woman is not made conscious, it creates mischief—the overflow makes mischief. If you don't use your libido, you are bored to death and must start some kind of nonsense. The real thing is not done, but it is always expressed in some other form.

The woman's flirtation with the man was already the creative libido, the overflow of energy not satisfied in marriage and children and not parked in creative work. She realized that the flirtation was not the right thing, but the energy was again not invested; neither in the mischief nor creatively, which was why the dream used that theme. It was the first symptom that some energy wanted to overflow out of the marriage situation. The dream picked it up where the thing stopped. But when she woke up, she projected the conscious view and felt it to be a horrible and awful dream. My first thought was also—is it objective? But she was not repressing a wish for that flirtation. You have to watch the patient and see if there is still emotion, something which you cannot do for yourself. While you are telling the story you cannot look to see whether you are emotional. Then I ask myself—what is the motive in wishing to divorce? I had in mind all these archetypal and alchemical motifs which one must know and which give one a background on archaic processes. Then I referred the dream to the actual situation. What had happened the day before when she had made an attempt at marrying her mind? The ego had united with certain spiritual and mental impulses, but it needed a certain amount of detachment from the shadow.

Thus the unconscious is not really a trickster. That amount of energy which wanted to make mischief has now found its goal. The dream just states an actual fact, although consciousness, with its morality and prejudices, experiences it as if something awkward was insinuated. That is the difficulty in interpreting dreams and fairy tales. To identify with the hero or the heroine is so obvious that we are at once identical and cannot, with a certain amount of scientific objectiveness, ask the question as to who they are. In archetypal stories one must be able to see the images in a transpersonal way. There is nothing in the story to show that it tells about an actual human being; nothing is said about the girl's inner subjective life. She has been born miraculously, has fallen asleep, has woken up, and has married. It is an abstract pattern.

The folklorist Max Lüthi wrote that all figures in fairy tales are abstract.[6] We would rather say they are archetypal figures lacking human amplification. An abstract is something from which life has been abstracted, thus the archetype is transhuman. We would say that fairy-tale figures are not human individuals; they are not filled with actual life. The heroine is a feminine schematic figure—what shall we call it, an ego? A good way, and the way out taken by many psychological interpreters, is just to talk around it without pinning it down to what it is. Literary persons and those philosophically interested in Jungian psychology often do not use the Jungian terms. They avoid calling the figure the anima, or the Self, but talk around it. That I think is sheer cowardice. Why should we not

make an attempt and admit that Jung has discovered such facts as
the anima, ego, and Self? The difficulty, of course, is that Jung's
terminology can lead one into thorny difficulties. We may go
through the hedge which makes one fall asleep—it does not
penetrate mentally anymore. Women love to talk about a concept
brought out by a great man and forget to penetrate into it. They
are mentally asleep, though this does not apply only to women!

If we try to penetrate that problem we must say that in one way,
for instance in regard to the fairy godmother, it looks as though the
girl would be a human being and the unconscious (the godmother)
threatens her ego. If one amplifies mythologically and compares the
figure with Persephone, or other such Spring figures, then you
must say that the girl is an aspect of a goddess and ought to be
called by the Jungian name of the Self. And what is collective and
what individual? That the girl is not an individual feminine
figure—Mary Miller or Ann Smith—is obvious. But why does she
behave like an ego? And why do we assume that the ego is
completely individual?

If you ask, "What are you as an individual?," most people point
to their bodies. But put the question to yourself, "What is individual in my ego?" The fact that I have an ego is not individual; it is
the most common and most normal complex among human beings.
That the ego helps in adaptation—"I notice," "I combine things,"
etc.—is not individual. One person does one thing less well and
others better. Some have one faculty of association and some
another. Functions which adapt to outer reality are usual for all
individuals. The ego has such a tremendous number of general
features that it is a puzzle to know what its individual essence is.
This essence can only be discovered through a thorough analysis,
which is not exactly what all egos go through. But there is an
archetypal "I," a collective disposition which is similar in everybody, and one aspect that occurs in some way in every human
being.

How is this archetypal aspect of the ego related to the Self? If
one has read Michael Fordham's writings on childhood problems[7]
and Erich Neumann's *The Origins and History of Consciousness*[8] or
has worked with a young analysand, one will have seen that many

neuroses in early youth show an ego consciousness backward in its development. If one looks at the unconscious processes in children, one will see that there are play impulses, dreams, and fantasies that tend to bring forth the ego maturity the child should have. So we could say that it is the unconscious which wants the improvement in the ego. The infantile ego does not want it. It is the impulse from the unconscious that causes the neurotic disturbance in its attempts to get the child onto a higher level of consciousness, to build up a stronger ego complex. The school technique—being able to concentrate and overcome fatigue—is inadequate without the instinct from the unconscious, which expresses the tendency for building up such things. Therefore the urge is a general human disposition, i.e., archetype, which comes forth from the Self. Fordham discusses the dream symbolism in early childhood as a tendency to build up a stronger ego consciousness, a completely different role from that of the second half of life.

Young people in the bisexual phase of puberty sometimes develop a crush on an older person of the same sex. If one analyzes them, the unconscious seems to support this admiration and imitation, this clinging to a person of the same sex. Looking at it superficially, one might interpret this figure in dreams either as indicating a homosexual tendency or as a symbol of the Self, for the older brother or uncle figure appears with magic qualities, as the saving factor or teacher. He is a projection of the Self. The natural reaction of the young admirer is that he would like to be like the object of his admiration. So the figure functions as a model of a more adult way of existence or behavior. It is a projection of the Self. As long as the ego complex is weak, this projection functions as a model to be copied and followed. It assists in building up a more adult ego complex. If you take all these practical facts into consideration, you can say that the ego has an archetypal foundation, and that it is the Self which builds up the ego complex. It is this aspect that is meant by the hero or heroine of a fairy tale: the archetypal foundation of the individual ego, or the pattern of an ego which functions in harmony with the Self.

2

As an illustration of ego formation we might remember certain processes in a frog's egg. At a given stage a gray spot is produced on one side of a frog's egg. Experiments prove that this gray spot later develops into the head. If you cut into this with a thread, a double-headed frog will be produced. If you remove it, the frog will have no head. Thus you can prove experimentally that the gray spot in the frog's egg is that part of the plasma which later develops into the head. If you remove the spot, and then drop a little hydrochloric acid onto the plasma, a grayish spot will grow. The correct plasma will be formed; a new head will grow, and a whole frog will hatch out. This process is similar to ego formation. The ego would be the center of the field of consciousness formed in it, but produced by a total reaction of the whole psychic system, which is a self-regulating system. You can say that the latent impulse to produce the ego is expressed by the image of the mythological hero. He has qualities which do not coincide with the actual ego, but have more to do with the archetype of the total psyche.

Most human difficulties, including neurotic and psychotic dissociation, are linked with an ego that is not functioning in accordance with the total disposition of the psyche. There is a kind of disharmony between it and the makeup of the psyche. In a certain type of schizophrenia there is an enormous fantasy production in the unconscious and an impoverishment in consciousness of either thinking or, as Eugen Bleuler pointed out, of emotion and affect. The conscious personality is in disharmony with the wealth of vitality of the unconscious. The overflow of the unconscious falls into too narrow a vessel. One of the main tasks of therapeutic treatment, therefore, is to try to enrich the range of emotional reactions so that the vessel is larger and more solid and can receive the emotional impulses from the unconscious. But there are various forms of disharmony. Not every neurotic split is due to this cause, though it is a frequent form of dissociation.

Especially the ego complex tends to dissociate from the rest of the psyche and to get out of harmony with it; it tends to act autonomously. Therefore one of the most essential problems of the human race is to build an ego which functions in a healthy manner, that is, in accordance with the instinctive makeup of the total anthropos. On the one hand, we are distinguished from the other animals by having a strong ego complex; and on the other, our greater consciousness presents us with the danger of a split.

The mythological tales in which hero or heroine behave in a specific way express an unconscious attempt to produce an ideally functioning, model ego complex. The hero represents the ideal ego complex in accordance with the requirements of the psyche. He is the one who cures the sterility of a country and restores collective health through a flow of life in healthy forms. Every tale has a different meaning, with the model hero functioning in accordance with his instincts. When the heroine functions in accordance with the instinctive requirements of the psyche, she is the pattern of the conscious feminine personality. It is a kind of model of an archetypal connection of ego and Self, which has to be filled out by actual realization in each person's life. You could say the totality, or what we call the Self, is a dormant, inherent possibility. It is like an egg, a mass of possibilities that needs actual conscious life with its tragedies, conflicts, and solutions to bring the totality into reality.

Thus the ego is the instrument by which psychological potentialities can become real. For instance, if I am of an artistic disposition but my ego never discovers it, and does not do something about it by trying to use those possibilities, they might just as well not exist. Obviously, therefore, the ego is the instrument of realization of all the different psychological, inborn dispositions of the human being. Expressed mythologically, the ego is the instrument of incarnation for the Self. The hero and heroine in fairy tales

22

illustrate the way in which such instruments of incarnation must function. The ego has an infinite number of different functions to fulfill, and every tale emphasizes one aspect, generally the one which is at that time lacking or needed in the collective situation. A striking example would be the Son Godhead. The central religious god of our civilization is a helpless man hung on the cross. He is condemned to suffering and complete passivity, and that is what the very active self-willed Western man worships and prays to, what he needs to meditate upon.

There is, however, another problem: there is an infinite range of the symbols of the Self—for instance, a golden ball or a treasure which must be found by the hero. If we jump to the conclusion that these are symbols of the Self, such an interpretation might fit a dream. But it is not a mythological interpretation; for example, you cannot say that one symbol of the Self finds another. Technically it is true, but it does not make sense. We must differentiate our interpretation and ask: what would be the difference between the symbol of the Self, such as a golden egg or ball, and the hero or heroine who also represents an aspect of the Self? The simplest statement would be that the hero is a human being and the ball is not, which is banal enough but has to be taken on the right level. In some material the totality appears in certain impersonal symbols: a tree, for instance, and sometimes in a half-human personification, that is, the hero. What is the difference? One aspect, the ball, is that of a material symbolization of the Self; that is, a symbol which refers to the totality of the psyche in an impersonal way which tends to turn up in moments of dissociation and disorientation.

When one feels lost in a chaotic situation, as far as I have seen, especially when the ego tends to take its miseries, complexes, and involvements too personally, a material abstract symbol has generally the effect of objectifying the experience, and of achieving a detachment which at times is badly needed. If someone thinks he or she is the only person who ever had an unhappy love affair, then life has to be seen in a less personal perspective. In other cases when the symbols of the Self appear personified as human beings, they contain a hint of the required personal attitude; a certain type of human reaction is needed to meet the situation. It is not sufficient to be detached or philosophical; a specific human attitude is required.

Our fairy tale "The Sleeping Beauty," or "Briar Rose," belongs to the pattern of the daughter goddess disappearing—in our story, in a deathlike sleep. In the Demeter-Kore myth, Kore, with her bridegroom the god of death, disappears temporarily, fading out of life and then returning again in a springlike reawakening of nature. This pattern of the divine girl who disappears and reappears is paralleled on the masculine side. There is a divine son who disappears into the underworld and is brought back in spring, like Tammuz and Adonis. This is a universal theme. There is also a daughter goddess who disappears in this way, who, *mutatis mutandis,* has the same meaning. This type of Kore (maiden) is closely linked up with the archetypal mother figure. In our story the girl is blessed by a certain number of mother figures and cursed by one of them; she is blessed and cursed at the same time. In the Kore myth, Kore's disappearance is not directly connected to the mother, Demeter. The latter has a changing double aspect—standing for fertility, for help in childbirth and for the grain in corn, but when she has lost her daughter, she becomes the goddess of revenge and sorrow. Demeter changes from one aspect to the other, depending on her relationship to the daughter.

In the antique tale "Amor and Psyche," the girl goddess is badly persecuted by her future mother-in-law, the goddess Venus, characterized as the Great Mother figure, like Ishtar and Atargatis. Here we have an interesting variation, for Venus persecutes out of jealousy because Psyche is said to be more beautiful—as in "Snow White." People worship the girl Psyche instead of the mother Venus. Psyche is thought to be an incarnation of Venus. But because Venus resents the existence of a living human incarnation of herself, she persecutes her. This is an interesting development in Western and Mediterranean civilization. A mother goddess produces a more human incarnation, a daughter figure to whom she has a very ambivalent attitude. It is a vague parallel to the same tendency in the famous story of the love affair of Aeneas and Dido.[9] Dido is a goddess, since she bears the name of a Phoenician goddess, but in the Aeneid she is a human queen. Venus and Juno decided that Aeneas should love her. They arranged the affair and then Zeus on Olympus decided with them that Aeneas should leave Dido, who then committed suicide.

This famous and impressive tragedy shows the ambivalent attitude of the gods in the collective unconscious toward a more human personification. This seems to be still a present-day problem. Erskine wrote a book, *The Lonely Venus*,[10] in which he too discusses it. Venus is the mother goddess acting in accordance with her affects and emotions without much reflection and so getting into a mess, then recognizing that the goal would be to become human. The same tendency that took place in the religious systems of the late Roman Empire has taken place in Christianity. This is borne out in the Judeo-Christian tradition by an ambivalent God-father figure who produces a Son, not a mythological divine son, but a human being with historical reality. So the incarnation of the Father in the Son has taken place as a tremendous religious collective experience.

The same tendency can be seen in the development of the antique mother goddess who wants to incarnate in a human daughter, but the impulse remained abortive. It has nowhere been carried through and become a religious event. The cult of the mother goddess got stuck and suppressed and then reappeared later in the cult of the Virgin Mary, but with great mental reservations and precautions for disinfection of her dark aspect. She was once more admitted, but only insofar as the Church Fathers approved, and if she behaved. The dark aspect of the antique mother goddess has not yet reappeared in our civilization, which must leave a question mark in our minds, because naturally something is lacking.

If we study the antique mother goddesses who disliked their own human figures of incarnation, we see that the conflict may be characterized in the following way: the mother goddesses depict absolutely unreflecting femininity. They simply personify elemental emotional feminine reactions. If their husband had a love affair with another woman, they made a terrible scene (like Hera). We women must admit that without the brake of consciousness we should do the same, for that is the elemental reaction. The mother goddess always behaved like that. But, at the same time, she behaved with charity; everything poor, lamed, and unhappy was taken on her lap and loved and nursed. Elemental unchecked charity is typical for a mother goddess. Sexual behavior as in Baubo was absolutely natural. The mother herself was the great whore who gave herself to every unknown man she met. There was infinite fertility and generosity, unstinted charity, infinite jealousy and vanity, and so on.

All these goddesses are characterized by the total reaction which is in every woman, for it is a part of her natural emotional and instinctual structure. If you compare the daughter goddesses with these mother goddesses, according to Greek mythology, they are identical with the mother (just as the Son is with the Father). Usually, though, they are a little more human—that is, capable, as Psyche was, of sacrifice and of not simply following an impulse, of the ability to fulfill the task and not to show charity to the beggar man in the underworld, of restraining themselves from helping the dying and the poor, and of judgment, which meant being more reflective and restricted and human, more formed and less primitive and chaotic in reaction, but more human and steadfast.

This progressive tendency within the pattern of feminine life appears in the collective unconscious in an effort to produce a new form of femininity in woman, and also a new model of eros in man—a more balanced attitude. Man in our civilization is ahead of woman in the civilizing process. In South India, the humanizing of woman, and of eros, seems to be ahead of the West. There, women are proud of their femininity, and there is a more differentiated attitude to eros. In the West, there is toughness, vulgarity, and lack of differentiation of the eros level, and far greater logos differentiation than in the East.

The king and queen in our fairy story had no children, but the frog says to the queen, "Your wish shall be fulfilled. Before a year passes you shall have a daughter." Before the birth of the hero or heroine, there is often such a long period of sterility; and then the child is born supernaturally. Put into psychological language, we know that before a time of outstanding activity in the unconscious, there is a tendency toward a long period of complete passivity. It is, for instance, a normal condition in the creative personality that before some new piece of work in art or a scientific idea breaks through, people usually pass through a period of listlessness and depression and waiting; life is stale. If one analyzes them, one sees that the energy is meanwhile accumulating in the unconscious.

I remember a time when I felt desperate in this way. Then I dreamed that I was looking at a big railway station where shunting was going on, and new trains were being composed. The dream showed that the energy in the unconscious was readjusting itself; energy and instinctive patterns were rearranging. Before the outburst of a psychotic interval, there is also such a time when everything becomes stale. But then comes the explosion. Libido has been accumulating in the unconscious and comes out in a destructive explosion.

So these periods of sterility mean that something specific is in preparation in the unconscious. Here it is foretold by the frog. The frog sits in the Queen's bath—the Freudians would certainly have something to say about that! In folklore the frog is looked upon as a rather unchaste animal. It was used in olden days in love charms in which its bones had to be worn in a certain form. It appeared at the beginning of many prescriptions having to do with fertility, sexuality, and bisexual love. One thinks of it as the male member fertilizing the queen. But if you read folklore, you find that it is a maternal animal used to help women at childbirth and to bring fertility. In many countries, the croaking of frogs in springtime is said to resemble the cries of unborn children, and therefore represents the soul of the not yet incarnate child.

In many countries the frog is believed to be poisonous and is called a witch's animal. This is borne out by Hildegarde von Bingen, a medieval mystic and learned writer, who says that especially in spring when everything is so beautiful, the devil likes to put frightful ideas into the heads of human beings; the devil "likes the croaking of frogs." Here again is a connection with sexuality, sexual desire, a "spring mood," a mood of exuberance in nature. Naturally, from a Christian standpoint, the frog can only be attributed to the witch and the devil. But it has also to do with the birth of children and the ending of a stage of psychological sterility; it indicates a spirit of nature, or a vital impulse.

Jung has said of the frog that it looks like an attempt by nature to form man on the level of the cold-blooded animal, because of the striking similarity to the human structure with the little feet and hands. This idea that the frog is an imperfect human being is very widespread. People call a child a "little frog." The frog is a cold-blooded creature, not yet a human being, and therefore represents, especially in dreams, an unconscious impulse that has a definite tendency to become conscious. There are impulses which resist consciousness—you have to push them, so to speak. The complexes themselves, if left alone, would remain unconscious. But sometimes there are complexes which have a strong energetic drive toward consciousness; they force realization of their existence upon people. The frog represents such an impulse—that which imposes itself upon you; so it is only a question of acceptance in consciousness and a realization of the content. If an analysand dreams of a frog, I know that I must only have a receptive attitude, and that then the rest will follow by itself. In many other tales a magic figure says that something must be done, or eaten, and then you will get a child. But here nothing is required; it is a natural process. The queen has only to wait and perhaps knit some little things for it!

So a little girl is born who is very beautiful. Then there is a big party for the baptism of the child where something terrible happens. Fairy godmothers turn up in a certain number, either seven or eight, or twelve or thirteen, or six and seven, or two and three—but always one is forgotten, or left out, who then curses the child. So we come to the motif of the forgotten godmother. Sometimes she is not invited because there are not enough golden plates, sometimes because she had retired for fifty years to a tower where she lived alone, and people had forgotten her—she had lived too introverted a life. Or she may have been forgotten without any reason; but then she turns up without further ado and has to be given a different plate, which she takes as a personal insult, so she curses the newborn child.

This motif of the forgotten god or goddess, more frequently the goddess, is an archetypal one. When Agamemnon wanted to leave for Troy, there was no wind to take the ship across. It was discovered that Artemis was angry and demanded the sacrifice of Iphigenia, so that Agamemnon had to sacrifice his own daughter to get across the sea. Artemis was wrathful at being left out, a typical motif for the hurt goddess, since it is usually the female who resents being ignored. (But I must admit that there is also sometimes a male god who revenges himself if he has not been included in receiving sacrifices.) This reminds me of a story: at a children's party a little girl ran crying to her mother, "The little boys are pinching my bottom." The boys were duly scolded, but then she came crying, "I'd rather be pinched than not looked at."

What does this mean psychologically? It is obvious that gods represent archetypal contents in the unconscious, or collective complexes—normal complexes which everybody has, not pathological complexes. As Jung says, complexes are normal in our society, for example, ego and shadow complexes. They are different dynamic factors in the psyche which belong to the normal structure of man and which are generally personified in gods. You see this best in the astrological gods: Mars = aggressivity and self-defense, Venus = sex, and so on. Each god represents a specific pattern of behavior. If a god or goddess has been neglected, it means that a specific natural psychological way of behaving has been omitted. It has either intentionally or stupidly been left out of consideration.

Especially in early childhood, a new tendency first coming to life appears exaggerated for a time. Then, in the course of time, it forms a part of the general functioning. For instance, some children can, for a time, only play with the dog, or a train. They have phases where they are completely absorbed in one particular thing, which is then suddenly dropped for something new. This behavior strikes us sometimes as rather obsessive. There is always some new craze. In a boy it may be fighting or climbing trees, but it represents the awakening of a new element of consciousness, which throws the whole balance a little bit off. The awakening of sexuality is one of the strongest of the phases. Usually, at such a time, it swamps and dissociates the personality until it reaches its normal level.

So complexes are not harmonious in human beings. They can fight each other, and may even push aside other instinctive drives.

If a god is forgotten, it means that some aspects of collective consciousness are so much in the foreground that others are ignored to a great extent. The archetype of the mother goddess has suffered that fate in our civilization.

For the development of Western civilization, it was perhaps necessary for the Western mind to have to ignore the mother goddess for a certain length of time and to put the whole emphasis onto male development. But ignored organs of the psyche behave in the same way as ignored organs of the body—if you eat irregularly, your stomach is upset. Our physical organs need a certain amount of attention; we cannot afford to ignore their needs by one-sidedness. And the same is true of the organs of the psyche. If we ignore certain vital nuclei in the psyche, they will cause an illness in the system. Just as stomach trouble can result in complete destruction of health, so can one complex that does not function properly disorganize the whole. Then there is a neurosis, or worse, and one has to find out what has been ignored and is now "cursing" the whole personality. That is a very optimistic interpretation, because indirectly it says that if one were always to behave rightly, and sacrifice to all the gods, then nothing could happen to us and we would all be psychologically healthy. The different variations of the fairy tales, however, do not quite confirm this—in some of them the godmother turns up just because she likes to cause trouble. Sometimes the outbreak of a neurosis is a just-so story. It would be wrong to say that it was brought about by guilt. Sometimes it is due to one-sided behavior, but one must also reckon that nature can be spontaneously deficient. The gods sometimes create trouble; it is not always just man. In nature herself there are deficiencies, incompletenesses, and disharmonies.

In a French version the bad godmother is called Misère, the goddess of misery. Something which is nobody's fault falls upon people, and one cannot accuse anyone of a moral deficiency. This has happened to many of us, for we have been brought up with the idea of a benevolent Godhead; if evil comes, it is our fault, or that of old Adam. The fault lies in some human being. But you can just as well say that the guilt lies with God—an idea that is not obvious to us, though it is to some other civilizations. God may get into a terribly bad mood, which then falls on mankind. It is important to keep this in mind to balance the Christian view with that of the immorality of nature. If the myth tells the story in different versions, as does ours, then some uncertainty exists about the problem.

Why does Briar Rose come under such a terrible curse? One version says that it is a just-so story, and the other version that the goddess was angry because she had been ignored. There may have been real uncertainty about the problem. It is like the modern theory of light. One theory has it that light is made up of particles, the other that it is waves. It would seem that if one is true, the other could not be. Similarly, either neurosis is caused through some transgression and cured by an ethical change of attitude or it is bad luck caused by nature and changed by good luck. Each view excludes the other, yet apparently both are true. One should see the double aspect and treat the neurosis from both sides, even though the aspects radically contradict one another.

The mother goddess who has been ignored appears as a personification of hurt feelings, vanity, or resentment. She is the personification of feelings which have turned sour—milk which has turned sour—and that, I think, throws light on a problem that has a lot to do with the problem of women. It is why I have chosen this fairy tale for my discussion on feminine psychology. The source of evil and of things going wrong in women's lives is often a failure to deal with and to get over hurt feelings, for hurt feelings open the door to animus attacks. The source of things going wrong, and of evil in women, in a tremendous number of cases, is that archetypal reaction of not getting over a hurt, or resentment, or a bad mood, through being disappointed in the feeling realm, and then being overpowered by the animus. Suddenly one is in an upset or possessed mood. It is very helpful to ask, "Where have I been disappointed or hurt in my feelings and have not sufficiently noticed it?" Then you will frequently find the cause. If you can get back to the origin of the hurt and where you have not worked it out, the animus possession will stop; for that is where it jumped in, and that is why in animus possession there is always an undertone of the reproachful hurt woman.

Animus possession in a woman annoys men madly; they go up in the air at once. But what really gets the man's goat is this undertone of lamenting reproachfulness. Men who know a little more about this know that eighty-five percent of animus possession in women is a disguised appeal for love, although unfortunately it has the wrong effect, since it chases away the very love that is wanted. Underneath the animus there is a feeling of reproach and at the same time of wanting to get back at the one who has hurt you. It is a vicious circle, and arguing develops into a typical animus scene. Thus the ignored femininity which plays up in a woman's anger is something archetypal.

Naturally, women who have a negative mother complex are those most liable to this form of reaction, since they are in such need of warmth and attention which they have not adequately received from the mother. Here I must refer to C. G. Jung's paper "Psychological Aspects of the Mother Archetype,"[11] where you find a much more detailed description of the different aspects of the mother complex in women. This paper is the basis of my lecture. Women who have not been properly attended to by their mothers tend to be especially touchy and constantly feel ignored. If one has sufficient self-esteem, one need not be hurt. If a man ignores a woman who is sure of herself, if he runs after another woman in her presence, she only thinks he has bad taste. She is so sure of herself that it does not annoy her. But if she has insufficient self-esteem, the abyss of hurt feeling and resentment wells up. A woman with a negative mother complex is always threatened with the resentful, hurt feeling that keeps welling up on every occasion when a man does not agree with her, or if another woman steps on her corns. Her greatest task is to overcome her resentful anger. Such a woman will nurse a hurt for years, put it in a drawer, and bring it out again and again; she follows the archetypal pattern of the goddess.

As our story is a collective and not a personal story, we have to find out where it is typical of our civilization, where some aspect of the mother goddess, of feminine nature, has been consciously ignored in Christianity. The most obvious fact, which has become a problem in modern times, is sexuality. Under the ecclesiastical law of social order, it is said to be dangerous and the cause of much trouble; it destroys marriages and so forth. It should be brought under control by law and be permitted only in marriage. That is the Catholic view, which also says that total abstinence would be better, or that sex should be allowed only for the procreation of children and anything else is sinful. But you cannot just decide by sitting at a round table how a god (sexuality) has to be ruled, which is a tremendous error in the Christian system, resulting in the god's starting to develop autonomous activities. This ruling as to sexual behavior has never been observed. Either people have kept to the law and become neurotic, or they have lived a double life, or fallen into sin and regretted it afterward.

Monogamy among animals works as long as there is an equal number of males and females. Baboons go about in groups of twenty to thirty and are monogamous as long as the sexes are equal. If by some natural catastrophe the males are reduced, however, then the surplus of females is distributed among the males and it is ignored that females outnumber males. But in our civilization the law of monogamy rules, and as a result some women have no sexual life and many go into convents; they are out of the game. But nobody takes any notice of the natural fact of their biological needs, which has to be faced, and the goddess is ignored. One pretends not to see some natural and vital organic archetypal need which is right there and wants to function; rather, laws are laid down and enforced with bad effect.

Not only the god of sexuality—if one can use such a term—has been ignored, but also some of the needs of feminine life. It is well known that there is far more trouble over chastity in convents than in monasteries, so that the possibility of giving up the woman's side of the order has been seriously discussed. Apparently women have greater difficulty in this respect. Men can more easily do some hurt to their nature and are less harmed than women. Military service for women is also a problem, for women seem to digest the regulations imposed on them less well than men—their nature revolts more. They need to be more natural and less one-sided in their development. It seems to me that here there is a concrete feminine need. A man's *élan* for spiritual interests can carry him along and away from his body.

This difference between men and women is symbolized in mythology by the gods of the sun and moon: the sun being the masculine mind and the moon the feminine. Looked at naively, one can say that the sun is reliable. It rises regularly, whereas the moon is moody. It comes up every evening an hour later and fades and wanes and disappears. In Egypt the moon is the male god Min; it probably has a connection with primitive man, since the moon is so moody and irregular in its behavior. In most civilizations, however, the moon is feminine. In the Western Christian civilization, one could say that the solar principle is exaggeratedly ruling and that the lunar principle is not recognized enough. In our story it is the godmother, a part of the feminine principle, who has been ignored by the king.

So the girl is cursed, either because the goddess is angry or because her feelings are hurt. In one of the many versions she is not cursed by a goddess but by a rejected, unpleasant lover. A disagreeable man turns up at the king's court and is refused. In revenge he curses her and puts her to sleep for a hundred years; he is a magician. Here the dangerous power who curses the girl is a male figure. He would represent, in the context of feminine psychology, an animus figure, that is, the personification of a negative spirit which is not accepted at the king's court. The rejected lover who curses the girl is a semidivine figure, which touches again on the just-so story; for nobody can pretend that she should have married him. The girl does the right thing in refusing him, but all the same the curse falls on her. We cannot assume, however, that this unpleasant lover is the personal animus of the heroine. It is much more probably that he represents a mental attitude which has been rejected by the father king. The latter represents the collective principles of a civilization, and the unpleasant lover would be all that which has been rejected by the collective.

It is sometimes possible that the collective does not represent normality and then the *Zeitgeist* is ill. Then the right instinctive behavior can come up in an individual against the collective; there are collective neuroses. A whole family may be neurotic, and then a child is born who, by God's blessing, has a healthy disposition and, instead of adapting to the family neurosis, opposes it. Or there is a psychotic woman. She is married, but according to the Mendelian laws, does not necessarily have a psychotic child. She can have a normal child, but the latter is born of a psychotic mother and will be allergic to her and will react negatively to the mother's illness. To hate the mother is a healthy instinctive reaction in this case. That is a genuine tragedy which occurs over and over where the healthy nature collides with the neurotic family attitude. The instinctive right behavior causes undeserved misery. It is the theme of an infinite number of hero motifs. What is pathological hates what is sound, and what is sound is disgusted by and hates what is pathological—just as animals fight against the sick animal. A normal child born into pathological surroundings will not be able to say that he is right and the others are wrong, for he will have doubts. The others will say he is wrong, that he is the devil, and that is the inevitable tragedy in many young lives. Sometimes in analysis it is enough to say: "You were right, why do you doubt it?" Just the confirmation suffices.

In marriage also, one partner may be neurotic, a mass of repressions, and will always accuse the other. Let us say that one partner has a sexual perversion and wants to force the other to cooperate, but the other refuses. The former will accuse the latter of lack of feeling and love, but the other partner will still be disgusted. Who is neurotic? In such cases they will always accuse each other, and sometimes it is very difficult to find out where the fault lies.

I remember a case where the wife had terrific hysterical symptoms but only when the husband was around, and was quite normal when she was away from home. In analysis it was discovered that the man was completely contained in the mother complex. As far as feeling and love and affection were concerned, he had never married. When he was sixty-seven and she sixty-two, he was still writing to his mother whether he should not divorce! They were grandparents, and the husband had not made up his mind yet if he should say yes to his partner! Every time she went home, she got seasick. It was a normal reaction and a good sign that her healthy nature vomited in such surroundings. You can innocently fall into misery—an important truth to remember, especially for those people who tend to be moralistic about the question of neuroses.

3

At the beginning of Nazism in Germany, I was several times asked by Germans in what respect they were abnormal, for though they were unable to accept Nazism, not doing so made them doubt their own normality. Those who stuck to their instinctive reactions and, in a higher sense, remained normal and on the right path, yet fell into misery and complete disaster. They were impressed by the collective impulse, though they were right in not joining the movement. In that case, misery fell upon people who had done the right thing.

I want to look at this question from another angle. Many fairy tales start with the motif of a king, or a merchant, who crosses the sea in his ship or goes through a wood and gets stopped by an evil spirit, or perhaps a black dog, or even the devil himself, who will let him go if he will give the devil whatever he meets first on his return home. The king agrees, thinking it will probably be his dog, but a child, born in his absence, runs toward him and he realizes that he has sold his child to the devil. Generally this child turns out to be a hero or heroine who has the task of freeing him- or herself from the devil by the performance of heroic deeds.

Because the king or merchant is stopped by the devil, we can say that the collective conscious attitude has become stuck. In such a case, renewal can only come by discussion with the other princi-ple—the devil, or the principle of evil—whatever was hitherto excluded. Naturally the devilish, hindering principle wants to be guaranteed that, in the future, life will be continued on its lines. In an individual neurosis that would be when one is stuck and cannot go on: one has to (a) enter into discussion with the unconscious and (b) to promise that life in the future will be conducted on new lines. Naturally, the devil's conditions are too extreme and one-sided, so that the child's task will be to liberate itself and get beyond the opposites.

Jung tells the story of a very correct businessman, a gentleman, educated as a Christian, who behaved very decently with his wife and children at home, who neither smoked nor drank too much nor ran after women. When the man was about forty or fifty, however, he developed the classical neurosis of such people—bad dreams and the usual manager's disease. In the middle of a sleepless night at about 3:00 A.M., he woke his wife up by shouting, "Now I have it! I am a crook and a bum, O.K.!" Being a man, and a real man, who had wholehearted reactions, he went over to the opposite side from that moment, spent all his money, and lived a dissolute life from then until his death. It was a complete enantiodromia. It needed a certain amount of courage but was no joke for the family and the children, who had to go into analysis; but the man had gotten stuck, as the king was stuck. The devil presented his bill and life went on on the devil's path, for the man could not free himself and get on the middle path, to himself.

A fairy tale which begins in this way, in showing the necessity of a change to the opposite, could be paralleled with our story in which the frog speaks to the parents who have gotten stuck. They have no children and their land is no longer fertile; here, though, the frog does not threaten to steal the child, but to give it. The tension is not as great as in the first case, and the unconscious offers continuation of life with no conditions attached; it offers a new possibility to the existing conscious attitude. But nevertheless we must expect, and can see from the story, that payment will be exacted; the demands of the dark world will probably still come up, as they do at the baptism. Then the dark side of nature appears asserting its claim on the child.

There are other variations. In a medieval version, three fairy godmothers bear the names of Lucina, Venus, and Themis. (I spoke earlier of this Quattrocento tendency to give the names of known classical goddesses to the contents of the unconscious.) The rewriter of the story chose to call the evil fairy godmother Themis, and I think his intuition quite remarkable. Lucina is a name of the Roman goddess Juno. She was particularly the goddess who helped women in childbirth. The name of Venus speaks for itself. Themis (Justice) is the one who is hurt, who curses the child and has the function of the bad fairy godmother. She represents an aspect of the mother goddess which has been very much forgotten in our civilization, but which exists in many primitive civilizations, and in antiquity, that is, a feminine principle which contains a strange kind of severity and revengefulness, and which does not coincide with the parallel male attitude. When we think of revenge or punishment—revenge is an older form of punishment—we think of the law, of its transgression, and of punishment according to established laws, for that is our custom.

To make laws and decide what is to happen to those who break them is in our countries a man's way of dealing with the problem. Our laws are based on Roman law and patriarchal mentality, so that we always think of punishment as having to do with the masculine world, and of women as representing the principle of charity and the making of exceptions. In medieval times, the Virgin Mary was represented as taking under her cloak the sinners, who, under divine law, would go to hell or purgatory, but for whom she obtained better conditions from God. That men make the laws and deal with worldly matters and women have the role of pleading for leniency fits the old patriarchal family pattern, where father does the punishing and insists on schoolwork, and mother begs for leniency, saying that father is too severe. Though this pattern often does not fit with reality, it is the pattern all the same. The problem of justice and punishment in the male world is linked up with the idea of "just" laws, and justice means that everybody gets the same punishment for the same sin. It is based on statistical thinking, and there are no exceptions, unless there is a regulation to cover them.

That is a defense against an overgrowth of evil, but it is a one-sided way of looking at the problem. According to mythological standards, there is also feminine justice, and a feminine principle of revenge. What would that be, according to the rules of law and justice as we see them? It would be more individual and personal.

One might say that, as we look at it, the law represents the logos principle; there is a basic idea that a certain order must prevail in the family and in life. Certain rules have to be made and those who do not keep to them must be punished. It is a protest against chaos and typical of a rational attitude toward life. But there is another process of revenge and punishment which I would like to define as the *revengefulness of nature*. If for twenty years a person eats hastily and without even sitting down to do so, eventually he will probably be punished with stomach disorders. It cannot be called a legal punishment; it is the natural consequence—wrong behavior is followed by bad luck or illness.

Punishment and revenge are not brought about only by humans, but also by a process of revenge in nature. Sometimes the same thing happens psychologically too. A wrong attitude, not necessarily immoral but one not in accordance with nature, is also avenged, and the person will have bad luck, though no moral law has been broken. It could be called punishment by natural processes, or revenge by the natural process of things. In most primitive mythologies, there is an aspect of the feminine goddess of nature known as Nemesis—Revenge, Fate; and Themis—Justice. The principle of justice in the Jewish Kabbalah belongs also to the left, that is, to the feminine side of the Sefiroth tree. So justice is a feminine quality according to Jewish symbolism, which seems very strange.

Nature is sometimes harsh, severe, and cruelly revengeful. There is neither judgment nor rule, but the revenge of the dark aspect of the feminine nature goddess. The Quattrocento Italian writer who gives the dark mother the name of Themis, justice, illustrates how nature rectifies masculine law in a complementary, natural way. Women tend not to think so much along the lines of justice and law, but react against what they do not like with nastiness, more like nature, as it were. (These are dangerous statements to make because every woman in the animus will justify what she does by referring to my book!) In the anima there is also a certain nastiness, for the anima is primitive woman. Women, and man's entire anima, have a way of reacting to disagreeable situations by being downright nasty. Instead of being thought-out, or just punishment, nastiness is a kind of overflowing of a mood and is not, in all circumstances, unjustified; in certain situations, just to be nasty is the right answer. The vixen who bites the cub at a certain age does the right thing. By that she puts it on its own, which is how mothers sometimes can shake off children who cling too much to them; they just become like the animal mother and growl! At bottom that is the revengefulness of nature in a positive aspect, though seen from the outside it is ugly. If the woman is in Tao and functioning according to the inner laws of her being, she can afford that kind of feminine nastiness, and it is not animus possession. The animal who wants to be fed by its mother too long gets the nasty mother in revenge. The functioning of this feminine rule is not recognized in our patriarchal civilization, and therefore we think things must be "just."

I know the mother of an eight-year-old girl who is very lively and rather lonely, and always wants her mother to play with her. On her free afternoon the mother parks the child out. At the last minute, however, the child always wants something. For instance, she is clever enough to say that she has done her sums—which she hates doing—and wants her mother to check them. From a rational point of view, the mother should help the child with her school-work. But in this case, from the feminine standpoint, the mother is right, for on the child's part it is a calculated trick to keep her mother at home. Outwardly, of course, it looks completely wrong, if the child's request seems rational and just. When the situation is rationally on the side of the child, it needs a certain subtlety to be able to say that the mother is right. There comes the great question of whether she should follow the motivation underneath and just be nasty, or the upper, which is wrong for her. Women who have too great a sense of duty have difficulty in such a case, for they are apt to deviate from the instinctive reaction and think that a good mother with a Christian education should help the child with her schoolwork. It is a "should" and therefore, from a feminine standpoint, an animus reaction, a well-meaning one, but still animus. The healthy reaction would be to say no.

You see how terribly subtle the problem is, because you can take every word I have said to justify animus ideas against real instinctiveness. One needs to be very downright and honest to know what the unconscious says. But such Themis revengefulness in nature brings us to a very serious situation, one of the greatest present-day problems of our world: namely, that created by the great improvement in medicine due to the rational and technical development of the white man's civilization. This is basically due to the domination of the white races. Pretty soon the world will be hopelessly overpopulated; in a couple of hundred years the situation will be absolutely hopeless, but the United Nations and other organizations continue to improve hygienic conditions in India and other Eastern countries and to help overpopulate the earth. Possibly nature will invent a new virus—and a virus is capable of fantastic mutations—or bring about such a state of irritation that Russia or the United States or some other country will use the atom bomb, because somehow humanity has to be reduced.

All the well-meaning charitable enterprises in the world are built up on a *Weltanschauung* that does not take the dark side of Mother Nature into consideration. They are based on Christian ideas. But if one ignores a goddess, she manifests herself again. At one time nature and her dark side were in harmony, but from the twelfth and thirteenth centuries onward—as can be seen for instance in mythology, in poetry, and in religious movements—natural compensation was no longer on the lines of the one-sided light attitude. From that time onward, there was a wrong persistence in an attitude that had hitherto been right. There was no realization that a further evolution was necessary, that an alteration was required and an awareness of the dark side. Instead there was a stiffening on a general scale throughout Europe; what had been right developed into a neurotic attitude, and defense mechanisms were set up against the unconscious compensation.

Supposing a child, a girl, grows up in unfeeling and cold surroundings at home. In consequence she develops great independence and her animus gets activated—which is quite right and the only solution in accordance with nature at the time. But then the parental situation fades and the child leaves home. If she persists in her independence and is unapproachable on the eros side, she might develop a neurosis. The stiff animus attitude, which was a defense method and in accordance with nature at one time, has to be softened.

Persistence in an out-of-date attitude creates an impossible situation. It is a tragic fact that the structure of man is such that perseverance is necessary to maintain the principle of consciousness. But it is just this persistence which brings about dissociation. The only issue here would be the Jungian attitude: to know of these difficulties and try to develop a greater flexibility and a more open attitude within one's conscious attitude, to follow one's instinct only until one has a clear message to the contrary from the unconscious, which may indicate that one should move over a little to the other side. Here the difficulty is that this flexible attitude may be confused with infantile unsteadiness. There is a kind of infantile incapacity for sticking to things. The person changes and wobbles, which denotes a weak ego consciousness, an either/and/or attitude incapable of steering a steady course. To people who act in this way, the wisdom of Jungian psychology—that is, of balancing between the opposites—is sheer poison; for it is used to justify a lack of backbone and a weak consciousness. It becomes an attempt to justify the infantile unsteadiness by quoting Jung and the principle of opposites.

In the second millennium of Christianity in Europe, the collective conscious attitude has been too stiff and inflexible in its devaluation of the feminine goddess, especially its dark nature side. This is why our century has been characterized by a protest of women against this fact. Sleeping Beauty has woken up!

To return to our story. The angry fairy godmother curses the child, saying that she will die on her fifteenth birthday; but another godmother softens the curse into one that she should sleep for a hundred years. Sleep and death were two gods who in antiquity were looked upon as divine brothers: Hypnos and Thanatos. The ancients saw sleep as a kind of death, and therefore in this story they have to be taken relatively. If I dream that such and such a person dies, it means that the complex represented by that person is completely repressed—so repressed that I have no further hunches about it. It has died, it has ceased to participate in my psychological life and so is represented as a dead person. That is why in a psychosis there is so much symbolism of ghosts and cemeteries and corpses coming out of graves. They are autonomous complexes which have no connection with the ego. About the godmother's curse, therefore, one could say that the dark side, the evil side of nature, threatens to cut off this girl from all surrounding life. That will happen at her fifteenth birthday at the age of puberty.

Puberty is an age when neurotic attitudes often break out. It then looks as if a part of femininity was allowed to develop as far as the juvenile plane and not beyond. The feminine element which does not quite fit in a civilization is allowed to live through childhood, but not when it gets to the age of being taken seriously in the adult world. In the Basel Fastnacht, a god of sexual liberty rules, a god with whom the Christian civilization does not know how to deal, though other civilizations also have some trouble with it! The Christian civilization has rules governing moral behavior, and at certain festivals, like Carnival, these rules are relaxed, but this must not be taken seriously; it is only childish fun. That is, we let such things live as child's play, but as adults do not take them seriously. We say that is for the child, or for Carnival, or that one was just having fun. We allow it in the harmless disguise of having fun, but when we should take things seriously, we repress them again.

One of the best historical examples is the romantic way of playing with the feminine principle. The romantic poets, especially among the Germans, rediscovered the anima problem and gave the most wonderful descriptions of the anima, as for instance, in "Der goldene Topf" by E. T. A. Hoffmann, whose interpretation by Aniela Jaffé has unfortunately not yet been translated into English.[12] Hoffmann wrote a story that really got to the core of the anima problem and brought up its deepest problems. But in romanticism generally things got so dramatic that some poets snapped, and others became converted to Catholicism. The majority, however, used a trick known in the history of literature as "romantic irony," which meant that at the end of a marvelous story, suddenly someone says, "And it was all a nice dream!" Many modern artists will laugh off what they have written. They write or phantasize also about the most serious problems, but themselves say that "it is all art" or "play," so that it is quite impossible to take the phantasy seriously and apply it to oneself. Development to the age of fifteen is permitted, and then the lid is put on.

The romantic poets probably thought it would break them if they took it seriously, so they said it was phantasy or art. That would mean that the content was repressed again, for things were getting too serious. In the Renaissance the whole problem of antique paganism came up again, and people said they preferred Venus to the Virgin Mary, but it remained an artistic play and for that reason was not persecuted by the Church; it had gotten stuck at a certain moment, and the contents were never really admitted and taken into serious consideration.

The good fairy godmother turns death into sleep for a hundred years, which makes a long period of sleep and repression. This happens in reality. An individual's problems do sometimes disappear, but often one has the awkward feeling that they are somnolent rather than solved. Generally, the conscious attitude is such that the problems cannot come up for some reason, and therefore fall asleep—although one feels they will recur. The king has everything removed from the court which might consummate the curse. He removes every spindle from the court, but, typically, the one forgotten thing gets the girl. Obviously the old woman whom she finds in the tower is the forgotten godmother who had not been invited. She had been living for over fifty years in a remote tower. But this time she seems to be an ordinary old woman, who is so old and had lived in such a retired way that she had been forgotten, and now the curse fulfills itself. For the time being, we can say that she is the dark side of the feminine principle forgotten in our civilization, and also the dark, imperfect side of Mother Nature.

We should go into the problem of the spindle, which is a symbol of femininity. In medieval Germany one speaks of "spindle kinship," just as one speaks of the "distaff side of the family" in referring to relations on the mother's side. It was the sign of Saint Gertrude in the Middle Ages, who took most of the qualities of the pre-Christian mother goddesses such as Freja, Hulda, Perchta, and others. The spindle is also the attribute of the wise old woman and of witches. The sowing of the flax and spinning and weaving are the essence of feminine life with its fertility and sexual implications. Flax was also regarded as having to do with feminine activities. In many countries women used to expose their genitals to the growing flax and say, "Please grow as high as my genitals are now." It was thought that the flax would grow better for that. In many countries flax is planted by the women, for it is linked up with their lives.

A colleague, Carol Baumann, collected dreams of pregnant women and the dreams occurring immediately before and after birth, and published her results in a little paper which appeared in the first volume of the *Festschrift zum 80. Geburtstag von C. G. Jung* under the title "Psychological Experiences Connected with Childbirth." Here you will find that in some of the dreams the motifs of threads and of weaving appear. I recently met with such a motif. A pregnant woman dreamed that a lot of women took her on a boat, although she begged for her husband. A very positive woman then turned up and showed her a piece of silk, explaining that it had been combed so that the threads went this way and that way, giving a chameleonlike effect. The dreamer felt this was very numinous. Then two young women, twins, led her by the hand onto the upper part of the boat. Owing to a negative mother complex, this woman had some difficulty with having a child, and thus the whole unconscious centers on the maternal instinct and on giving her a positive, instinctive pattern by which to meet the birth. This pattern is symbolized by the chameleon cloth and the many threads in it. I must confess I do not know what this refers to in plain words. I think one can only say that the mystery of giving birth is basically associated with the idea of spinning, weaving, and other complicated feminine activities in bringing together natural elements in a certain order. The biological analogy which imposes itself upon one's mind is that every child is the coming together into definite patterns of the Mendelian inherited units. We know that every human being is a complex factor. We could call it a woven cloth of all the ancestral units, both biological and psychological, which make a single person, so that producing a child is like weaving it together from all the different elements, chemical, biological, and psychological.

Konrad Lorenz has talked in his lectures of the patterns of behavior in animals being inherited according to the Mendelian laws. Patterns of behavior in animals are subdivided into single actions—those fragments of patterns follow Mendelian laws.[13] Similarly, in every new child there is a living mixture of psychosomatic elements which reorder themselves according to a certain pattern and make a new being in a most mysterious form. This mystery of the way in which a child again becomes a whole from inherited psychological and physical patterns is what is referred to in feminine weaving. To this tremendous opus, the woman does not only contribute consciously, but with her whole being, and through her psychological substance. It also seems to me, from the little I know, that it is essential and positively important for the child that the phantasy of a pregnant woman and mother should in the early stages be centered around the child. I would say that if a mother thinks a lot about the child to come, prays, and has phantasies about it—that is, spins and weaves for it—this phantasy activity prepares a nourishing ground for the child to be born into. The mother's attention does naturally circle around the mystery of the child to come, wondering about it, and this affects both her feeling and the psychological and physical health of the child.

The woman who dreamed of the chameleon cloth was a professional woman and was very proud of herself that she could have the child "by the way," that is, work to the end. She was proud of her good health and of her other activities, and was a very lively person, but I think she really missed the inward weaving for the child. Due to her negative mother complex, she had not realized that she must weave a web around the child with her phantasies and feeling expectations. Therefore she had the dream to tell her that she must have the psychologically right attitude.

Everybody who has knitted or done weaving or embroidery knows what an agreeable effect this can have, for you can be quiet and lazy without feeling guilty and also can spin your own thoughts while working. You can relax and follow your phantasy and then get up and say you have done something! Also the work demands patience, which for an animus temperament is quite an exercise. Only those who have done such work know of all the catastrophes which can happen—such as losing a row of stitches just when you are decreasing! It is a very self-educative occupation and enhances our feminine nature. It is immensely important for women to do such work and not give it up in the modern rush. But it can be abused, like all psychological activities. I once knew a painter who forbade his wife to knit. He said that women knitted in such a desperate way, putting all their sorrows and disappointments and anger into their knitting—and there is this side to it, for women do sometimes knit like mad. It has a double aspect. This man had had such a mother and had experienced the negative side, and so forbade his wife to knit, in spite of the fact that she was not like his mother. When knitting or spinning or weaving is characterized as negative, one can make a guess that the woman is making plots, that she is spinning a yarn or some kind of intrigue. Wishful thinking is being spun into the evil web of the witch. If the mythological context of the dream or fairy tale connects this activity positively with the conscious life of a feminine figure, it symbolizes the creating of the right atmosphere, an inner activity typical for a woman.

A woman's task is to create a certain atmosphere, for she is mainly responsible for the ambiance in the home, for the invisible feeling tone and the phantasies she has about her family. If that feeling tone is right, she can nourish the right attitude and adaptation of her family. If the wife trusts her husband and children, without overvaluing them, the atmosphere is fertile, which makes the family want to live up to that trust. To have trust in her family, and expectations for it, is one of the tasks of the maternal attitude and will invite compliance. Nothing is more difficult for a child than to feel itself mistrusted, for it then feels itself to be a miserable creature. On the other hand, there are women who imagine that all their children are either a Savior or a Jesus Christ or the blessed Virgin Mary, and this truly destroys the child. The savior phantasy in mothers is very often at the bottom of the destruction of the son, for it affects the boy. The mother must spin the right kind of phantasy, neither overvaluing nor undervaluing the child, keeping it rightly in her mind and heart, and then it can go its own way.

Such things have been too much ignored. We hear much about pedagogics and preventing complexes and putting the child on the pot at two years old, et cetera—as if the outer rules were the whole thing. We tend not to see that the phantasy and feeling life of the mother is what must be attended to, not just the carrot juice and the bottles! Women generally do know this and realize that if the child is upset, it is because the mother is disturbed. It is being discovered that while a child is still in the womb, something may happen to prevent its normal development. Secret phantasies of the mother have much to do with the creation of a life situation. Naturally this refers also to the anima of the father, whose neglected eros can also destroy the child, so that the father, one step removed, is confronted with the same problem.

In the culture of India there are strong matriarchal tendencies. There the child is regarded as a reborn soul, and the threads, the chameleon cloth, are the karma of the generations. You might say that we, in the West, think of ourselves more as single units. But we also speak figuratively of a chain of generations, or a thread going through a family. In India, where they believe in reincarnation, they would say that they were all a part of the great web of the Godhead. As threads return to the same position again and again, the eternal thread appearing and disappearing—human beings go and return and always a thread goes through; they claim that they can count the links in the chain of their incarnations. Whether that theory has been built upon observation, or whether it is an explanation, remains a question; but it is how they interpret the same fact, the recurring patterns.

The way in which the father's unconscious phantasies affect especially the daughters is well known; it is evidenced when the man who does not come to terms with his anima problem parks his phantasies on the daughters, by expecting them to live what he did not, or by incestuous desires, and so disturbs the daughters' natural development.

Because of his mother complex, a certain man married very late and then made his wife into his mother. When about fifty years old, he became very restless and had numerous sexual phantasies about women, although, being "a perfect gentleman," he did not make them conscious. He had a recurring nightmare in which he saw his daughter standing by a lamppost in the street waiting like a prostitute for men. His whole eros problem was projected onto his daughters. One ran off and led a wild life and became ill and died. A second daughter, for a while, did the same thing; and a third became very prudish. All had an unsolved love problem. It clearly referred back to the spinning and weaving of the father's anima, which had never been shown up. He had left it to the next generation, and the daughters inherited it.

Within the weaving activity, which is essentially feminine, the spindle is a phallic thing. It is what penetrates, goes back and forth, and around it everything revolves. In Plato's *Timaeus,* the cosmos is said to revolve like a spindle, around an axis in the womb of the goddess Nemesis. In our story, the spindle acts like the sleeping thorn, or needle, with which witches and magicians used to prick people so that they passed out. In many folklore tales there occurs the motif of putting the sleeping needles, which the magicians have, into the head or eye or behind the ear or even into the finger, and making the person fall asleep or pass out at once. A pointed thing is a stinging remark. (In German, *eine Pointe* is a stinging remark.) Such a remark expresses the habitual aggressiveness of women, and of the anima. Women do not habitually bang doors or swear, but make some subtle, gentle, pointed remarks— the soft-voiced, wounding witch remark that hits right on the other person's tender spot.

Generally one speaks of the natural mind of women in a positive sense. The mind of woman, being closer to nature, has the advantage of being able to see things realistically. My own great-grandmother, every time her children went off into adolescent romanticism, is supposed to have said: "Children, go and make your beds!" thus bringing them back into reality. Or there is the famous story by Anatole France about a saint who went on a boat to the northern isles and saw, as he thought, a crowd of people who had come to meet him, all dressed up in their best clothes. He had no spectacles on and gave them a collective baptism, but unfortunately they were penguins! When they died, heaven was confronted with a problem, for, having been baptized, they had a right to go to heaven, but, on the other hand, animals were not admitted. What was to be done? The Father, the Son, and the Holy Ghost assembled, and it was such a difficult question that they had to ask all the Church dignitaries and saints. There was a tremendous theoretical discussion as to whether baptism could confer an immortal soul on a penguin! They tried to solve the problem cleanly and exactly. But as no decision was reached, they called in Saint Catherine, who considered it for a short time and then said, "Oh, well, give them a soul, but a little one." It was no problem for a woman with her natural mind—the penguins were a small kind of human being, so they should have a small soul! She was good-natured and practical about it! The negative aspect of the natural mind, on the other hand, can get at people's complexes in a destructive way. It is a misuse of the natural mind very common among women, and it is what happens here—a negative phantasy on the part of Mother Nature hits the girl and puts her to sleep.

4

The spindle is even more dangerous when turned against oneself, because then it does not come outside and cannot be caught. Seemingly, it does not cause trouble, but it destroys the woman herself. Frequently one comes across women who say, "Well, you see, I somehow assumed that I should never get married," or "I was stupid, for I never managed to do anything in life." One asks, "Why did you assume that?" God knows! In early youth such a self-destructive conviction was arrived at and never discussed with anybody or expressed in any way. From then on, the whole inner development with the possibilities of creating or of becoming something or somebody vanishes, just as Briar Rose vanished after pricking herself. You can only see that something has stopped in such people; they seem asleep and move along under a dark fate, one does not know why. Everything has stagnated. Generally they do not talk about it, for they themselves do not realize it. Speaking of it to the analyst would imply that there was a problem about which they had doubts. But if they are really in a bewitched sleep, they are not being dishonest; it simply never occurs to them that there is anything to discuss. Such women simply fall out of life one day, just as happens in the fairy tale. Perhaps it is the negative mother complex, or perhaps the mother's animus. The old woman in the story is a kind of mother figure or grandmother, and the spindle would stand for the mother's animus.

I remember the case of the pronounced psychological illness of a woman who could not digest anything and had to take all food in the form of pills. Half starved, she came to analysis, because her doctor had finally come to the conclusion that her illness must be psychological. The woman's mother had been a nurse in a hospital and had lived the Christian, self-sacrificing attitude of considering her life valueless and wanting nothing from it. Life should be given to the service of others, and with this went a suicidal tendency, a real problem which many nurses in hospitals have—although this self-sacrificing attitude did not stop her from catching the head doctor of the hospital. After marriage her animus came up again, and she would moan to her husband and children that she should not have married or had children but should have remained a nurse.

So the children grew up in an atmosphere in which the mother's animus informed them from morning to evening that their existence was a mistake, that it was wrong for them to be alive. The daughter gave in to whatever was asked of her, since she felt she had to propitiate her surroundings. She was frightened of everyone, her basic attitude being that she had no right to be alive—"but please do not kill me, and I will do anything you want!" She had been pricked by the deadly spindle of her mother's animus opinion, which she herself had also adopted, namely that she should not be alive! She was just such another Briar Rose, stung by the mother's negative animus, and did not know it.

The strange thing was that when she first came into analysis, I felt as if something had been put over my head and I was falling asleep. I always let myself go into such phantasies when I get an impression from an analysand. My feeling in this case was that I should get up and put my head under the cold water tap. There was quite a pleasant atmosphere, for she was like a little duckling in my hands and never contradicted or opposed me in any way. She interested me, and I felt sympathetic and yet had this sleepiness, which depicted her own situation. She had not woken up to the fact that she had the right to live. For years the analysis consisted in showing her in all the events of her life where she had unconsciously, continually given in. We always came back to the same thing. But she had fallen into an abyss of unhappiness and was completely unable to digest anything. To digest is to react. But this woman had no reaction to what happened to her.

In a broader collective sense the same motif would mean that certain factors in feminine psychic life have been devaluated by some unconscious reflection. In our civilization one of the most widespread unconscious reflections—perhaps not quite unconscious, but still at the back of people's minds—is an association between Evil and woman. In the story of the Garden of Eden, Adam told God that Eve was responsible. She had talked to the devil. Over and over you come across that negative connection and the identification of evil with the woman's problem. Men with a negative mother complex do it frequently. Since our civilization is mainly patriarchal, such a thought is at the back of the minds of many people. A high-ranking Catholic priest once said to me, "Why is there always this problem with women?" His remark was quite justified because once again a hysterical woman had tried to seduce him in the confessional and had behaved disgustingly. Such women afterward go around saying that the priest had tried to seduce *them*.

A priest wears a robe, which proclaims his desire to have nothing to do with women. That irritates certain women, who make up their minds to seduce him; they are irritated by the woman's dress. Naturally, seen from the priest's standpoint, it is disgusting to be always surrounded by hysterical women. There is no love in it; it is just a power drive, and of course the man says, "My God, women!" But what he does not see is that by wearing a robe and being representative of a patriarchal order, with a Pope at the head but no female counterpart, there is a kind of declaration of war against the feminine element. It is a very ticklish problem because it calls forth this reaction in women. Of course it is very unreasonable, but behind it is the question: "Why do we have no priestesses?" In three cases the dreams of women who misbehaved in this way have said that there should be priestesses, which shows they felt insulted!

In many primitive civilizations both sexes are represented in the religious ceremonies, and women can attain higher ranks as religious guides. In actual fact, the Catholic Church is not as bad as it is theoretically, for there are many women who assume the role of the priest through the spirit of their personality; then men give in to it. Superiors in convents were of course such priestesses; though they did not have the title, they had the role. Saint Teresa of Ávila is a striking example. But the basic problem comes from the more patriarchal attitude. Women who do not take the trouble to think about such things get a hidden feeling of inferiority that they compensate by being disagreeable, and so attracting attention. If one cannot attract men's love, then one must provoke their anger. At least the priest must think about one whether he likes it or not!

When the prince appears after a hundred years, the thorny hedge growing around the castle blossoms suddenly into beautiful roses. The rose, says one medieval author, belongs to the goddess Venus and means love, for "there is no love without thorns." They also say *"Ubi mel, ibi fel,"* where there is honey, there is also the bitter gall. You can refer the meaning of the thorn to the terrible involuntary hurts loving people always inflict upon each other. There is the expression "a typical lovers' quarrel." We would call it an anima-animus quarrel, the sword crossing of animus and anima, which consists in a most horrible way of hurting each other in the most vulnerable spots. Just where the man has a most uncertain delicate feeling, the woman places the thorn of her animus; and where the woman wants to be understood or accepted, the man comes out with some anima poison dart.

Such hedges of thorns in dreams refer to exaggerated touchiness, which is always combined with aggressiveness. If a very touchy analysand comes, I know that I shall get a lot of very bad stings, so I put on an armor. Touchy people are proud of their sensitiveness, by which they tyrannize others. An unkind word provides tragedy for months. You cannot open your mouth because you might hurt the other person. They get into tempers over everything and sulk and are hurt in their wonderful delicate feelings; it is just plain tyranny.

Such people usually have a very vulgar hidden power complex which comes out in the shadow—an infantile attitude toward life through which those around are tyrannized. What should be a receptive, loving attitude becomes a thorny hedge, where every man who tries to penetrate gets so torn that he just retires. A man cannot get at such a touchy woman who is hurt by the most harmless remark. It is too complicated, and naturally he gives up, like the men in the fairy tale.

The solution in the story is strange, for there is no merit and no dramatic event anywhere. The situation just changes after a hundred years. The prince comes, but does not do anything special; he just goes through at the right time. Several conclusions can be reached. One could say this illustrates that the problem of touchy domination has to be treated with patience and waiting. If you try to get through and show such a touchy person that she is a tyrant, you generally get just kicked into the thorny hedge and entangle yourself, and the relationship goes to pieces. I have often failed in such cases, and the patient has walked out deeply hurt that I dared to touch that problem and misunderstood it as domination, when really it was the great delicacy of an incredibly delicate soul! The only thing to do is not to attack the problem directly, but to wait until people are so lonely in their power complex that they are at the end of their rope. The passivity of the prince shows that the collective images of the fairy tales recommend such an attitude.

There are situations which belong to the feminine principle—that is, the anima of man and the feminine in woman herself—where time is the essential thing; nothing else can help and all interference is wrong. We can take for example the anima problem: certain men with a positive mother complex marry late, because they become the type of oversensitive literary bachelor with a very delicate flowerlike anima and are so touchy and oversensitive that they never know how to go out and get a woman. They are imprisoned in their own sensitivity. If a kind of vital physical drive does not force them, they stay outside marriage and the woman's problem for too long, but often such people suddenly wake up without analysis. I have seen this happen at thirty, thirty-six, or forty. They just leave their touchy cage and marry happily—and the thing goes quite well, without analysis. It is just as though they at first waited too long, but then caught up. It is like a delayed or late development due to their delicacy or sensitiveness. Analysis would not help such people; they just had to sleep and then wake up. Sometimes the best thing to do with such a bachelor type is to send him away and say he is O.K.—he should just wait until he finds a woman who suits him. One day he will wake up. He has been under the veil of a too-delicate feeling side which has developed in the positive relationship with the mother. With women who have the idea that they have no right to exist, the same thing happens. Under the influence of such thoughts they give in to everybody, and then suddenly wake up, without becoming conscious; the phase of sleep has come to an end.

I remember a friend, much older than I, a very delicate, sensitive, quiet woman who first came under the tyranny of her stepmother and then of her elder sister, who thought she would replace the mother. This poor woman did what she was told. They had no money, and she went to work and behaved. The only thing one could say was that she was rather boring, and one felt that she should not be. Suddenly at the age of forty-three she woke up and married and had a child and developed slowly into a lively and interesting woman. When the hundred years were over, her life began to constellate. One would not get far by analyzing such a person. There are many cases, especially among sensitive people, who develop better without the interfering operation of an analytical treatment, which sometimes only gets them out of their inner rhythm.

If taken on a personal level, the story of Briar Rose is that of the negative mother complex in a woman, and also of a man's negative mother complex when his anima goes to sleep. Now let us look at the counterpart, the pattern of a positive mother complex, of which this story is an example.

Snow White and Rose Red[14]

Synopsis of the Tale

There was once a poor widow who lived alone in her cottage with her two children, who, because they were like the flowers blooming on the rosebushes which grew before the house, were called Snow White and Rose Red.

[Rose Red was the more lively and more extraverted of the two and Snow White was the quieter. They were good girls and always did what their mother told them. The story is very long and sentimental, which is very typical of the positive mother complex. There is an effort to describe a wonderful atmosphere.] The little girls never quarrel, are obedient, and lead a wonderful life and help their mother, etc. They sometimes do risky things—such as going into the woods and playing too long and forgetting to come home, and then falling asleep under a tree, close to the edge of a pit, into which they would have fallen had they walked a couple of steps further in the dark. But, according to their mother, an angel had watched over them, so all was well.

One evening while they sat spinning at the hearth, there was a knock at the door, which Rose Red opened, and there appeared a bear. After some flutterings and bleatings by a dove and a lamb which live in the house with them, they let the bear in, since he said he did not want to harm them, but was half-frozen and wished to come in and warm himself.

"Poor Bear!" said the mother. "Come in and lie down before the fire, but take care you do not burn your skin." So the bear came in and told the children to knock the snow off his coat, and then grumbled out his satisfaction and lay down before the fire, and stayed the whole winter. The girls played with the unwieldy animal, pulled his long, shaggy skin, stood on him and rolled him to and fro, and even beat him with a hazel stick. He bore it all good-naturedly, but if they hit too hard he cried out:

> Leave me my life, you children,
> Snow White and Rose Red,
> Or you'll never wed

—which was the only indication that he had some other intention; otherwise he behaved like a big, good-natured toy.

But as soon as the spring returned, he said he had to go and could not return during the whole summer, for he was obliged to go into the forest and guard his treasures from the evil dwarfs, who stay in their holes all the winter but come out in the summer and steal all they can find. Snow White was so sad at his departure and opened the door so hesitatingly that when he pressed through it, he left behind on the latch a piece of his hairy coat. Through the hole made in his coat, Snow White fancied she saw the glittering of gold, but she was not quite sure and thought it must have been a hallucination.

One day, when sent into the wood to gather sticks, the two sisters came to a tree, on the trunk of which something kept bobbing up and down. When they got nearer, they saw a dwarf with an old wrinkled face and a snow-white beard a yard long. The end of the beard was caught in a split in the tree, and the little man kept jumping about like a dog tied by a chain, for he did not know how to free himself. He glared at the girls with his fiery eyes and said, "Why do you stand there? Are you going to pass without offering me any assistance?"

"What have you done, little man?" asked Rose Red.

"You stupid, inquisitive goose!" he exclaimed. "I wanted to split the tree in order to get a little wood for my kitchen; for the little food which we use is soon burned with great faggots, not like what you rough, greedy people devour! I had driven the wedge in properly, and everything was going well until the wedge sprang out suddenly, and the tree closed so quickly together that I could not draw my beautiful beard out; and here it sticks, and I cannot get away. There, don't laugh, you milk-faced things! Are you dumbfounded?"

The children tried their hardest to pull the dwarf's beard out, but without success. "I will run and fetch some help," cried Rose Red at length.

"Crack-brained sheep-head that you are!" snarled the dwarf. "What are you going to call other people for? You are already too many for me. Can you think of nothing else?"

But Snow White said she had thought of something and pulled her scissors out of her pocket and cut off the end of his beard. As soon as he was freed, the dwarf picked up his sack filled with gold and, instead of thanking them, insulted them further and ran off, calling them stupid for having cut off a piece of his beautiful beard. But they did not mind, or were too stupid or innocent to notice anything, and forgot about it.

Some time afterward, Snow White and Rose Red went fishing, and as they neared the pond they saw something like a great locust hopping about on the bank, as if going to jump into the water. They ran up and recognized the dwarf. "What are you after?" asked Rose Red. "You will fall into the water!"

"I am not quite such a simpleton as that," replied the dwarf. "But do you not see that this fish will pull me in?" The little man had been sitting there angling, and, unfortunately, the wind had entangled his beard with the fishing line. So, when a great fish bit at the bait, the strength of the weak little fellow was not sufficient to draw it out, and the fish had the best of the struggle. The dwarf held on to the reeds and rushes which grew near, but to no purpose, for the fish pulled him where he liked, and he must soon have been drawn into the pond. Luckily, just then the two maidens arrived and tried to release the dwarf's beard from the fishing line; but both were too closely entangled for it to be done, so Snow White pulled out her scissors and cut off another piece of the beard. When the dwarf saw this, he was in a great rage, and exclaimed, "You donkey! That is the way to disfigure my face. Was it not enough to cut it once, but you must now take away the best part of my fine beard? I dare not show myself again to my own people. I wish you had run the soles off your boots before you had come here!" So saying, he took up a bag of pearls, which lay among the rushes, and without speaking another word, slipped off and disappeared behind a stone.

Not many days later the girls were sent to the next town to buy thread, needles and pins, laces and ribbons. On the common they saw a great bird flying around and then dropping lower and lower until at last it flew down behind a great rock. Then they heard a piercing shriek and to their horror saw that the eagle had caught their old acquaintance the dwarf. The compassionate children thereupon laid hold of the little man and held fast until the bird gave up the struggle and flew off. As soon as the dwarf had recovered from his fright, he began to abuse the girls again and say that they had torn his beautiful coat by holding him so roughly, although by now they were accustomed to his ingratitude. Coming home, they returned over the same common and, unaware, walked up to a clean spot where the dwarf had shaken out his bag of precious stones, and stopped to admire them.

"What are you standing there gaping for?" asked the dwarf, his face growing as red as copper with rage. Suddenly a loud roaring noise was heard, and a great bear came crashing out of the forest. The dwarf jumped up, terrified, and tried to run away, but the bear overtook him. Thereupon he cried out, "Spare me, my dear Lord Bear! I will give you all my treasures—see these beautiful precious stones which lie here? Only give me my life—what have you to fear from a little weak fellow like me? You could not even feel me beneath your big teeth. There are two wicked girls, take them. They would make you nice tender morsels, they are as fat as young quails—eat them!"

The bear, however, without troubling himself to speak, gave the bad-hearted dwarf a single blow with his paw, and he never stirred again.

The girls were then going to run away, but the bear called after them, "Snow White and Rose Red, fear not! Wait a bit and I will accompany you." They recognized his voice and stopped, and the bear's rough coat suddenly fell off and he stood up, a tall man dressed entirely in gold. "I am a king's son," he said, "and was condemned by the wicked dwarf, who stole all my treasures, to wander about the forest in the form of a bear till his death released me. Now he has received the punishment he so richly deserved."

They went home, and Snow White was married to the prince and Rose Red to his brother, with whom they shared the immense treasure the dwarf had collected. The old mother lived happily with her two children. The rose trees that had stood before the cottage were planted now before the palace, and every year produced beautiful red and white roses.

The beginning of the story is characterized by a kind of innocent childhood paradisiacal situation, the mother-daughter paradise. Everything is all right, but a bit too beautiful. It would be marvelous if it were like that! There are three persons, so from our point of view it is incomplete. From the average statistical viewpoint, four is the usual number of the totality and here there are only three. The fourth thing soon appears as the bear, so in the wintertime they are four—three women and a bear. But in the beginning the male element is completely lacking. There is no father, for he has died. It is the feminine atmosphere which is described as ideal. As long as the children are young, it is all right, but they live so isolated a life that they never see a man; they are out of life.

If you apply this to a collective situation, you can say that the masculine and the feminine world are not in the right connection, so to speak, on the human as well as the spiritual level. One of the ways in which the feminine world defends and establishes itself in its own right is by creating a feminine paradise. You see this sometimes in women's clubs where the women sit together and talk about their little concerns, ignoring or excluding the man's world. You can see it also in families where the mother and daughters get together and play among themselves, scorning the father and brothers a little, saying that men must get out of the kitchen; men are big babies, or fools. In the same way that men have clubs to reinforce their self-esteem and role in society, there is no reason why women should not have a parallel in which they can assert their femininity in their own right and realize their differences from men and their different needs.

There are primitive tribes where young men are initiated into men's secret societies and young women into women's secret societies. The men learn certain men's arts, such as speaking in council and the use of weapons, and the women learn weaving and certain feminine arts and are instructed in feminine adult behavior and love magic. In Greece there was a cult of the goddess Artemis of Brauron, who was a bear goddess. Young girls of good families were given to serve the goddess from their twelfth to sixteenth year. In the awkward time when girls are just as difficult to keep at home as boys, they were given into the service of the goddess. They behaved like tomboys—neither washed nor cared for themselves in any way, spoke roughly, and were called bear cubs. Thus the bear cub societies of the mother goddess served to reinforce the feminine under the veil of protection. In this way, the feminine personality could develop unharmed by the problem of sexuality and go into life with a certain amount of maturity, gained in security under the bearskin. Otherwise, often only half-developed girls would fall into sexual life and at thirty would be old and worn out. Naturally, such women cannot develop anymore mentally, for the vital substance is exhausted; they are just tired old women.

Particularly if girls have a rather delicate, feminine nature underneath do they hide it behind tomboy manners. I taught boys and girls of that age for a long time, and observed that the girls who wore such bearskins were much more alert and interested in school and that their marks went down as soon as they started a love life, dating boys, and became more interested in love. Those to whom this happened later had a better chance of developing a certain amount of personality than those who went into the other side too early.

If the feminine group clings together and makes a certain hedge against the masculine principle, it is not, *eo ipso,* always negative, but rather reinforces the feminine so that the two can meet on a better level later on. One must not forget that there is not only the great attraction of the sexes, but they are genuine opposites which have always threatened each other—the women pulling the men into their feminine ways, and vice versa. That forms a kind of constant tension between men and women which is not abnormal; the otherness makes the attraction.

In our society women were more concerned with their neighbors, with births, deaths, and marriages, with the personal things. It is their task to create the atmosphere of connectedness between those near at hand, while the men must know of what is happening outside and take measures to meet the world. One meets with this in Chinese philosophy too. In chapter 20 of the *I Ching* you will find that to look through the crack of the door is right for a woman but harmful for a man. To look at things narrowly or intimately is not shameful for a woman, for that is her natural outlook, but a man should have wider and more objective interests, and look at things from a wider angle. In China, therefore, there is the same distribution of areas of interest. An only feminine world lacks the breadth of horizon. It is too narrow and personal if not in contact with the masculine principle. Everybody knows what happens if you have flocks of woman together—girls' schools, and homes for nurses. One thinks of the enormous tower which was built in Zurich for nurses—only for female nurses! Think of the atmosphere in girls' schools where the girls congregate together and discuss the teacher's tie, etc. The story illustrates the feminine scene—innocent and charming in its own way but it lacks the other side.

The woman with a positive mother complex naturally tends to have self-assurance and those personal interests her mother had, but also, naturally, there are the dangers and disadvantages. Here there is a normal development. On a winter's day the bear, the fourth element, walks in. We should therefore look at the symbolism of the bear. I have been told that if you skin a bear and hang it up in a butcher's shop, which is something people used to be able to see, it looks exactly like a clumsy human being. This simple fact may account for the projection that bears are bewitched or cursed human beings. Everywhere in folklore the bear tends to be the bewitched prince, or the man who has been cursed to walk about in a bearskin.

Among the followers of Wotan there were the Berserks (*beri* = bear, *serkr* = skin or shirt: bearshirts). To "go berserk" was thought to be a gift in certain families. If a battle was taking place and the duke or the count sat at home, suddenly he would give a terrific yawn and then fall into a deathlike sleep, while on the battlefield there appeared a bear who killed everybody. After a while the bear disappeared, and the duke woke up and was very tired. He had "gone berserk" and in the form of an exteriorized soul, a bear's soul, had fought the battle. These Berserks were looked on as the ghost-bears who did great deeds, and the proof that it really was the duke himself was that the bear was wounded in the right paw, and the man when he woke up at home was wounded in his right hand. In olden times in Germany this was looked upon as a positive quality inherited in certain families, but later this changed, and now to "go berserk" has a negative implication and means to be capable of getting into a great rage which touches on an ecstatic religious experience. That is why many people do not want to give in to their fits of rage. When one is in a rage, one feels possessed by the plentitude of life; one has a feeling of completeness and of being one with one's own purpose; one has no further doubts or uncertainties and one feels warmed through. It is like a stove on a cold winter's day! One can work oneself into a feeling of being fully and marvelously alive and afterward say, "*I* told them." Waking up from the ecstasy and paying the bill is less pleasant. Then one feels less divine, and a bit awkward! It is only in anger that we really know what anyone thinks of us; only in anger do we give voice to our true opinions.

Giving up the capacity for expressing one's rage is as hard as giving up any other neurotic symptom; for people are often in love with their berserk quality and won't give it up in order to become sober and reasonable. The idea of holy wrath was even admitted in Christianity, where it was permitted, for instance in the Crusades where one fought for Christ, or for the priest who might work himself into a holy rage in the fight against sin and wickedness. That, of course, is an excuse to continue the berserk rage. Rage is just barbaric, but it still exists in us all, and if a nation is unjustly attacked, the whole nation will rise up in a so-called holy rage. Should one get into such a rage if one is really seriously attacked? Are there times in life when it is justifiable? The question is connected with your deepest outlook on life. Has a person the right to defend himself in certain crucial moments? From the Christian standpoint it is generally not permissible, since Christians should be only good, but it is another question when it comes to fighting Nazism and the like. There one comes to a place where it is a question of religious conviction. One has to make up one's mind and stand by that.

Our decision will depend on the image we have of God. If we believe that God is only good, it is clear that we should be only good, but if we think of a black as well as a white side of God, then the blackness has its meaning too. That might mean that one had the right, that it is instinctively right to use claws and teeth if really unjustly attacked. A son devoured by his mother may be a decent fellow who tries to be reasonable and says that he is grown up and wants to go out with a girl and have a flat of his own. But the mother won't give in, even though the son suggests that she should see his analyst, which she refuses to do. She does all she can to destroy him. Has he not the right to say that he intends to walk out? She will call him cruel and wicked, but the onlooker will see that it is a matter of life and death for the son, who has the right to be harsh. It is not necessary for him to "go berserk," but in the innermost corner of the personality something rises up and the fight *is* necessary. If people have no conviction of their right to live, you can get them nowhere in an analysis. There is such a thing as having the right to defend oneself and to fight not to be overthrown by the animus of the mother or some other wickedness in the surroundings, and those who cannot do it are really sick.

Christ himself was not so lamblike as some people like to pretend. There are indications of this, such as the fact that he "brought a sword" and that the sin against the Holy Ghost was not forgiven.

A world in which nothing on the harsh side is ever allowed, is not on the side of life, and here we come to a typically feminine problem. The more feminine a woman is, and the less aggressive her animus, the more she will tend to be overrun by her surroundings. You probably know such gentle daughters in families who have always done what father and mother wanted and who did not marry. They nursed their parents until they died and then took care of other people's children. If they tried to get married, all the family was against it, saying that they could not be spared.

Such women, with their gentleness and femininity, are just killed, run over by a truck, and they are the fools. In modern life this is not so frequent, for the poison of being aggressive has gotten into women, but formerly there were many women of this nature. In Berlin one used to speak of "Tante Einsprung" (the aunt ready to jump in and help). She was an institution in practically all families to be phoned when anybody was ill and to be at everybody's beck and call—the poor old maid, just called upon whenever wanted, and whom everybody looked down upon while making use of her. Though it is a great thing for a woman not to be aggressive, she can be too one-sidedly feminine, and then she is out of life and will not be able to cope with it. The one-sidedly feminine world, where everything is so gentle and rosy and nobody quarrels, needs the bear. He comes in wintertime and is a good-natured animal; but later, when he catches the dwarf, he kills it with one blow of his paw. Though not a disagreeable animal, he knows they have come to the end of the road and that it is the right time to take action and put a stop to the dwarf's nonsense. That is the turning point of the story, where the bear instinctively kills the dwarf, over whom the girls have been sentimental.

So it is the question of integrating the masculine side into the feminine world without going a step too far, and that is a great problem. A woman who wakes up after being too passive, too feminine, faces the possibility of being too aggressive. But no one hits the bull's-eye the first time; it takes practice, and the fact that she at first shoots wide of the mark accounts for the many typical exaggerations, when too little or too much aggression and insufficient adaptation are replaced by outbursts of affect.

The bear illustrates the ideal reaction. He has not been bad-tempered and angry like the dwarf, who worked himself up into a rage and a state of constant irritation. He simply kills his enemy when he meets him, in contrast to the weak, nasty irritation shown by the dwarf. In a woman, the bear and the dwarf would represent two animus figures. The dwarf always reacts in the wrong way, being irritated and irritating those around him. He perpetually creates little quarrels all over the place over any little stupidity—a nail or a louse! These little irritations flame up, and everybody gets caught in them; the voice rises or drops, and everyone around jumps in. The dwarf does a whole series of idiotic things—catches his beard in the tree and in the fishing line. If a dwarf—who in mythology is supposed to be a good craftsman—does not know how to free his beard and catch a fish without getting entangled, he deserves what he gets. The girls should have laughed and left him.

So we have a marvelous picture of the annoying and irritating side that a woman's animus can produce. It shows how a grown-up, intelligent woman can entangle herself in such a silly idiotic quarrel or discussion. The irritated animus loses his sense of humor and is ungrateful and full of power. The dwarf demands that the two girls get him out of his entanglements, and then he shouts at them. His demands on them are annoying, which is also a classical aspect of the negative animus. Everything is formulated from the hidden standpoint of having the right and the need to be served. It is the compensation for the too yielding feminine nature of "Tante Einsprung," who is always ready to say yes. The dwarf is an overcompensating figure of the girls' sweetness who is completely egotistical and ungrateful and who, in a nasty way, compensates their exaggerated femininity. But the dwarf had to come up; they could not get to the prince without him as an intermediary. The early suffragists inevitably got into such exaggerated attitudes and were overmasculine and egotistical in their demands. One cannot get to the right instinctive balance at once. It has to come by detour and by first suffering the overcompensating attitude.

If one makes a study of dwarfs, one will find that ninety-five percent of their nature is positive. They collect treasures, are wonderful goldsmiths, can weave, make golden goblets, and are great craftsmen. In folklore, children who are blessed by being born on a Sunday go to the dwarfs' hill and are given hats which make the wearer invisible, or invisible fetters like silk, by which even dragons can be fettered.

Allwis was the one who knew everything in German mythology. The Kabiri in Greek and Cretan mythology were the companions of the Great Mother. They were smiths and craftsmen; thus dwarfs are extremely positive and creative figures. They refer to the creative impulses of the unconscious, so one very rarely comes across destructive dwarfs in mythology. Only in the German story "Rumpelstiltskin," there is a wicked, destructive dwarf who twice tries to steal the child, though he has also helped the miller's daughter to spin gold out of straw. Then he suddenly develops his other side and has to be destroyed. Dwarfs have a lot to do with the feminine world and occur more frequently in women's than in men's dreams. They often represent the first creative impulses in the unconscious and some kind of creative activity still hidden in the womb of nature.

If a dwarf who, *per definitionem*, is such a good craftsman, is very clumsy, as he is in our story, then he is a contradiction in himself and should not exist. He demonstrates an irritating quality, which is typical for unlived creativity. If a woman has this "hit the ceiling," irritating animus, it is generally a sign that she really has creative gifts that she has not yet used. The overflow of the creative energy is not rightly employed and therefore gets into destructive mischief and entanglements. Such women have destructive effects, and the cure is in some creative activity in which the dwarf can come into his own and do something where he really does know how to work.

Many women who have worked with Jung engaged themselves in some kind of creative work, and people sometimes resent this because they think it is something artificial and looks like occupational therapy. But if you look more closely at such situations, you will see that it is not necessarily a case of outer ambition but what the animus needs to do. If the woman does not help her animus, he goes off and creates mischief. He must have his chance to live. It really means complying with the unconscious needs.

The bear gets into a holy rage, which can be negative or positive. Only if one gets into such a rage that it becomes a cold rage is it dangerous, and it can mean murder, for then the climax of the rage has become silent and cold. In Greek, *arctos*, the word for "bear," takes the feminine article. It is the animal of the mother goddess Artemis in Greek mythology and according to medieval writers is also the animal of the Virgin Mary. In a matriarchal situation naturally it would be an aspect of the animus and, in general, have a more positive aspect. The bear knows why he acts as he does; there is no trembling or panic of uncertainty. If one knows that this time one's aggression is in the right place, one does not need to shout; the element of rage has been transformed, there is calm, and the rage has been integrated.

Usually, when one is in a rage, one feels that it is holy, for subjectively one feels right, and for this reason it is very tricky to find out whether it is really right or one only thinks so. In mythology the gods' rage was not always holy. Think of Ares in the Trojan war, or the goddess Kali in India, who might slaughter a few thousand people and drink blood on the battlefields, or Hathor in Egypt, who goes off into the desert and kills everyone and has to be pacified with beer. Then, when she is drunk, she is peaceful again.

In our language a mythological god is an archetype, and an archetype is always at the same time an instinctive pattern. For the archetype of the mother, the biological basis would be motherhood; for the archetype of the *coniunctio,* it would be sex. You could refer every god to a biological instinctive dimension; the god represents its meaning, or spiritual aspect. One could say that every instinctive dynamism is correlated with an archetypal image. Thus gods are representations of general complexes. Ares, or Mars, is an image of the instinct of aggression and self-defense in nature. In animal life, self-defense and aggression and fear dominate a whole part of life, and we are not exempt from this. Every archetypal god image is a dynamic, explosive load of psychic energy and humanly uncontrollable. Here, however, that great power is in its right measure: with a powerful stroke of his paw the bear puts an end to the destructive mischief of the dwarf.

5

The girls have pity for the dwarf, by which they only harm themselves and their future bridegroom. The same motif crops up in the story of "Amor and Psyche" in Apuleius' novel, *The Golden Ass*. When Psyche has to go into the underworld, she is told that there will be an old man in the waters of the Styx who will ask for help, but that she must try to remain firm and not help him. Women often overdo maternal pity; I call it the Salvation Army sentimentality. To be immediately moved by something helpless and in difficulties, anything up against the wall and cornered, belongs to the archetype of the maternal instinct, and such things always arouse a woman's pity. But every virtue, if overdone, is against instinct and can become its own opposite. Again and again one sees how women suffer unconsciously through the virtue of pity.

As an analyst, it has often happened to me that when I had cornered a patient, one of my feminine colleagues would ring me up and say, "Have a little pity." And I had to reply, "No, no pity!" Pity can have a completely destructive effect, keeping the person infantile. Women should check their natural maternal impulses and cultivate a certain amount of objectivity and detachment, which would enable them to see what is really good for the other person.

Another aspect which one meets with very often and which is at the back of many conflicts is that a woman may have a husband or lover of the type of the dwarf—that is, who is neurotic, or suicidal, or a sadistic kind of man with a negative mother complex. But every time the woman has had enough of it and wants to tell the man the truth and to clear out, pity for the poor fellow overcomes her and she cannot "let him down." If the dreams agree, you can say, "Throw him out!" But usually there is a projection of the woman's destructive animus onto the man. Even if there is no man on the outside to torture her, the woman will get it from within, for when she is alone her animus assures her that she is lonely and nobody and nothing and will never get anywhere—the sadist within tells her that. Therefore the two contact each other again, for to have it outside seems better than to have it inside. So one gets nowhere!

Pity for the outer figure really means indulging in one's own blind spot. People want neither to realize that they have such a figure within themselves nor to put an end to it. So the situation gets twisted into having pity for the outer figure and self-indulgence in one's blind spot. That is the wrong kind of pity. It occurs much less frequently with men, though it does happen with them too.

The heroine in fairy tales often makes the mistake of showing the wrong kind of pity, thus letting loose destructive powers. It is typical for a woman to have Salvation Army ideas for the wrong people. Of course there are rotten things in society that should be eliminated, but this type of woman often attaches herself to that which cannot be changed and, in a sense, actually lives off it. An example of this is the widespread problem of the martyr wife and the drunken husband.

I know of a family in which there were several sons. Both father and grandfather were heavy drinkers, and the sons, with one exception, were the same. The nondrinker had a disagreeable wife, and the first time he came home drunk she told him that if that happened again she would divorce him. She was the only one to save her husband from the destructive family pull. All the others had nicer, better-natured wives, but they showed the wrong kind of pity, with which they contributed to the destruction of their own husbands. Some maternal women sit on the china egg, like the dummy egg given to swans, always hoping to hatch out the phoenix—but only a big stink results! There is a crucial time in woman's individuation when she must liberate herself from inappropriate pity.

The destructive dwarf is also a thief who steals the bear's treasures. Technically, this destructive kind of animus steals the possibilities, the treasures and values of the positive animus. The very maternal woman adores mothering a young man—the misunderstood genius—to whom she will give the mother love he never got at home. A woman of fifty lived alone in her flat and took up with a young man of twenty who had had a hard time in his youth and who had cheated with money and forged checks. She was filled with pity for the poor fellow, because he had had such a horrible youth, and she let him live in her flat for nothing. She gave him employment in her business, where he cheated again and accumulated fifty thousand francs in debts on her account. But that was not enough, she still did not go to the law but covered it up and pardoned him again, because he cried and said he was ashamed of what he had done. Then he lived with a girl for a time in her house, and then started putting arsenic into the older woman's food.

That was a striking instance of pity in the wrong place, pity which amounted to absolute stupidity. She was a very intelligent woman, but the unhappy, unmarried type who does not know where to apply her maternal feelings and wastes them on such a creature. There the values of the positive animus, which the woman could have used, had she been more objective, were wasted—her greatest values and her capacity of understanding. The fairy tale says that this is because she has such a negative animus herself.

We must assume that the woman who wasted her money on the crook and murderer had such an animus herself. People are blind outside and look so decent that it needs a lot of actual police work to discover the same figure within them, but you will find it if you make a direct attack by saying, "Now, put your foot down and throw him out." Then it is interesting to see how, at the crucial moment, the woman will begin to lie, so that you discover the crook within. It transpires that there is a very subtle kind of self-deception going on, for all instinctive warnings against the thief have been overlooked. It is impossible for a normal woman to live beside a man like that without becoming suspicious. So she deceives herself—the crook animus refuses to listen to the warnings and the hunches she gets from the unconscious. It is highly symbolic that it is a man who poisons her slowly: the wrong ideas of the animus give her the daily small doses of poison. In analyzing such a case, sooner or later there is a showdown, and the woman has to face that she is lying to herself and not listening to the warnings.

The *puer aeternus* type of man is often a crook who deceives maternal women. Such men are cruel and destructive to them. Most men with a positive mother complex are lazy, for the mother is the symbol of matter, and matter is, among other things, inertia. The positive mother is like a big feather coverlet which always incapacitates the man, who will naturally tend to be lazy. As a boy he does not do well at school and will not equip himself by work and study. He lacks the ability to face the fight in life, or earn enough money, and then later comes the tendency to become a crook and to ask the woman he loves or the insurance company to pay for him.

Stealing is an ambiguous, double-faced factor. In itself, it is comprehensible, for the thief is the man who has the good instinct to get what he wants, which shows a healthy attitude. For to want something is natural and healthy and helps to keep one alive and able to enjoy life. But what is wrong about theft is that it is an infantile shortcut brought about by laziness, from the inability to work and save money to get what one wants.

All those neurotic people who cheat their way into high positions without any real work or action come into this category. There are thieves and robbers even in the government, where high positions have been obtained by trickery—through an aunt or uncle, perhaps. Such men have intrigued like women. In a woman you can say, *mutatis mutandis,* that it is a similar thing: there is an animus figure who wants to get things by a shortcut. The maternal woman who nearly got poisoned wanted to escape loneliness, to have contact with people, and to find an object for her maternal feelings. But she cheated herself into thinking that this young murderer was all right. If she had thrown him out, she would have been back again with her own problem and would have had to figure out a way to get what she wanted legitimately, and that would have taken a lot of effort of feeling and thinking, so she preferred to spill her mother's milk on the crook. That is the mechanism of cheating oneself.

Every dark thing one falls into can be called an initiation. To be initiated into a thing means to go into it. The first step is generally falling into the dark place and usually appears in a dubious or negative form—falling into something, or being possessed by something. The shamans say that being a medicine man begins by falling into the power of the demons; the one who pulls out of the dark place becomes the medicine man, and the one who stays in it is the sick person. You can take every psychological illness as an initiation. Even the worst things you fall into are an effort at initiation, for you are in something which belongs to you, and now you must get out of it.

Why does the nasty dwarf get entangled with his beard? The beard is mentioned in many fairy tales. You know the story of Bluebeard, the great woman murderer. You could say that that was a wonderful image of the destructive murderous animus par excellence. There is also the tale of King Thrush-Beard, which shows the transformation of the negative into the positive animus. A third story is another Grimm's tale called "Oll Rinkrank," in which a king does not want his daughter to marry, so he builds a glass mountain and says that any suitor must first walk over the mountain. All those who try to do this disappear. Then a prince comes whom the princess says she will help, and they go together to the glass mountain, but the princess falls into a ravine and disappears. In the mountain lives a devil called Rinkrank, the old Red Knight. This old man forces the princess to call him her husband, and he calls her his wife. He is with her during the daytime and goes out stealing in the night and returns with sacks full of pearls. After a time the princess has enough of it. When he puts his head in through the open window, she catches his beard and says she will not let him go until he promises to set her free, which he is obliged to do, and she marries her prince.

Here when the beard is caught it is positive, while in our main story it is negative. In the one instance, the animus is set free; and in the other, he is caught. So what is the beard? The hair which grows on the different parts of the body is reminiscent of our animal nature; it is the remains of the fur which we have lost and which most other animals still have. Hair evokes the idea of something primitive and instinctive and animal-like, but the meaning varies according to the part of the body on which the hair appears. The hair on the head carries the projection of unconscious involuntary thoughts and fantasies, because these grow out of our heads.

In a certain African tribe the initiation of a young man before he can be married consists not only in circumcision and instruction in tribal matters, but also in the creation of a headdress. He has to go into the desert and construct his own headdress. This consists of innumerable little plaits made out of his hair, into which he introduces sticks and shells. At night the neck is supported so as to leave the head free because this wonderful coiffure has to remain day and night. Until this cathedral, or temple of hair is constructed, he may not marry—that is, he has to acquire spiritual maturity and to have his own point of view. His task is to express in symbolic form his whole spiritual being, after which he is an adult member of his tribe. He must not only be sexually but also mentally mature, and that is expressed by the construction he builds with his own hair on his head.

The Freudians argue that Delilah castrated Samson by cutting off his hair. But did she actually do that? In cutting off his hair, Delilah destroyed Samson's soul or his creative conceptions, his thoughts and ideas, and therefore castrated him in a psychological sense. A woman can make a man completely stupid so that he loses his creative power. In medieval times of chivalry, a knight might not *verliegen* (lose by lying too long). If a medieval knight gave up his deeds and masculine adventures and stayed with his lady in the castle, then she had caught him, for he remained at home with his beloved and so lost all his ideals and enterprise and further spiritual development. This is what happened to Samson; he lost his masculinity in this way.

But what is the beard? It stands for something involuntary; it is the growth around the mouth. Thoughts and words bubble out of the mouth without your ever having thought them—they talk themselves. Automatic nervous talking is a typically neurotic symptom especially of women, though not only of women. A kind of constant nervous talking goes on and on, but without anything being said. "Brain declutched, mouth running on automatic," says a proverb from Berlin. It goes on continually and is completely automatic; it is a logos flow which is quite uncontrolled and unconscious and creates a lot of trouble. Language invites such a thing. The grammatical structure of a language affords the suggestion; that is, if you begin a sentence in a certain way it is difficult not to end it typically. A French teacher once remarked to me that the *clarité* (clarity) of the French language was a disadvantage, for it invited you to let the words make sentences on their own—the sentences begin and end in a classical way.

I caught myself in this once. During my studies, I one day happened to see an elderly woman in a hallway giving her hand in a sad and tragic manner to a young man, who looked a bit embarrassed. I thought to myself that it was probably the end of a love relationship and friendship. I knew neither of the two. Later, this woman and I attended the same course and got talking. Afterward we had a cup of coffee together, and I spoke of building something. Looking into her cup, the woman said, "You are building up," and "it" replied, "And you are pulling down!" She had begun a sentence, and I had just finished it! She asked why I had made that reply, and I explained that I had not meant anything, that the sentence had been left suspended and I had just finished it. But she pressed me so much, saying that I must have something in mind, that in the end I told her the impression I had gotten from what I had seen, whereupon she asked if I were a fortune-teller! It had been the great tragedy of her life. I blamed myself there for having spoken so thoughtlessly.

That is the animus beard, the thoughts which bubble out unconsciously. Jung has told a story of a husband who suffered so much from his wife's scenes, but the wife could never be convinced afterward that she had said the things. Her husband once made a recording without her noticing it and in a favorable moment played it back to her. She swore she had not said the things, in spite of the recording of her own voice. "It" had talked, not she as a conscious person; the things had said themselves. Seen from the feminine angle, she was right in saying that she had not said them. That is an aspect of the animus, the wordiness of the animus, in fairy tales expressed as the demon's beard. You have to pin him down, as in "Oll Rinkrank," and say, "I will only let you out on such-and-such a condition." The beard has to be pinned down. One has to ask oneself, "Who was talking, if it was not I?" One can best catch the animus at work in such thoughtless talk. In our story, the dwarf entangles himself. He catches himself, and the only thing for the girls to do would be to leave him in his own trap.

When the animus is rattling off on the wrong track, he generally contradicts himself. He generally gets caught out by the unconscious flow of thought. It would be sufficient to leave him there and realize that one has contradicted oneself and detach from it and say, if I can contradict myself so terribly, then I must find out what I really mean. If I do not know what I really want, I say this and that. Then it would be a question of stopping and saying that I had been contradicting myself and must stop and see what I really meant. But the girls pull the dwarf out, and he goes on doing the same thing. But here, in the end, the bear destroys the dwarf— that is, an animus-inspired emotional reaction in the woman herself. Usually women in the end get slowly sick of their own negative animus. If they don't, they can probably never be cured— but a normal woman usually gets sick of her neurotic side and one day puts an end to it.

At the end of the story the bear marries Snow White, and a brother of his, who suddenly turns up, marries Rose Red. The story ends with the motif of the marriage quaternity—which in Jungian terms is a symbol of the totality. In *The Practice of Psychotherapy,* in his paper on the transference, Jung speaks at great length on this subject.[15] He shows there that the archaic sociological pattern of cross-cousin marriage serves to hold the society together in a balanced form. This pattern is no longer valid, but it returns within us on a higher level. In every couple relationship there are actually four figures involved: the man and his anima, and the woman and her animus. In alchemical symbolism they appear as the alchemist and his woman friend, and the king and queen in the retort. Only when the two partners can relate to all these figures can one speak of a complete relationship, and therefore love in modern terms becomes a vehicle of the process of individuation and the development of higher consciousness.

In our story there are two male figures: the dwarf and the bear. If the dwarf had not been such a nasty creature, one of the girls could have married him, and the other, the bear. But the former is replaced by the bear's brother. We might ask whether this brother might not be the dwarf transformed.

When someone dies in a dream, it shows that that specific personification is coming to an end. The psychological energy invested in it will appear on a different level, though sometimes, unfortunately, it reappears on the same level. How many people dream that a shadow has died, but unfortunately it is still alive and appears again. But if one can succeed in bringing the transformed energy onto another level, the figure stops functioning in this way, or forever. Here the transformation seems to have taken place, for the dwarf disappears and the two girls find the two bridegrooms.

The mother is the fifth figure; she represents the matrix in which the totality forms. To a certain extent the totality is still in the vessel, in the matrix of Mother Nature; this means that an instinctive possibility has constellated in the unconscious, which indicates possible progress. When somebody has a dream with a positive solution, within the layer of instinctive life possibilities, such a possibility is constellated. One is now fishing in waters where there are fish, whereas before there were none.

A positive dream shows in what direction one should fish and that there is a fish to be caught. But naturally there is still the slip between the cup and the lip—between the positive dream and the concrete realization. At least progress has taken place if you know where the pond is, and where the fish is. If a cross-cousin marriage occurs at the end of a fairy tale, and it does relatively often, this does not mean that modern man has realized psychologically what it means. For the moment this motif is more like a program for the future, the image of a goal which has not yet been realized. It is an intuitively perceived goal, but there is still a long way to go until we will understand it fully. We have to realize that an intuition is not yet a fact.

A hedgehog had a race with a hare. But the hedgehog took his wife, who looked just like him, and put her at the other end, and every time the hare arrived at the end of a lap, the hedgehog said, "Here I am!" In the end the hare died, worn out! The intuitive puts a bit of his intuition at the end of the race. He generally marries a sensation type, the slow type, and if this partner one day says, "I have realized something; I have noticed such-and-such," the intuitive replies, "I told you that five years ago!" which is probably true, thus taking all the wind out of the other's sails. But the intuitive should be careful, for he is always in the place of the hedgehog's wife, taking intuition for realization.

Why did the dwarf get his beard entangled in his instruments—the tree and the fishing line? It looks like pure stupidity, but even such little details are quite meaningful. I have often observed that women who make a first attempt to use their mind, say at the university, show an animus especially inclined to mix up the instrument of the mental work and its meaning. It is typical for a kind of half-baked animus. Such women will learn bibliographies or lexicons or certain grammatical rules by heart and get absolutely lost in that. It is as though they could not get beyond the instrument. I know of a woman who for forty-five years collected certain indications on excavated bricks by which one could draw conclusions as to the layer, or the age, to which they belonged. Thus she made a very important archaeological contribution, but she had put her whole mental activity into this detail and could not get beyond it.

In any kind of study you have to have your instruments. But if the study is to become meaningful, it has to have a revivifying effect on the mind. Particularly at the end of the nineteenth century, nearly every German scientist got stuck in such introductory studies. Not only preliminary studies were made, but pre-studies to pre-studies. You cannot talk about a subject without a certain preliminary study, but one should not lose sight of the fact that it is only the instrument. Paderewski, the president of Poland, related that a competition was once started for which everybody had to write a book on the elephant. A Frenchman went to the zoo and then wrote a booklet entitled *L'Eléphant Amoureux*. After plenty of vodka, a Russian wrote a book entitled *L'Eléphant, existe-t-il?* ["Does the Elephant Exist?"] An American wrote a book with a lot of figures and photographs called *Bigger and Better Elephants.* The German never looked at an elephant at all, but went to all the libraries and then wrote ten volumes entitled *Introductory Pre-Remarks to the Study of the Elephant.*

That is what getting entangled in the fishing line means. Since the mind of woman is a kind of natural mind, it easily gets caught in techniques because they are new to it. I have seen innumerable studies in which the female writers have become entangled in their fishing lines, and then have given up because they could not get away from the problem. Their professors had told them to learn this and that, but they could never realize that that was only the instrument. Such difficulty is the symptom of a primitive and not a developed mind. You find it among primitive women who have not yet developed their animus, or the man who has not developed his anima. When the man's mind is in the course of awakening, it generally goes through this phase of entanglement and needs a thorough realization that a further awakening is necessary. Women take the instrument for the goal of the study, a typical error which keeps them from their creativity but makes them useful to men. They are good secretaries for creative men, for then they need this function. They collect, and the man gratefully uses the material, but then the woman is reduced to collecting for the man and can never be creative herself.

The dwarf who entangles himself is an image of the negative animus in woman, who is, however, in the story eliminated by the bear, the positive animus. This leads us to the next story, which centers totally on the theme of the destructive animus.

The Girl without Hands[16]

Synopsis of the Tale

A miller had fallen by degrees into great poverty until he had nothing left but his mill and a large apple tree. One day, when he was going into the forest to cut wood, an old man, whom he had never seen before, stepped up to him and said, "Why do you trouble yourself with chopping wood? I will make you rich if you will promise me what stands behind your mill."

The miller thought to himself that it could be nothing but his apple tree, so he said yes and concluded the bargain. The other, however, laughed derisively and said, "After three years I will come and fetch what belongs to me."

As soon as the miller got home, his wife asked him the origin of the sudden flow of gold that was coming to the house. The miller told her that it came from a man he had met in the forest, to whom in return he had promised what stands behind the mill. "For," said the miller, "we can very well spare the great apple tree."

"Ah, my husband," exclaimed his wife, "it is the Evil Spirit whom you have seen. He did not mean the apple tree, but our daughter, who was behind the mill sweeping the yard."

The miller's daughter was a beautiful and pious maiden, and during all the three years lived in the fear of God. When the day came for the Evil One to fetch her, she washed herself quite clean and made a circle around herself with chalk, so that he could not approach her. In a rage he said to the miller, "Take her away from all water, that she may not be able to wash herself; else have I no power over her." The miller did so, for he was afraid. But the next morning, when the Evil One came, the girl had wept upon her hands, so that they were quite clean. He was baffled again and in his anger said to the miller, "Cut off both her hands, or else I cannot now obtain her."

The miller was horrified and said, "How can I cut off the hands of my own child?"

But the Evil One pressed him, saying, "If you do not, you are mine, and I will take you yourself away!"

The miller told his daughter what the Evil One said and asked her to help him in his trouble and to forgive him for the wickedness he was about to do her. She replied, "Dear father, do with me what you will—I am your daughter." And her father cut her hands off.

For the third time now the Evil One came. But the maiden
had let fall so many tears upon her arms that they were both
quite clean. So he was obliged to give her up and after this lost
all power over her.

The miller now said to her, "I have received so much good
through you, my daughter, that I will care for you most dearly
all your life long."

But she answered, "Here I cannot remain. I will wander
forth into the world, where compassionate men will give me as
much as I require."

Then she had her arms bound behind her back and at sunrise
departed on her journey. In time she arrived at a royal garden,
and by the light of the moon she saw a tree which bore most
beautiful fruits. She could not enter the garden, for there was
water all around, but she was tormented by hunger, so she
kneeled and prayed to God. All at once an angel came down,
who made a passage through the water, so that the ground was
dry for her to pass over. So she went into the garden, but the
pears were all numbered. She stepped up and ate one to appease
her hunger, but no more. The gardener perceived her do it, but
because the angel stood by he was afraid, and thought the
maiden was a spirit.

The next morning the king found that a pear was missing and
asked the gardener whither it was gone. He replied, "Last night
a spirit came, who had no hands, and ate the pear with her
mouth."

The king then asked, "How did the spirit come through the
water? And whither did she go after she had eaten the pear?"

The gardener answered, "One clothed in snow-white garments came down from heaven and made a passage through the
waters, so that the spirit walked over on dry land. And because
it must have been an angel, I was afraid, and neither called out
nor questioned it; and as soon as the spirit had finished the
fruit, she returned as she came."

The king said, "If it be as you say, I will this night watch
with you."

As soon as it was dark, the king came into the garden,

bringing with him a priest. At about midnight the maiden crept out from under the bushes and again ate with her mouth a pear off the tree, whilst the angel clothed in white stood by her. Then the priest went toward her and said, "Art thou come from God or from earth? Art thou a spirit or a human being?"

She replied, "I am no spirit, but a poor maiden, deserted by all, save God alone."

The king said, "If you are forsaken by all the world, yet will I not forsake you," and he took her with him to his royal palace. Because she was so beautiful and pious, he loved her with all his heart, ordered silver hands to be made for her, and made her his bride.

After a year had passed, the king was obliged to go to war and left the young queen to the care of his mother. Soon afterward a boy was born, and the old mother wrote a letter to her son containing the joyful news. But the messenger rested and fell asleep on his way, and the Evil One changed the letter for another saying that the queen had brought a changeling into the world. As soon as the king had read this letter, he was frightened and much troubled, but he wrote to his mother that she should take great care of the queen until his arrival. But the messenger again fell asleep on the way and the Evil One put a letter in his pocket saying that the queen and her child should be killed. When the old mother received this letter, she was struck with horror and wrote another letter to the king, but received no answer. Rather, the Evil One placed another false letter for the mother into the messenger's pocket, saying that the mother should preserve the tongue and eyes of the queen as a sign that she had fulfilled the order.

The old mother was sorely grieved to shed innocent blood, so she cut out the tongue and eyes of a calf and said to the queen, "I cannot let you be killed as the king commands, but you must remain here no longer. Go forth with your child into the wide world and never return here again."

Thus saying, she bound the child upon the young queen's back, and the poor wife went away, weeping bitterly. Soon she entered a large forest, and there she fell upon her knees and prayed to God. The angel appeared and led her to a little cottage, over the door of which was a shield inscribed with the words: "Here may everyone live freely."

Out of the house came a snow-white maiden who said, "Welcome, Lady Queen," and led her in and said she was an angel sent from God to tend her and her child. In this cottage the queen lived for seven years and was well cared for; through God's mercy to her, on account of her piety, her hands grew again as before.

Meanwhile the king had come home again, and his first thought was to see his wife and child. Then his mother began to weep and said, "You wicked husband, why did you write me that I should put to death two innocent souls?" And showing him the two letters which the Evil One had forged, she continued, "I have done as you commanded," and she brought him the tokens—the two eyes and the tongue.

The king then began to weep so bitterly for his dear wife and son that the old mother pitied him, and said, "Be comforted, she lives yet! I caused a calf to be slain, from whom I took these tokens; but the child I bound upon your wife's back, and I bade them go forth into the wide world, and she promised never to return here because you were so wrathful against her."

"So far as heaven is blue," exclaimed the king, "I will go; and neither will I eat nor drink until I have found again my dear wife and child—if they have not perished of hunger by this time."

Thereupon the king set out, and for seven long years sought his wife in every stony cleft and rocky cave, but found her not—and began to think she must have perished.

But God sustained him, and at last he came to the large forest and little cottage. Out of the house came the white maiden, and leading him in, she said, "Be welcome, great king! Whence comest thou?"

He replied, "For seven long years have I sought everywhere for my wife and child, but I have not succeeded."

Then the angel offered him food and drink, but he refused

them both and lay down to sleep, and covered his face with a napkin.

Now went the angel into the chamber where sat the queen, with her son, whom she usually called "Sorrowful," and said to her, "Come down with your child. Your husband is here." So she went to where he lay, and the napkin fell from off his face.

So the queen said: "Sorrowful, pick up the napkin, and cover again your father's face." The child did as he was bidden, and the king, who heard in his slumber what passed, let the napkin again fall from his face.

At this the boy became impatient and said, "Dear mother, how can I cover my father's face? Have I indeed a father on the earth? I have learned the prayer, 'Our Father which art in heaven'; and you have told me my father was in heaven—the good God. How can I talk to this wild man? He is not my father."

As the king heard this, he raised himself up and asked the queen who she was. The queen replied, "I am your wife, and this your son, Sorrowful."

But when he saw her human hands, he said, "My wife had silver hands."

"The merciful God," said the queen, "has caused my hands to grow again"; and the angel, going into her chamber, brought out the silver hands and showed them to him.

Now he perceived that they were certainly his dear wife and child and kissed them gladly, saying, "A heavy stone is taken from my heart." After eating a meal together with the angel, they went home to the king's mother.

Their arrival caused great rejoicings everywhere; and the king and queen celebrated their marriage again and lived happily together until the end of their lives.

There are many international variations of the story in which the miller realizes that he has sold his own daughter to the devil, or to the evil spirit, or, as this variation says, to the Evil One. The motif of not having hands, as far as I have seen, is one that only occurs to heroines; it is very widespread and has different causes. Here it happens because the girl has been sold to the devil.

The theme of the miller is very ambivalent in folklore. Looked at from a naive angle, the peasant's angle, he is the only peasant who does not do any hard work, a primitive kind of Mercurius who has the trick of making water work for him. The use of water power is one of man's earliest inventions. Formerly, grinding had been done either by animals or slaves turning a stone going around and around, which was terrible work. The Greek word *mechane* means "trick," and the water mill is the technical trick by which the work is eased. There are innumerable stories in folklore in which there is a rich miller who exploits the hardworking peasants in the neighborhood by putting up the price of flour. He sets the price for both sale and repurchase; he knows the trick by which he can torment the primitive peasant, and is therefore at enmity with him. The peasants say: "He sits there and through his water trick can put up the price." He thus carries the projection of being the working devil and a power fiend.

On the other side, the invention of the water mill is a very ingenious one, both creative and clever, and the wheel is a mandala. So the miller is also a constructive figure, a Hermes-Mercurius, and belongs in that mythological family. In folklore, the benevolent miller—who stores the flour in times of plenty and gives out from the reserves in times of scarcity—often appears, and is then the benefactor of the country. So he can be said to have the mercurial quality of human consciousness, which can be used for good or evil. Here he has come to the end of his tether and therefore sells something to the devil; you could say that the devilish quality is very close. Though he acts half innocently, in a moment of difficulty he lets something within his realm fall into the devil's hands. This would refer to the misuse of intellectual consciousness for an unethical goal, which naturally is something which every intelligent person is tempted to do in a moment of difficulty. If you are stupid and honest and get into difficulties, then you need help; but if you are dishonest, you will help yourself and immediately the intellect, or this higher capacity of consciousness, is misused.

I do not wish to speak here of the demoralization through technology in our civilization—that you can think about for yourselves; but the problem is there constellated in its nucleus, the abuse of getting oneself out of a difficulty by a conscious trick. What we now lose on the scale is our own soul; we are doing the same thing as the miller, thinking that we are just sacrificing a bit of nature. We plan to build a new power station in the Alps, thinking that thereby we shall only lose a few trees and fields. We do not sufficiently realize our own carelessness in regard to nature and are selling our souls to the devil, whereby certain psychological values get lost. In a town the view does not vary. There are electric lights and cars and houses, but we miss the breathtaking moment of reality—the uncanny feeling of a dark, rainy night, or the beauty of a moonlit landscape—the ever-changing aspect of nature in its natural surroundings.

No longer have we a share in the emotional experiences of our ancestors, which have been a part of man since he first came into being: the full moon, the whistling of the wind in the trees, link us to instinct and the life of the unconscious past. There is a whole scale of emotion which enriches our lives and links us with our ancestry. Industrial technology steals that, and we never notice what we are losing unless we go back and pick up the threads, for at least a part of the year. Most people are conscious enough to be stirred by the loss of the apple tree and the meadows, but what is still much worse, and is linked up with the apple tree which we cut down, is all that life of the psyche which we destroy—those experiences which belong in the whole pattern of nature.

So, from the miller's standpoint, his daughter would represent his anima figure—that is, a part of his feeling and emotional life which is now sold to evil and falls into the devil's hands. If we take it from the feminine standpoint, one could say that this represents the case of a woman who through a negative constellation of her father complex has fallen into the greatest danger. What would it mean if the father sells his own daughter to the devil, because he is at the end of his resources? If a miller gets into such difficulties, it is the result of a general collective catastrophe where, with a thoroughly asocial attitude, he wants to save his own skin at the expense of others; or, if his difficulty is individual, then something must be wrong at his mill. He either overcharges or is a bad workman, or something like that. Otherwise why should he be in difficulty? In such a case, he should ask himself why his mill and his business are in such a bad way. Why is it only he who suffers, what has he done wrong, what laws of life has he ignored? It looks as though it was his own individual trouble. In parallel stories the miller is replaced by the figure of an old king who got stuck. This refers to the widespread motif of the king's need for renewal; he represents the central principle of collective consciousness which wears out periodically. In our story the father is not a king but a rich merchant, so he would more likely represent the commercial outlook of collectivity which has exhausted itself. All intellectual qualities of the human mind have the quality of wearing off after a certain time. One aspect of consciousness has been used too long and become routine, and then it becomes meaningless. Consciousness needs a certain regularity, but can degenerate into routine—and that entails a loss of soul.

Therefore the miller who slowly comes to the end of his usefulness could be a professor, a schoolteacher who abuses his abilities in the same way, or a carpenter. In any case the superior function is running down through routine. It might be a nurse, who can turn into a smiling automaton, who hands over the soup and takes the temperature; her kind nursing has become just a habit and a mechanical trick. She turns on the machine and underneath is deadly bored—a malady of the overuse of her extraverted feeling. So it is not only the man, but anywhere where mental activity has become a trick, which naturally runs down—then comes the devilish turn when the miller, instead of facing poverty and discovering something new, wants to continue in the old way, and therefore sells his daughter's soul to the devil. That is the wrong move. If a father does this, his anima and his eros faculties degenerate, and the daughter will grow up with a father who may be successful in business or science but will have no heart. He neglects her on the feeling side. He never talks or plays or flirts with her, which he should do to a certain extent, but has to carry on with his business and has no time for her.

A woman who has such a father has not been nourished by his eros function. In our story the daughter shows that such a woman is sold to the devil, which would mean that, since she was not nourished on the feeling side, a destructive, devilish intellectualism, a devilish animus of some sort, will take possession of her. She will either be very ambitious or very cold, or she may do the same thing as her father, continuing his life pattern in the calculating, cold way of her animus. The girl in the story reacts in a very typical way to such an inheritance by realizing that there is this negative possibility and trying to keep herself out of the terrible danger.

I am reminded of a typical case which illustrates my point. The father was a tremendously powerful businessman, very enterprising and active in politics, but cold as ice and with no married life at home and no love for the children. He went through the house like a bull or a thundercloud, without any human relationship; his eros was completely degenerated. When he died, his daughter took up various mental interests. She went in for art and tried to study philosophy. But every time she touched any field of masculine activity, she became completely manic. She took up philosophy and read books like mad, as though she were a machine; she was possessed by the devil. She was sensitive and tried to change, for she realized that this was all destructive and saw that the devil had gotten her. When she tried to play the piano, she got possessed by it and fell in love with her sadistic music master. She practiced day and night and he pushed her on. She lost all her friends and relationships, but, being more or less normal, she woke up to what was happening, realized the possession, and dropped it all. In the end she was not able to do anything. Whatever she did was done in a destructive way, so she developed into a completely passive, feminine personality. She had the choice either of falling into the devil's hands or of refraining from all activities—that is, of losing her hands. She passed forty years of her life in such passivity. It was like someone sitting up a tree with a monster waiting below. If she came down into life, she would be caught by the devil of ambition. In our story the girl chooses to keep clear of the devil, and to sacrifice participation in life, rather than fall into his hands.

6

The girl without hands has to suffer because her father did not solve his own problem decently, but avoided the conflict by selling her to the devil. Seen from a woman's standpoint, she is threatened by a terrible animus. As soon as she touches anything on the side of life activity she may fall into animus possession or a power drive and become as cold, ruthless, and brutal as her father was. All she can do is to keep right out of the life of the spirit.

That is what the girl in the story does. She cries so much that the devil cannot get at her. She protects herself by a pure attitude; the tears wash her hands and she remains clean, but the devil has tried to get her, and her father has had to chop off her hands. She is thus mutilated and unable to take up any activity in life, just like the woman who tried playing the piano and studying literature, but in such a possessed way that she could not go on.

The animus is a kind of primitive man, just as the anima in men is a kind of primitive woman who overdoes things and then collapses. Among primitive civilizations, human activities are not regularly distributed. There are times when they work like mad, hunt, or go to war with tremendous activity, but then they go to sleep for a long time. The irregular rhythm is typical for primitive man, and the animus in general tends to have such features, but where a powerful father complex is constellated, it is much worse.

The girl then leaves home, comes to a royal garden, and is so hungry that she wants to eat some of the pears. The gardener sees that she is not just an ordinary thief, as an angel stands by to protect her, and he tells the king, who finds her and marries her and gives her silver hands.

Remember that the father thought it was an apple tree he sold to the devil. Apples, mythologically, often have an eros connotation, and they also represent fruitfulness and the continuity of life. The king or father figure who owns an orchard, a tree, or a stable is an archetypal motif which comes in quite different connections when it illustrates masculine psychology: a fairy tale may say that a king has a beautiful garden in which there grow golden apples; he discovers that a golden bird steals one every night, and sends his sons to find out about it; or a sheik has a mare which produces a beautiful foal every year, but the invisible hands of a *div* come and steal it, and the sheik sends his three sons out on a complicated quest. The motif of the king who has a garden with beautiful fruit in it which invisible powers steal is very widespread. In general, as Jung says in his chapter on the king and queen in *Mysterium Coniunctionis*, the king represents the dominant content of collective consciousness, generally a God-image, and therefore is usually a symbol of the Self, but he is only a partial aspect of it, namely that which is relatively understood in collective consciousness.

Such representations of the Self, as seen in collective consciousness, always risk no longer expressing the totality of the Self, but only one or another aspect, just as individual consciousness is constantly threatened in that it does not adequately express the total psychological situation of the person. Life is so rich and continually changes so much that there would need to be great flexibility in consciousness to be capable of expressing all that is going on within. Consciousness is rarely capable of such an ideal condition and always tends to be too narrow, or to stay too long on one track, which is probably why we need dreams to keep us informed and adapted to the new conditions of life. The individual has constantly to adapt, as does collective consciousness. In mythology there are so often impotent or sickly or helpless and aged rather than brilliant kings, for these represent the no longer adapted collective attitude.

The thief is the personification of an unconscious factor that attracts energy from consciousness. If you are depressed, you get up in the morning in a bad mood, and everything begins to be boring and flat; something is stealing your energy. The primitive man who gets up in such a condition actually says that somebody has stolen the fat of his kidneys, or one of his souls, and he goes to the medicine man to find it again. These losses of energy and interest mean that life is fading from the realm of consciousness, which is generally due to a complex constellated in the unconscious that attracts the energy. In the conscious one feels bored and stale, while the dreams slowly become enriched. A lot of life has accumulated below, but you cannot pick it up. When the feminine aspect of the Self, or the anima, begins to damage or steal energy from collective consciousness, a kind of sullen opposition in the collective unconscious appears. This atmosphere of inertia indirectly forces the man to change his attitude. When a woman cannot make the evolution necessary to meet the situation, it is natural for her to adopt the feminine reaction of becoming nasty and sullen, and of spoiling the man's pleasure by always saying no. She ruins the atmosphere by a nasty passivity, at the back of which stands the half-unconscious intention of forcing the man to change.

Jung often quotes the Hopi creation myth in which it is told that the Hopis originally lived in deep layers below the earth. Every time a layer became overcrowded, the women would make the situation so intolerable that the men were forced to find a way of getting up into the next layer, so that the women, who did nothing themselves, by their nastiness forced the Hopi men into the world of consciousness. Another form of the same thing is when a woman begins to be very demanding on the feeling side. Because she did not receive enough feeling when young, there is a kind of psychological hunger which makes exorbitant demands on the man. This can go so far as to change into a constant infantile attitude; but otherwise, within bounds, it has quite a good effect on the relationship, because the man tends to be lazy in eros matters. If the woman does not put forward her claims, he may let things go, with the idea that he has more important things to attend to. But if the woman gives a reminder from time to time that she needs a certain amount of attention and care, this has a positive effect on the man's anima, which he will recognize if he pays close attention. Being unable to become active, the heroine in our story attracts the king's attention by stealing the fruit of his garden in this secret way.

Apples are generally looked upon as a masculine symbol and pears as a feminine symbol. One is reminded of an analogy to the Garden of Eden, where Eve was induced to steal the fruit and eat and give it to Adam. But there it is not the angel but the devil who gives it to her. As you know, in the story in Genesis, the apple stands for the knowledge of good and evil, which would make men equal to God; that is, to steal and eat the fruit would be to break into the realm of the divine totality, and it is the Promethean sin to want to go beyond the natural unconsciousness of Paradise—the sin of wanting to become conscious, which is resented by nature, or in this case by God. Later philosophies, and some of the Church Fathers, started to think a little bit differently about the story in the Bible. They said that if Eve had not eaten the fruit and given it to Adam, man would not have fallen into sin and been driven out of paradise. Then God would not have become man; Christ would not have been born and lived as a man and been crucified on earth. And since, from a Christian standpoint, that is the highest act of divine grace, one cannot help thinking that what happened to Eve in the Garden of Eden was a *felix culpa*—a fortunate sin, a sin with a favorable outcome.

In the medieval legend of the Holy Grail, there is in the story of Parsifal another contrast to the story of Adam. Parsifal does not transcend the taboo against gaining knowledge and ask about the Grail vessel. He asks neither about the king's wound nor of the service of the Grail vessel, because he had been told that to ask was childish. Parsifal there is likened to Adam and is often called the third Adam, in contrast to Adam primus and Adam secundus. His sin is in not asking, whereas the first Adam ventured into the realm of knowledge and ate of the fruit. This mirrors a slow transformation in man's attitude toward consciousness. It is as though now it is a sin not to become conscious, whereas originally it was felt that it was a sin to become conscious. In a different form, it is still a conflict for many people who, when talking of depth psychology and analysis, say that one should not dig up such things, one should let sleeping dogs lie, and that to follow one's common sense and the general rule would be enough, for to want to know more is to sin. But we know that to remain unconscious is also a sin against nature. If someone remains below his level, or pretends to know less than he should, feelings of guilt and other neurotic symptoms appear. We are still confronted with the paradox that it is a sin to become conscious and a sin to remain unconscious. Since we cannot remain in a state of innocence, it is a question of choice and attitude which sin we prefer.

Here certainly the theft in the king's garden has a positive result because it draws the king's attention to the girl, and he marries her and gives her silver hands—which are not as good as she gets later, but with which she can function halfway. Later she gives birth to a child but, when the king is away at the war, the letter that should announce the birth falls into the hands of the Evil One as well as the king's reply, with the result that the queen and her child are driven away into the forest. This exchange of letters has several variations, and generally it is not the devil who exchanges the letter, but the cruel mother-in-law does it because she is jealous.

Taken from one angle, you could say that the girl represents the type of woman who has to live a completely passive life and, in the positive sense of the word, only a feminine life, because she is threatened with falling into a pathological drive as soon as she leaves the frame of passivity. But the solution of keeping out of the devil's hands by keeping out of life is only a temporary one. Sooner or later the problem will return, and very often, as it does here, it comes up in marriage. Many young girls refrain from studying or developing their minds, because they rightly feel that if they did they would fall into animus possession and that would prevent them from marrying. But if the girl marries and her wish to develop her mind is not appeased, the problem will return. She has avoided animus possession and has married. But her secret longing also to develop the other side within her still remains, and very often a kind of unsatisfied restlessness and depression overcome her. So the devil reappears and this time interferes with the marriage situation.

In this part of the story, the negative father complex of the woman is confronted with the negative mother complex of her marriage partner. The girl is condemned to passivity and isolation, to inactivity in life, in order to save herself from the devil, but if she marries a man with a mother complex, the mother or the mother-in-law will interfere. Since the daughter-in-law is passive, rather lame, and incapable of taking a definite stand, the mother-in-law will step in and arrange, for instance, what has to be done for Christmas, and what the baby needs. The girl can do nothing about it, for the mother-in-law has stepped into a vacuum. Generally, the young girl is able to defend herself against the older woman, but if she has also to defend an inner area within herself, then she will not have the energy or ability to defend herself on the outside. It can be said that wherever the woman is forced into too great passivity in order to avoid her devil, she will become a martyr, for those around her will take advantage of her. The fact that she is too passive and isolated, and does not grab what she wants, attracts others to take advantage of the situation—the devil is attracted on the outside. But the pattern thus created has a meaning, for unless she were persecuted by her mother-in-law, she would never get her hands back and would have artificial hands to the end of her life. The action of the whole story circles around this problem.

If we interpret the king on a subjective level, not as the husband but as an inner figure in the heroine, he would represent a collective dominating positive spirit. The woman would then adopt all the prevailing ideas concerning religion and duty and behavior, and would live in accordance with collective standards. That would be replacing a personal attitude by a conventional one in which the woman would do the right thing, because that is what's done. She would behave normally, but without spontaneity. Her positive eros quality would not be fully alive. You can see this, for instance, in the case of women who have been injured either by a negative mother complex or a demonic father imago. They have difficulty bringing up their children, since they apparently lack spontaneous reactions toward them. Children bother or annoy them, for they have insufficient positive maternal instinct to accept the daily chores and routine of changing the baby's nappies and keeping the place tidy, and so forth.

From one standpoint children are terribly boring, but the woman with a normal mother instinct can take this in her stride. If she gets too mad, she can shout at the child and the thing will not go too far and will not get beyond the warmth of the maternal relationship. But the woman with the negative father or mother complex has an unredeemed negative side within her which would let her go too far. Because she cannot be spontaneous, she compensates by being an especially good mother, putting up with all the irritation of the children instead of exploding. Or the resistance may be unconscious and may cause such a mother to drop the child, for no reason—an unconscious murder act, which is even more frightening. They cannot admit to themselves that in a sense they hate the child. Rather, they overcompensate by reading books on how to bring up children and try to be as perfect as possible. Instead of spontaneity, collective standards are adopted.

Such a condition does not refer only to the bringing up of children. Wherever a woman has an unredeemed demonic side within her, all her activities connected with the eros relationship, with her husband and children, will be performed in an artificial way. What cannot be produced spontaneously is brought about by force of will, which leads to an unfortunate situation, according to the story. There is insufficient spontaneity, symbolized by the silver hands, which replace those which have been cut off. Instinct is replaced by the rule of the collective. But such people will be aware of a dead corner within them, of something unredeemed; and the restless seeking remains, as though the devil stirred in the background and would not leave them alone.

In our story the devil interferes again and works up a plot of misunderstandings between king and queen so that she is accused of having given birth to a changeling and is driven out to the forest, where she lives in a lonely hut, but protected by an angel. She is driven into nature, where she has to find the connection with her positive animus within, instead of functioning according to collective rules. She has to go into deep introversion. The forest could equally well be the desert, or an island in the sea, or the top of a mountain. She is cut off in the stillness of virgin country, which would imply that she has to retire into her own loneliness and must realize that, for though it looks as though she had a husband and children, or a job, she is not yet really alive. Most women, since they depend so much on relationship and long for it, have great difficulty in admitting to themselves how lonely they are and in accepting that as a given situation. To retire into the forest would be to accept loneliness consciously, and not to try to make relationships with good will, for that is not the real thing. According to my experience, it is very painful, but very important, for women to realize and accept their loneliness. The virgin soil would be that part of the psyche where there was no impact of collective human activities, and to retire to that would be to retire not only from all animus opinions and views of life, but from any kind of impulse to do what life seems to demand of one. The forest would be the place of unconventional inner life, in the deepest sense of the word. Living in the forest would mean sinking into one's innermost nature and finding out what it feels like. Vegetation symbolizes spontaneous life and offers healing to the woman destroyed by a negative animus or negative mother complex.

In many stories women badly injured by the negative animus or negative mother complex are persecuted not by the devil but by their stepmother. All the second half of this story is concerned with the negative mother complex and the demonic father as well— it is the same development. In both cases the girl is doomed to passivity and has to go back to the unhurt virgin ground in her soul. In practical life if you ask such a woman what she would do if she could rid herself of all the demands of outer life, usually she says despairingly that she does not know—she just feels like sitting on the edge of the bed and crying. You can ask if she would not like to talk to somebody, to listen to music, to contact friends, but there is nothing!

If one regresses into this primitive inner layer, it is because one cannot live on the ordinary level with other human beings. As long as one is on that level, one has to be a part of it. But the forest is the place where things begin to turn and grow again; it is a healing regression.

Thus the girl was forced to go into the forest and there met the angel. If there is such a zero point where life is reduced to absolutely nothing, the fairy tale says that one should then go completely into nature, and, in my experience, this is often the right thing. Frequently women say that the only way in which they can enjoy life a little and not feel so bad over their difficulties is by taking long walks in the woods, or by sitting in the sun. This is a genuine tendency, for it seems as though only nature in its virgin beauty and essence has the power to heal in such a case. Women have a very deep relationship to nature in its positive form. Relationship to animals can also effect the cure, and many women make a relationship to a pet, which at that time may mean more to them than anything else because its unconscious simplicity appeals to the wounds within them. Relationship to a human is a differentiated task; but relationship to an animal is simple, and in feeling for it, the lost tenderness may be discovered.

At first glance it might seem that the angel had been added to the story at a later date, but apparently there is always something resembling the angel, even in countries where they do not believe in angels, or it may be a bird sent by God. In Russia it is an old man; God himself comes down to help the poor girl. So divine intervention seems to be a genuine aspect, and not just to have been inserted in this version. God himself, or one of his messengers, intervenes. Practically, this means that only a religious experience can help the woman out of her difficulty.

One could say that that is the typical experience of the hermit— the animals make friends with him and bring him to the inner spiritual life. In the Middle Ages there were many hermits, and in Switzerland they were called Wood Brothers and Sisters. People who did not want to live a monastic life but who wanted to live alone in the forest had both a closeness to nature and also a great experience of spiritual inner life. Such Wood Brothers and Sisters could be personalities on a high level who had a spiritual fate and had to renounce active life for a time and isolate themselves to find their own inner relation to God. It is not very different from what the shaman does in the circumpolar tribes, or what the medicine men do all over the world, in order to seek an immediate personal religious experience in isolation. This story indicates that it is the only way to heal the deep split and hurt suffered by this woman. Collective standards do not help. She has first to reach the zero point and then in complete loneliness find her own spiritual experience, which would be personified by the angel.

In the supreme moment of loneliness and sadness, it is as though activity began in the unconscious, for in that moment the hands are healed. The text says that "her hands grew again as before." The variations are sometimes more detailed, but they always refer to healing by nature, not by doing something special. In many versions the hands are healed by putting her arms around a tree; that is, she gets healed by a process of inner growth, the tree being a symbol of the process of individuation. In the quest of the hero, it is responsible action that brings about the process of individuation. The heroic deed and tremendous suffering are aspects of the process. But sometimes also, without anything being done, things change and become better. There is a natural process of growth, of maturing and transforming in the psyche. There are such situations where one has to wait, and noninterference is the healing factor.

In a Russian parallel there is a very striking story of how the hands are healed. In this story the woman wanders through the country with her little son upon her arm and comes to a spring and wants to drink, but is afraid the child might fall into the water. Then the water slowly rises; she looks again and gets so thirsty that she leans forward and the child slips from her arm and falls in. In despair she begins to cry and to walk around and an old man says, "Take the child out!" But she says, "I have no hands!" The old man repeats, "Take the child out!" Then she puts her arms into the water and suddenly grows living hands. At that moment she was about to lose the child, the last thing she had and the only thing she loved, but by saving it from drowning she herself is helped.

In real life I have seen that such passive women were not even able to make up their minds to enter analysis; even that would be too much effort—they would rather remain in despair and do nothing. But if it were a question of saving a child of hers from falling into the unconscious, if a son or daughter began to be neurotic, that would force a mother who would otherwise sink into total passivity to try to save the child, and so face her own problem. This can bring her to the humiliating step of having to ask the psychotherapist for help and can pull her out of sinking passively into depression. If not the actual child, it might be some activity or interest, which to her is like a child. I knew such an unmarried woman who was cut off from every kind of relatedness, except playing the piano. But then she had inflammation of the nerves of the arm and she lost that too. That was her inner child, her one activity in life, and at a crucial moment it was taken from her. That was the turning point. She went into analysis and came out of her problem. It could be losing some kind of employment, anything that was positive before. Even in the Russian story the woman cannot save the child she loves so much from drowning. God himself has to come and say, "Do try!" The fact that she is so limited and wounded makes the divine intervention necessary, and that, in my experience, is very true—an actual miracle is needed. One can only help people to the best possible attitude, but it needs a miracle to heal the deep wound so that she can stretch out her hands and then the waters of life bring the cure.

Jung writes that women with a negative mother complex often miss the first half of life; they walk past it in a dream. Life to them is a constant source of annoyance and irritation. But if they can overcome this negative mother complex, they have a good chance in the second half of rediscovering life with the youthful spontaneity missed in the first half. For though, as Jung says in the last paragraph, a part of life has been lost, its meaning has been saved.[17] That is the tragedy of such women, but they can get to the turning point, and in the second half of life have their hands healed and can stretch them out for what they want—not from the animus or from the ego, but, according to nature, simply stretch out their hands toward something they love. Though it is infinitely simple, it is extremely difficult, for it is the one thing the woman with a negative mother complex cannot do; it needs God's help. Even the analyst cannot help her—it must one day just happen, and this is generally when there has been sufficient suffering. One cannot escape one's fate; the whole pain of it must be accepted, and one day the infinitely simple solution comes.

Mutatis mutandis, the problem for men is similar where the anima has been hurt by the mother's animus. Such a man may be able to talk about it, but he cannot bring up from within the genuine chthonic masculine reaction and be of himself definitely masculine. He lives according to what he believes to be the masculine pattern. To find one's personal spontaneity is something so simple that those who have it cannot understand how difficult it is for those who lack it. A woman who has gone through such an experience of finding her hands again has missed a part of life, which the woman with the positive mother complex had, but the latter remains unconscious of certain deep healing processes. The former, however, who has had to go around the whole world to find life, will have also found the religious meaning of it. Simply to live is like a Zen experience for her. She will have the full consciousness of what she is doing and is therefore rewarded for her suffering, which is what Jung means when he writes that "a part of life is lost, but the meaning is saved."

The king comes to look for his wife, but does not recognize her. He then puts the napkin over his face and lies down to sleep. His wife, having been told by the angel that her husband is there, tells the boy, Sorrowful, to pick up the napkin, which had fallen off, and to re-cover his father's face. The king hears his wife talking to the boy and recognizes her, and the couple is reunited. If we interpret the king as the woman's real husband, it would mean that after a crisis in the marital life where she has to be cut off temporarily, the natural relatedness will come back after the healing. If the king represents, as he probably does here, the ruling principle of collective life, such a woman can then adapt to collective life and its activities. It is as though she had awakened in the second half of life to take a normal and adapted place in society, and the whole strangeness which cut her off before has disappeared, for she can now act spontaneously and from within.

The son was named Sorrowful—"Schmerzensreich," which means "rich in sorrow." He is the fruit of the woman's life that has passed through the whole experience of suffering and thus acquired serenity and wisdom. By knowing so much about suffering, such people generally can readapt to life and, having gone through a great deal in a mature way, will naturally be able to help others. She will have something that attracts; for others will recognize her sufferings, which will also make her more understanding for theirs. A Siberian shaman was asked by a traveler if, after the initiation, one could go as far as one liked. He answered yes, if one was ready to pay the price in suffering each time. Sufferings are steps within the inner processes. This woman knows more than anyone who has not lived in such a condition.

The motif that the king's face has to be covered in order to protect him from the sunshine is very meaningful. In mythology the king and the sun are much connected, as for instance in *le roi soleil* and the sun symbolism of the king in Egypt.[18] The king would be the earthly representative of the sun principle. If he represents the dominant of collective consciousness, the sun would be the archetype behind it. In general the sun has a positive meaning and brings light and warmth, but in certain circumstances it is also looked upon as demonic, for it burns up, like the "demon of midday" in the Bible when the sun burns in a destructive way, destroying all vegetation. Therefore one can say that if clarity of consciousness is too strong, it has a destructive aspect. It burns all those mysterious archetypal processes that cannot be pulled into the realm of collective consciousness. Every person who is on the way to individuation will discover, in some form, the necessity of keeping certain things entirely to himself, generally experiences in the realm of eros that cannot be told to anybody, sometimes not even to the analyst. There also are things one knows about other people, where it has happened that one learns another person's secret without ever wanting to do so, and one knows that one must always and at all times behave as though one did not know. There are things not even discussed with oneself—they must be left in the twilight and must not be looked at too exactly. There are secret things of the soul that can only grow in the dark—the clear sun of consciousness burns their life away. In mythology there are such fairies, trolls, and the like, even good ones, who have been struck by a ray from the sun and petrified. They have to live in the twilight, and if they are struck by the sun's rays, they turn into stone.

If you take the king as a real man, it would mean that he cannot reconnect with his anima—for the woman would represent his anima—without putting a napkin over his face, keeping himself away from the principle of collective consciousness. Only by shutting his eyes to the outside world can he unite with the sufferings of his anima. If he represents the collective principle in a woman, it would mean that within her, her collective religious ideas, and her ideas of morality have to be set aside so that she can react with her personal inner truth. The king gave her the silver hands and therefore forced her into a half right and half wrong kind of life. The napkin placed on his head would be covering a rational attitude, so that there is not too much of it. Collective principles should be a little bit discreetly relativized; one should not look at them too closely, which means that the principles of collective behavior in this special case do not become negative, because they do not go too far. Its rules are quite all right, as far as they go, because the animus is positive here. He gives her something that holds her on a certain line, a moral framework, and which protects her from being too weak or lost in life. The napkin on the face is a beautiful picture—the collective values should be protected from the sun of a too clear consciousness.

It is typical for the animus that, statistically seen, he is generally right, which is why we fall for him. But he is *not right in the actual situation.* You might say to such a lonely woman that she should introvert more, sink into her loneliness. Then she would say to you that she needs to relate more, introversion would make things worse still, she's already so cut off. She is quite right, but she says it at the wrong time! A thing which is usually right is now suddenly wrong, but one should not tell the animus that he is wrong. Say to him, "Yes, you are right, but just now the situation is different from what you think," and that is putting a napkin on the king's face.

Even if she has something of value to say, it might be better to keep her opinions to herself or express them only in private conversation or when asked. A woman who always gives advice irritates a man. It needs a veiling of the inner face of her animus. He first puts on the napkin, and when he lets it fall, the queen sends Sorrowful to replace it. The positive animus has the right feeling about the necessity for the veil. In this the king and the queen are united in feeling and attitude. That is the union of opposites. The handlessness which formerly was painful passivity has now been transformed into conscious discretion. That would be the positive aspect of the previous handlessness.

The motif of the veil is an archetypal one. You could say that the deepest religious experiences have to be kept secret and by nature remain secret, and it would be most destructive to tell them to anyone else. The person who knows more than the others is, by that very fact, unendurable for society and a black sheep—that is quite natural. For example, in a quarrel each party thinks he is right and the other wrong, but an onlooker cannot take sides, for he realizes that for both it is a shadow problem and that the shadow is being projected. The onlooker may be accused of cowardice, because he refrains from acting, but the person who sees further must keep out and be ready to accept the unpleasant role of a coward, because of the shadow projection in both parties. In collectivity this may look like a lack of backbone and an inability to take a stand on the right side, but no explanation is possible, for that would only bring an attack by both parties. There the veil has to be used. The process of individuation often imposes a certain discretion.

The Swiss saint Bruder Klaus had the greatest inner experiences and isolated himself and lived with them, and from time to time theologians would come and try to question him. He was not only a saint but a very clever peasant, and if he saw that they had no idea of real religious experiences, he would say that he was a poor, unlettered man who was very ignorant and would be so glad if *they* would help him in his ignorance. By veiling his whole inner life, he escaped the Inquisition. He had the instinctive healthiness which knew that one must not tell people of things they cannot grasp. There are mysteries that cannot be shared with everybody. Klaus spoke of his inner experiences to his friends, but some things can be told to no one, and a secret told to the wrong person is destructive and even irresponsible. An analyst also must interpret a dream carefully so that it may be within the range of the analysand's understanding, and not beyond it.

I was once consulted about a friend of my mother's maid who

heard voices. She was a cook and a primitive woman. The voices prevented her from going to communion. I was asked to take her on, but from a medical standpoint, she was just crazy. I saw that even if I used the most primitive language she would not be able to understand, so I referred her to an exorcist in Einsiedeln, and she has been quite all right ever since. In that case it was right to treat the voice as an outer experience. An enthusiastic beginner might introduce such a person to analysis but that would have been irresponsible behavior, for it would have taken her out of her natural place.

There are people who belong in the Middle Ages or even the Stone Age and who should be left there until there are definite signs that something within them needs to go further; otherwise, one acts destructively. I have met in Küsnacht a man belonging to the Stone Age! I had to buy some tools, axes, and saws, and let out that I was building a hut in the woods and that there would be no electricity. Next time I saw the man he said, "You are leaving civilization, and you are right. I did that long ago. I work about three or four months in the year, and then I go to one of the higher mountains in the Alps and buy bacon and wine and then go still higher and build myself a kind of nest of stone and wood in the rocks. I undress, and if there is nobody around I go naked on the glaciers and I search for crystals. Everybody," he said, "who goes to church gets ill. You must listen to the plants and stones because God is in them, and all the rest is junk. I am sixty-five and have never even had a cold." He was a kind of "abominable snowman" walking naked on the glaciers—not a person for Jungian analysis. So one has always to consider the historical age in which the other person lives and not expose that person to the "sun" of modern rationalism but leave that which should be veiled, veiled.

7

If we sum up the three fairy tales we have looked at so far, it is typical for all these heroines to live isolated in nature. In "The Girl without Hands," for many years the woman drifted more and more out of life and was cured only by accepting the fact that she had to stay quiet in the woods, and temporarily not go back into life. This is a very frequent motif, and being excluded from life for many years seems to me typically to illustrate a problem of feminine psychology. From the outside it looks like complete stagnation, but in reality it is a time of initiation and incubation when a deep inner split is cured and inner problems solved. This motif forms a contrast to the more active quest of the male hero, who has to go into the Beyond and try to slay the monster, or find the treasure, or the bride. Usually he has to make more of a journey and accomplish some deed instead of just staying out of life. There seems to be a typical difference between the masculine and feminine principles. The unconscious is experienced as isolation by the heroine, and afterward comes the return into life. What is also relevant is that the handless maiden in our fairy tale is also confronted with a deep *religious* problem, for she comes under the influence of both angel and devil. As you know, in the beginning of the story the devil tried to get her into his power, but she escaped and later was protected by an angel. She comes under two divine influences, that of the dark side, the devil, and that of the angel as the messenger of God. In the Russian version, even God himself helps her.

This is not typical for our civilization only. In primitive material you find exactly the same problem of the heroine's being confronted with the powers of good and evil as soon as she goes into the unconscious. In a woman this has to do with the problem of the animus. In masculine psychology you can say that the anima in man entangles him in life and its problems, in dealing with his instincts and drives, and so faces him also with an ethical problem. But the anima never directly puts the problem of his *Weltanschauung* to a man; rather she puts him indirectly into a situation in which he has to revise his whole religious attitude toward life. The woman, on the other hand, is directly confronted with the problem of good and evil as soon as she goes into the unconscious, because the animus has to do with ideas and concepts. When she goes on the journey within, she is at once confronted with God and the devil. Drifting out of life can also be dangerous for a heroine. It can happen that a woman does not find her way back into the human world. This is illustrated by an Eskimo fairy tale reported by Knud Rasmussen about a woman who became a spider. [19]

The Woman Who Became a Spider

Synopsis of the Tale

There was once a man and a woman who had a daughter, and they would have lived quite happily together if the daughter had not despised men. Her father wanted her to marry, but she always refused. Many young men came of their own volition, for she was a beautiful girl. It also happened that the father would bring home young men in the evening so that they might meet his daughter. But nothing helped; the mere mention of men made the girl bad-tempered, and if any came to the house, she went off on her own.

One day her father told her that he did not bring men to the house in order to make her sad or to hurt her, but that she should remember that they had no son, and that she was their only daughter and their only child. Her mother and he would soon be old and for many years he would not be capable of providing them with food and clothing, and who would help them in their old age if they had no son-in-law?

These words made the girl very sad, and she wandered out into the great uneven, undulating plains, on which were many small hills. Suddenly a head jumped out of the earth among the hills, a head without a body, but the face was that of a very handsome man. And the young man smiled at the girl and said, "You don't want to have a husband, but I come here to fetch you, and you must know that I come of a big and powerful race."

For the first time in her life the young girl was happy with a young man, and she lifted up the head and put it carefully in her fur coat and carried it home when it was dark. She slipped noiselessly into the house and put the head of the handsome young man beside her couch, and lay there and talked gaily and happily with the stranger, whom she loved because he was not like other men. Her father awoke and heard the whispering and giggling from his daughter's couch and could not understand what was happening there. It was repeated during the coming nights, and the father was happy, for now he knew that at last he had a son-in-law and a hunter in the house.

From now on the girl was always happy. Formerly she had stayed away from the village during the daytime so as to avoid the men, but now she often stayed at home and hardly ever moved from her couch. But the father and mother were very much surprised never to see their son-in-law.

One day when the girl was out, it happened that the father pushed aside the fur rug on her couch to find out who kept his daughter company during the night. When he found the living head of a handsome young man, a head without a body, he was very angry. He took a meat skewer and thrust it through the young man's eye and then threw the head out onto the rubbish heap, crying, "I have no use for a son without a body who could not hunt for us when we are old!"

The head rolled away and went farther and farther over the plains in front of the house and at last disappeared into the sea, leaving a bloody track behind it.

The following night the father and mother heard the girl crying and sobbing all through the night, and the next morning she asked where her husband was. The father answered that they had no use for such a son-in-law. "You are talking stupidly and you have behaved foolishly," answered the girl, "for he was a capable man and not an ordinary human being, and now I will no longer remain at home with you."

The girl dressed and went out and followed the bloody track, which led directly to the sea. She wanted to dive into the waves, but they were as hard as wood and she could not. Then she went inland looking for a white lemming which was supposed to have fallen down from heaven, for she knew that lemmings had special magic powers hidden in them. At last she caught one and threw it into the sea, and at once the waves parted and a road opened, which she followed to the bottom of the sea.

In the distance she noticed a little house. She ran to it and looked through the window and saw an old couple with their son. The son lay on the sleeping bench and had recently lost an eye. The girl called, "Here I am! Come out!"

The young man answered that he would not come out to her, and that he would no longer come after her, for her parents despised him. Even though the girl said she was never going back to her parents, the young man said he would never have anything more to do with her.

The girl was very much depressed, and without knowing what she was doing, she ran three times around the house in the same direction as the sun circles around in the heavens. Then she saw two ways—one led straight ahead and to the earth, and the second went up to heaven. She chose the way which led to heaven, but when the man saw that he cried out to her that she was going the wrong way and should turn around, that she was going up to heaven and would never come back again. "It's all the same where I go," said the girl, "if you won't live with me anymore!"

Now the young man regretted his words but too late begged her to come back, for she only went higher and higher up to heaven, until she disappeared out of his sight.

The girl went on without knowing herself how she did it, and came at last to something that looked like a lid with a hole in it. But it was difficult to get to the hole, and she did not know how to get on. At last she took courage and jumped and got hold of the edge and swung herself through the opening and once more found air and heaven and land. A little to one side was a lake, to which she went and sat down so that she might die here and her body disintegrate. She didn't want to think anymore. Life no longer meant anything to her. Suddenly she heard the splashing of oars on the lake and looked up and saw a man in a kayak. Everything he had—his kayak, his oars, and his harpoon—everything was of shining copper. The girl sat quite still and scarcely dared breathe. She did not think that anybody could see her in the deep grass in which she had hidden herself.

The man sang:

> A woman's breast tempts a kayak,
> Who crosses the shining lake
> To caress soft cheeks.

As the man finished his song, he raised one arm high up toward heaven and dropped the other down toward the lake. The girl saw that the upper part of her body was naked and that her fur coat lay across the strange man's arm.

Again the man sang the song, and as he finished it and raised one arm and dropped the other, the rest of the woman's clothing flew over onto his raised arm. The girl sat there naked and ashamed, and couldn't understand what was happening to her. For the third time the man sang his song, but this time the girl lost consciousness, and when she came to herself, she was sitting beside the man in his kayak. The man rowed far away with her, far over the lake with his bright copper oars, which glistened wetly in the air. They did not speak to each other until they came to a place where they saw two houses. At the entrance to the village was a big house and in the background a small one. Then the man said in a stern voice, "You must go into the big house, not into the little one."

110

The girl did what the man told her and went into the big
house, and the man rowed away. It was dreary in the big house,
not a soul was in it, but she had hardly entered before a small
woman ran in. She wore extraordinary clothes made out of the
gut of a bearded seal. She cried out to the girl to come into the
other house, for the man with whom she had come was dangerous and would kill her. The girl came out at once and went into
the other house. Here a little girl, with whom the extraordinary
woman dressed in gut skins lived, sat on the sleeping bench.

The young girl who had run away from the man she loved no
longer thought about anything much. Sometimes she thought
that she was already dead, but she heard what the others said
and saw them go around the house, and the woman came and
whispered to her that this time she was saved, but that the man
with whom she had come was not an ordinary man, that nobody
could resist him, and that soon he would come home and would
be very angry that she had left his house. But the woman would
help her, and she gave her a small cask filled with water in
which were four small pieces of whaleskin. She told her that
when the strange man came, she should hide at the entrance to
the house and throw the pieces of whaleskin in his face, for the
woman had sung a magic song over her present, so as to make it
strong.

Soon the man came back in his kayak. He sat down beside the
sea and called out that she should stay quiet in his house, that
he would not do her harm, and that she could never be hidden
from him. Then he came flying through the air like a bird, and
circled his house four times and then came to the small house.
There he picked up his bird arrow but cried out that he would
not kill her.

The girl stood hidden in the bend of the entry to the house
and threw the pieces of whaleskin in his face. In the same
moment he fell down out of the air and lost his strength. Then
the three women went into his house, which was the house of
the moon spirit, and it was the Man in the Moon himself which
the little woman in the skins had made harmless for a time
through her magic. The moon spirit is incalculable and can

become dangerous; he takes, but he also gives, and man must sacrifice to him in order to share in the things over which he rules.

The three women went into his house, and up in the rafters crowds of reindeer ran about. In the corner was a big water barrel, big as an inland lake. The women went to it and looked in and saw whales and walruses and seals swimming about.

In the middle of the floor lay the shoulder blade of a whale. The women pushed it to one side and saw an opening leading down to the earth from which one could see into the dwelling places of humans. One could see the people quite clearly and hear them calling out for all the things they wanted. There were some who cried out to be given whale meat. Others said they wanted a long life. The moon spirit is so powerful that he can give humans all these things.

The young girl looked at the countries of the earth and discovered far, far below, Tikeraq, the largest place she knew. Here there were many women's boats and many busy people. They were collecting water in small casks and throwing it up to the new moon so that they might have a good catch. It was all like a dream. She could not understand how she herself had got into all that, which she knew well from the stories that old people told. It was perhaps just a new moon, for the little woman in the skins had made the moon spirit unconscious. For as long as the moon spirit is weak, men sacrifice to him. They bring all their wishes before he becomes the big full moon, which can shine like copper.

Now the girl saw how the people prayed to the moon for a good catch. Some of the men had such strong magic formulas that their water ladles came quite near to the moon spirit's house. On the earth these water ladles were quite small, but here, through the magic words, they became enormous and were filled with cool, fresh water. These sacrifices are brought to sea animals, who often suffer from thirst. Sometimes a whale and sometimes a walrus and sometimes a seal was put into the ladles, which reached the house of the moon spirit. That meant that the man's prayer was heard and his sacrifice accepted and that he would have a good catch. But those ladles which re-mained near the earth, down by the people's dwellings, be-longed to the bad hunters who had no luck.

The young girl saw all that and remembered the pleasure that followed a catch, and she became homesick, she who a little while ago had only thought of dying.

The old woman in the skins and her little companion were sorry for her and wanted to help her get back to the earth. The three women plaited a rope out of the sinews of many animals, a very long rope which they rolled up into a ball as they plaited it. Soon it was finished, and the old woman said: "You must shut your eyes and let yourself down. But in that minute when you touch the earth, you must open your eyes quickly. If you don't, you will never become a human again."

The young girl fastened the end of the rope tight in the heavens and took the great ball of plaited sinews and began to let herself down. She thought it would be a very long way, but she felt the ground beneath her feet sooner than she had expected. It happened so quickly that she didn't open her eyes quickly enough, and she was changed into a spider. From her come all the spiders of the world—all come from the girl who let herself down from heaven to the earth by a rope of plaited sinews.

The girl in this story is out of the ordinary society since she rejects the usual human fate of getting married at a certain age and continuing the instinctual life of the tribe. The story ends badly, which is typical for many primitive stories, but not much more so than for those of our civilization. The breaking of a taboo, or the wish for something special, is evaluated negatively and leads to a fatal end. There is, for instance, an African story in which the girl wants to marry a man belonging to another tribe, which would be against the marriage laws of her own tribe. She marries the man from another country and suffers a terrible fate. The man, who owns a magic bull, is killed, and in the end she is killed also. This is typical for many stories where there is the wish for something special, against the ordinary rules of life, and the end is hopeless tragedy.

There is, however, the opposite idea in some other fairy tales, for instance in "Amor and Psyche" and "The Singing Soaring Lion-Lark,"[20] in which the girl wants a special husband. The father tells his three daughters that he is going on a journey and asks them what he should bring them. Two say jewelry, but the third wants a "lion-lark," which turns out to be an animal bridegroom, a kind of ghost-bridegroom with whom she finds great happiness after various tribulations and difficulties. Here we have the opposite pattern, in which the girl's special wish, after a long journey and various complications, leads to a beautiful union with a marvelous kind of ghost-bridegroom, and the whole story is told as a positive development. But in the Eskimo story the special wish leads to destruction. The story did not necessarily have to go wrong. When the girl came back to earth, she did not open her eyes quickly enough, and that simple mistake makes the whole difference. The natural conclusion would be that had she opened her eyes at the right time, she would have become a kind of shaman priestess who would have known about the mysteries of the Beyond through her own experiences and could have told her tribe all about things on the other side and would have acquired the reputation of a great shamaness—the woman who knows and who has had personal experience of the collective unconscious, the initiated person who, through her special experiences, would know what was happening in the unconscious. It is only this minor mistake of not opening her eyes quickly enough when she returns to earth which gives the story the negative outcome. Interpreted psychologically, it seems that if there is a situation in which consciousness is too weak, the experience of the unconscious turns negative instead of positive.

The great problem, and something we always have to keep in mind in psychological work, is whether the analysand's consciousness—or the substance of his personality, something we can feel but cannot describe—is strong enough to carry the experience of the collective unconscious. Some people are confronted with amazing experiences of the unconscious, even of the collective unconscious, but on account of a certain feebleness of reaction, they have no positive results from the experience. In the case of schizophrenics, nothing results from even the deepest experience. At the crucial moment where the material should be integrated, nothing happens. I remember once, for example, talking to a Polish-Mexican peasant woman in the Napa Valley State Hospital in California. She was a good-looking, middle-aged person. She sometimes produced the most astounding archetypal material from the collective unconscious and, unlike most schizophrenics, was pleased if she had a chance to talk about it. She had a kind of manic streak in her. When I met her, she immediately began to tell me what God and Jesus Christ had looked like when she had been on the moon and seen the heavens. It was quite interesting, but she had no connection with it. She told these things with great feeling, but was quite absent herself—she was just spinning like a spider who lets out a thread and runs up and down on it. She went along her own thread and was not human. One felt that there was nobody there to whom one could talk. In such a case one feels as though one were confronted with a vacuum. There is astonishing and interesting material, but nothing human in it.

The spider woman told the girl in the story to keep her eyes shut until she reached the earth. The journey to the earth was no great distance, and it does not seem that she had kept her eyes shut through fear. It is more likely that she did not want to face the return to reality; it might be a great comedown to be once more in reality after having been married to the moon god.

I knew of a very poor, miserable man whose mother was a whore and father a drunkard, and who went off his head and was put into the hospital with the most serious cases. A good doctor treated the case and got him into a relatively normal condition so that he could work in the fields, seemed completely adapted, and was put into the ward with the least mad patients. Then the doctor started talking to him very discreetly about leaving the hospital, and the man said, "Oh, no, Doctor, you are not going to catch me!" and off he went back into the worst ward and was as mad as before. He did not want to open his eyes and return to earth, where he had had such a miserable life. After his great experiences, he did not wish to become normal again.

There is very often such a tendency in people who do not want to come back, and there is a certain amount of conscious decision about it, for return to the misery of this world is a poor substitute for marriage to a ghost and the moon god. Also in the case of the Polish woman, I had the feeling that she was happy in her madness. She liked to clean the floors of the hospital, where she was quite free and worked very well. Neither do I think she was not humble enough to return to human life; she was just asleep. She was like a rabbit, which sleeps with its eyes open, and the intuitive feeling one had about her was just like that—a human being who was asleep, in spite of the fervor with which she related her experiences. Everybody in the hospital liked her, and you could ask her to tell you a story anytime. She would spin an archetypal yarn and then walk off again. She was a "spinster" (that is what the word comes from), or a spider who did not open her eyes onto this world.

The "head" people, according to the circumpolar tribes, are the people who lived under the sea—ghosts consisting only of a head. Certain African tribes also believe that there are "head" people—ghosts who roll about as bodiless heads. They are considered rather dangerous and are used for magic purposes. They constitute a powerful population under the earth or the sea and are supposed to be the spirits of the dead, the pure essence of the dead contained in the head. Sometimes they are the "skull" and sometimes the "head" people.

The girl is attracted to a ghost instead of a human bridegroom, and is very happy with him. It is a marvelous illustration of what we so dryly and technically express as "animus possession," which is an abstract formula meaning that the woman is married to a "head" bridegroom and unattainable and unapproachable on the human side. She is in constant conversation with this autonomous spiritual factor, with whom she has long inner conversations. If one could watch oneself when in an animus-possessed state (which one cannot), one would see, as one does in another woman, that one is constantly engaged in an inner conversation, thinking about and discussing things that one cannot tell other people. One cannot interrupt it, for it is completely involuntary; there is no Archimedean point outside from which the thing can be viewed. Only the onlooker notices that the animus-possessed woman is linked up in conversation with an inner spiritual process. She is so in it that she cannot see it. That is why such women appear not to be quite there, and as though they had something up their sleeve, for they keep something to themselves. The head is a wonderful image of the animus, with its opinions and musings going on all the time.

In this case the father hears the head husband talking, which is what often happens. Animus possession is especially irritating for a real man; a human bridegroom would have killed or hurt the head. It has an automatically irritating effect on the living man, who cannot stand this process going on in a woman. You can see this in life when a girl begins to have her own ideas. The father hears his daughter arguing and feels the animus growing, and having disliked and loathed that in his wife and in other women, when she too begins, he comes down on it. It is an age-old tragedy that the beginnings of mental activities in the daughters are smashed or doomed by the father's reaction. Many women are seriously lamed on the spiritual and mental side and in their work because the father in a bad moment had told them they could not do something. A woman of fifty once told me that she had wanted to learn Greek when ten years old, and her father had told her that she was not capable of that. Fathers should not discourage their daughters in that way, for that affects their development, and it is not the way to get the girl out of animus possession. Such paternal reactions have a devastating effect, for they affect the inner mentality of the girl.

Animus and anima, *in statu nascendi,* are not elegant; they are below the mark. For instance, boys at about sixteen, when the eros problem first comes up, suddenly do not work at school. They just stand around, and have acne on their faces and backs. One of our German teachers used to say, "Are you sitting in the boys' swamp again?" They have languishing fantasies, are swamped by feelings, physical reactions, and sexual and other fantasies of a most vague and stupid form. That is what the beginning of heterosexuality and the first awakening of the anima look like. If you get to know them better, you will find that they write terribly sentimental poems to girls, at which time the mother or sisters by their mocking remarks can hit or destroy something, just as the father does to the girls. It requires a superior attitude of consciousness to see and ignore such things discreetly. One should disregard these formative processes, which have to go through certain stages, and this applies to the girl's animus as well. When it first appears, it is unyielding and fantastic, and fathers should not attack it. But apparently even Eskimo fathers become irritated.

So the girl runs away into the sea, into the waters of the collective unconscious, but there too she is rejected. That comes from her own hurt, for, like the woman whose father had told her she could not learn Greek, the "it" in her did not want to learn anymore. The creative animus is so sensitive at that stage that one cannot regain one's enthusiasm, cannot get it back again, and then the same mistake takes place. Then the girl has two paths to choose from: she misses the path to earth, but goes up to the sky, in spite of the warning the head gives her. This time, because she has been warned, she is really responsible for her mistake, but she says to the head, "If you won't live with me anymore, it is all the same to me where I go!" That resembles the German saying: "It serves my father right if my feet are frozen and I get ill!" That is the reaction she falls into.

We know from other stories and from archetypal material that a tendency to marry a "head" is generally due to a father complex in the daughter. But this story does not say so. It is true that the very fact that she preferred the head bridegroom to a human one has probably to do with her father, but as it is not mentioned, I have not taken it up. In a story which we shall take up later, that the father is responsible is well illustrated. The mother's animus could also be responsible, but that would take a slightly different form. The mother's animus is seen in "Snow White." There it is the negative mother and her animus, and there the girl too has to go into the forest into a state of incubation. One might say that either the father's anima or the mother's animus could account for the daughter's being driven out of life, but, quite honestly, why should it always be blamed on the parents? For since mankind first existed, man has brought with him a certain amount of negative unconsciousness; that legacy is handed on from one generation to the other, and perhaps it was always so. Perhaps it is the general human condition—one is influenced not only by one's visible parents but by their unconscious, quite normally so, and every-where. I think it is a very rational, causal way of thinking always to say it is the father's anima or the mother's animus. Everybody is born of parents who have a conscious *and* an unconscious attitude. We know in fact that if parents are in connection with their unconscious, the pressure on the children might be less. But, even so, I would say that no human being escapes the condition of being influenced by the parents' unconscious. Why one girl is more influenced by the father's anima and another by the mother's animus depends, I think, on the original disposition of the child. One child will develop a strong father complex and the other, of the same family, does not. It is the effect of the inborn disposition that this daughter is more concentrated on the father and more affected by his unconscious. It is not quite so simple as that; but we know that a daughter who is more fascinated by the figure of the father than by the mother in her youth tends more to the fate of being separated from life.

The only way out is to take the responsibility for what one is, and to make an enormous effort to interrupt the curse or the chain which goes on from one generation to another. You see it even expressed in dreams. A patient was told by a dream to do a special thing which would redeem his father. If he did what his father did not do, he would interrupt the curse.

I knew a man who had never stood up against his mother's moods and was under the domination of his wife, whom he let do everything in order to have peace and a pleasant atmosphere. His son had great difficulty in asserting his masculinity but had to learn to do so. He married a girl with a rather powerful animus, and the situation repeated itself; for even in the first months of marriage she wanted her own way, and he had to stand up for things and the battle started again. He dreamed several times that he should redeem his dead father; that is, what his father had not done, he should now do. He had the responsibility of not continuing the same curse; otherwise his child would have the same problem. He had to stop the process of the ancestral curse, which in dreams was expressed by saying that he had to redeem his ancestors. The one who had to become conscious is the one who had to stop the curse that went on through the generations.

As mentioned before, one has also to consider the inborn disposition of the child, which either accepts or rejects the parental influence. One child, if told by her father that she would never be able to learn Greek, would say, "I'll show you!" It need not necessarily be as it was in the case of the woman mentioned. Already within herself was the thing which lamed her, so that long after the father had died she could not learn Greek. Whatever she tried to do, a voice said: "You are not capable of that!" She had the kind of animus that prevents every kind of development by discouraging thoughts. One could say that the father stepped into the trap of her expectations. It can happen that people have such a powerful complex, that it lays traps for you, and if you are not very conscious you fall into them. For instance, I do not tend to cheat or send analysands bills for the wrong amounts, but I once had a woman whose mother had always cheated her over money, and believe it or not, I sent the woman a bill for more than she owed me. Naturally, that constellated the whole drama, and I sat there flabbergasted.

If you are not on guard in such a case, you get pushed into the role of father or mother. One has to watch out day and night not to be caught, because if one is not sufficiently aware of one's own shadow, the analysand's complexes will force one to act in their pattern. It has such a collective effect that one is not quite conscious. All analysands try to push the analyst into their ancestral pattern. So it may be that the child's disposition invites the parents' reactions. The modern medical outlook of a causal relation of facts only is not a true evaluation, but a typical superstition in our civilization, which does not correspond to facts if one looks at them more closely.

The girl in our story goes up to heaven through a hole. Such a description is typical for the Eskimos, who think of heaven as being just the same as the earth, a mirror image of this earth, and where the moon god lives. The moon god is another beautiful animus figure but different from the head in the sea because he is not the single ghost of a dead person but the generally recognized god of the tribe, a god to whom the Eskimos do not show much love but to whom they pray for luck in hunting. When it is a question of survival, everything depends on a good catch, and he is therefore a god of fertility and the bestower of life. This is interesting, because people who have not gone into the details of mythological study tend to think that the male god principle has always to do with the spiritual, and that the mother goddess has always to do with the fertility of crops and animals, and so forth. In many Eskimo tribes the bestower of food is a feminine goddess. For instance, Sedna—who lives at the bottom of the sea and whom the shamans have to visit to rid her hair of lice or heal some wound, after which they will be lucky again—is such a goddess. Sometimes a woman goddess bestows the fertility of nature, but here it is a male god who has that function. One must not fall into a schematical way of thinking and say that the moon is feminine and that the goddess of fertility is a mother goddess. Even in Roman times the moon god was hermaphroditic. There existed a North African ithyphallic moon god; also, in the old Egyptian civilization the moon god Min had an enormous erect phallus and was a god of fertility in all realms. His animal was the bull.

So the moon is not always feminine, but it is a nature god and a spirit of fertility. You could therefore say that the essence of the idea of earthly fertility could be attributed to a feminine *or* to a masculine principle. One has to look at the whole context of a culture to find out why it is so. In China, in Polynesia, and in most of the Indian mythologies, they speak of "our mother the earth" and "our father the sky," but in Egypt it is the opposite. Geb, the earth principle, is a male god, and Nut, the sky goddess, is female. Now, how is the Egyptian civilization different from most others? In the Egyptian civilization, the concreteness of ideas is very striking. Like all peoples, for instance, the Egyptians hope for immortality, but only in Egypt has the idea been expressed by such a material preservation of the body. They tried to guarantee immortality by immortalizing the body. What in other civilizations is more a concept and a vision has become something quite concrete in Egypt. This fact also struck the Greeks. In Egypt the statues of the gods require renewal, so they were actually carried to the Nile and there washed and oiled. What normally belongs to the spirit or

The Feminine in Fairy Tales

the mind world, in Egypt belongs to the earth. That is the
psychological reversal expressed in the earth being taken as the
male principle and the female as the sky. What is not concrete in
Egypt are moods, feelings, and sentiments—they have a spiritual
connotation.

Now, what would it mean if the principle of fertility were
masculine instead of feminine? If the nature principle were masculine, what kind of attitude toward life would one expect? I think
there would be a compensatory kind of passivity toward nature. To
an active hunter, the wood, or the sea, with their animals, is a
simile for the woman; he penetrates nature and enters it and gets
nourishment there. He needs, of course, charm and luck, but in
the penetration of the hunting ground he has the feeling of active
life. In such a case, the "thou" in nature is a woman. Nature is
felt to be irrational, is loved and hated as a woman, and is regarded
as tricky and cruel and unreliable like a woman, and the fertility
and food bestower is therefore a goddess. But on the contrary, men
who have the introverted feeling attitude and do not believe in doing
things, or, if they do them, do not feel that it is the essential thing,
will experience nature more as an active male principle of life and
themselves as recipients of its gifts.

In this tribe they pray to the moon by throwing up ladles—a
feminine symbol; they want to receive passively. To go out in the
kayaks with harpoons is a minor thing, for it is the mysterious
something in nature which *sends* the animals and fish and reindeer.
The hunter is the wife, the woman, and nature sends the animal.
If a woman dreams about the moon god, that indicates her feeling
vis-à-vis the unconscious—she is passive and cannot realize that
she could do something. The unconscious is something active
which affects her, and she only asks for something.

The story then tells that when the moon god faints through the
magic of the spider woman, it is the moment of the new moon. We
can guess from the story that this passing out of the moon god
happens quite regularly, and that the spider woman is the great
power that makes the moon wane. So the girl gets into this play of
opposites between the moon and the spider woman, the feminine

122

and the masculine. The spider here is benevolent and the moon god a kind of moody creator.

The spider woman is a symbol of the Self for a woman, a positive and stronger figure than the moon. In spite of this, seen from the side of feminine psychology and as helping the girl against the destructive animus, who is a kind of Bluebeard, the girl cannot escape back to earth because of her inborn weakness and her inability to open her eyes. This theme belongs to many stories and is common in primitive civilizations where the process of individuation goes on in a kind of sleepy lethargy and unawareness. But we have to keep this in mind, for though we talk about primitive people, we have in some layers of our own populations the same kind of person, unawakened, animal-like people who cannot go into the unconscious or become conscious and for whom any contact with the unconscious is only destructive. Such people must be kept out of analysis. Beginners make a big mistake there, because these people produce wonderful archetypal material, and naturally, if one looks at the material alone, one can think that it is something exceptional. But one should not forget to look at the person and see whose dreams and visions they are, and whether there is any possibility of even a partial integration of the material. Sometimes one discovers that there is no possibility of such a thing and that one cannot lead such people on the path of individuation. You may ask whether it depends on the analyst's arbitrary judgment, whether he thinks somebody suitable or not, but it is the material itself which will show. The impossibility for the process of individuation to come about is to be found in the little details of the material, so you have to interpret the smallest details in dreams most carefully in order to be able to decide. In this story there are two such details. One is when the girl misses the right path, and the other when she opens her eyes a minute too late. In these two details the story deviates from the normal pattern of a shamanic journey, which is the pattern of initiation.

In Mircea Eliade's book on shamanism[21], one can see that in all the circumpolar tribes the shamans are initiated through experiences such as are related in our story. The shaman climbs a cord to heaven and then returns by means of it to earth. Afterward he carries the cord as a sign of his connection with the other world. They see the rituals from above and get initiated through what happens. Our heroine experiences a classical shaman initiation, but it fails. The Eskimos believe that crazy, possessed people and the shaman are the same, except that the latter can free himself again. Possession and mental illness and being a shaman are very close, but there are definite criteria as to which is which. Going up to heaven, meeting the spider, getting the four pieces of whaleskin, and so forth, could well appear in a person's material, but yet he could not go on the path of individuation. In the beginning of an analysis, when one has not yet made a diagnosis as to whether one is faced with a psychosis or with somebody temporarily overwhelmed by the unconscious, the dreams can look just the same. I have seen initial dreams which said that the sea flooded the whole land—that could be psychotic; or that graves opened up and corpses rolled around and came alive—that could also be psychotic. Actually, the unconscious only shows that the collective unconscious is absolutely on top of this person, but you can only say that this is a state which *looks* psychotic, though it is not necessarily so. But if it is, that will show in the poverty of the reaction toward the material, the lack of vitality, and reaction to such a motif will show either in extreme stupidity or in an entire absence of reaction. That is where you can find traces of a possible psychosis. If you see that, you cannot go with the analysand into the unconscious.

At the beginning of an analysis a woman dreamed that she saw the wedding or coronation of Queen Elizabeth. The dreamer was in a strange medieval town where the wedding took place and was milling around among excited crowds in the streets. A long procession came, headed by four black and then four brown horses, and the foreparts and the tails of the horses were like roosters. Afterward came the sun god, followed by the Queen, who was like a supernatural goddess. Then came numbers of elephants and lions, and so on. The dreamer was then back in the crowd and had to find a place from which to see the procession, and then realized that she had not cleaned her shoes and must do so. But then an infantile shadow figure came up and diverted her attention, and the dream ended. There is tremendous activity in the unconscious, and this could be healthy or not. She is in the crowd, that is, in the collective, but that could be healthy or not. Normal people too can be overwhelmed by the unconscious. That she cannot at once find her place shows that there is a certain weakness, but even that is not yet fatal. She realizes that she must clean her shoes, a very healthy thing. What is really important is that she has a clean standpoint, that she would not lie and cheat, would take her analysis seriously, and would take everything that came toward her in life. She was a great liar. But now an infantile figure, a childish girl, diverts her attention from the fact that she has to clean her shoes, and here the dream fades and has no solution. The whole thing, the dream says, will go wrong on account of an infantility, which the dreamer seems to be incapable of overcoming.

Because the dream seemed unhealthy or dangerous in only one place, I decided to take on the analysand, and for a few weeks or two months there was good progress, but I was always up against the infantility. She always complained and wanted to be babied and was always dependent on different people. She took a room and complained of the landlady, but went on being influenced by her. These were typical symptoms of infantility, and then something happened which brought the case to an end. Her former analyst, a woman, came to Zurich from another country, to fish her back. The analysand had written that she was satisfied with me, and that aroused the vanity of the other analyst, who talked to her and told her that I was an inappropriate person who would lead her to disaster, so the analysis stopped. Later the patient took up anthroposophy, and then developed a cancer phobia and became a hypochondriacal homeopathic in an effort to circumvent the supposed cancer threat. Finally she wrote to me that she would like to work with me again, saying that she realized that she had done something stupid and accusing the other analyst—as though she could not have resisted that interference. She said that she would come one day again, but I have heard nothing since—the petering out process in her dream came right into life through her infantility. It was not her fault; she just had not the strength to stand up against the other analyst. The dangerous element often shows in the last detail of the dream but is sometimes hidden in the middle, in some small point, and the beauty of the material is no guarantee against it.

This is a classical initiation dream, but it goes wrong and, as the Eskimo story says, it is because of the weakness of the personality. This woman was a primitive peasant girl, and she was not mature enough to swing it. That does not mean that people coming from a primitive layer cannot do it. Nature is aristocratic, but her system of aristocracy is different from our social ideas and goes through all the layers of society. It is very important to have the right feeling about this, as otherwise one lures people into a process which they cannot carry.

Jung mentions a dream in the "Children's Dreams" seminar, in which a little girl who later became schizophrenic dreamed that Jack Frost touched her stomach.[22] Jung said that the pathological element here was that the girl had no reaction. If the dreamer had woken up frightened, or if she had just said, "Then I woke up," that would have been equivalent to a reaction. But Jack Frost—the personified winter—came and touched her, and there was no affect. Sometimes people wake up with a cry, which is a vital reaction and a kind of lysis. Such a dream has a shock effect, but the amazing thing in the child's dream is that it has not even a shock effect. Jack Frost is a demon of the cold who should inspire fear. It is typical for schizophrenics that they will tell horrible dreams without any emotion; they speak of them as though they were rolls at breakfast and cups of coffee. That is a serious symptom. Or very often when there is a latent psychosis, there is a very narrow-minded rationalism which absolutely refuses a symbolic interpretation of dreams. Jung has observed that extreme narrow-mindedness can be a symptom of psychosis.

Such narrow-mindedness cannot understand symbols. I knew a psychotic case in which the woman had a compulsion: she always fastened papers together with clips. I asked her why, and she said that one day the window might be open and the wind might blow in and cause confusion. That was highly symbolic. The wind is the spirit of the unconscious, and one day that would blow in and she might never get out of her mental confusion again. So she pinned everything down. She was caught in a very narrow-minded, limited attitude about everything—a pure defensive mechanism. Such people have no spirit of adventure; they are frightened and caught by rationalism. Stinginess can be the same, it expresses the same thing. One cannot let go, cannot risk; one must keep everything together, because the frame might break loose at any minute. Thus the poverty of reactions is more important to watch than the symbolism itself. It indicates either a morbid disposition or—as in our story—a primitiveness, which prevents any further inner development.

The heroine returns to earth in the form of a spider. If she had kept her human body, she would have fallen to her death; so the spider woman turns her into a spider. The spider woman is a Great Mother figure who appears here in a benevolent form.[23] Within the psyche of a woman, she represents the Self. In Zuñi mythology there also occurs a spider woman who lives in the confines of the earth. She is sometimes helpful and sometimes dangerous to man. In Hindu mythology the spider is symbolic of a form of the goddess Maya, who represents that mysterious factor which makes us believe that the outer material world is the reality. The Hindu saint tries to overcome this delusion and thus transcend the world. In folklore the spider is often considered to be a witch animal because of its shrewd way of trapping its prey. As the Maya aspect revealed, the spider is connected with the source of creative phantasy in the unconscious psyche. A woman who had to turn within and, leaving outer activities, had to develop her creativity had the following dream:

> I was in a prison, a dark gloomy place. I received a parcel from whom I didn't know, but I knew that in that little white box was a spider. I wasn't sure if it was poisonous or not. I thought I must feed it through a little hole in the top of the box. I put a crumb in. That spider was God.

A prison symbolizes the introversion which was forced upon her but which she did not yet like. There she received a gift from the unconscious—the little white box with the spider. Then comes the surprising last sentence: the spider is God. The creative kernel at the bottom of the human psyche is nothing more or less than the presence of the divinity. This divine center spins, so to speak, the consistent thread of fate along which we move.

That is what the spider woman teaches the heroine in our story to do. With the help of this thread she can return to earth, but then she does not open her eyes and as a consequence remains a spider forever. She gets stuck in the inner world of phantasy and cannot return into human society. Viewed from outside, this could mean plain madness or only a mild case of remaining isolated and odd. It is the story of a failed shamanistic journey with all its tragic consequences. Our next stories will also represent such a journey but with positive endings.

8

"The Six Swans" and "The Seven Ravens"

I would like to discuss two stories together, because in both there is the motif of the sister who redeems her brothers, turned in one case into swans, and in the other into ravens.

Synopsis of "The Six Swans"[24]

A widowed king loses his way when hunting in a large wood, and an old woman with a nodding head says that she will show him the way out, on condition that he marries her daughter. The king agrees but has a very bad feeling about the new wife and therefore hides his children (six boys and one girl from his previous marriage) in a lonely castle in a forest, where he often visits them. In order not to lose his way, he uses a ball of cotton given him by a wise woman, by which, like the thread of Ariadne, he is able from time to time to get to the castle. But the inquisitive queen gets suspicious and finds out what he is doing and, having learned magic arts from her mother, makes some fine silken shirts, into each of which she sews a charm. Then, with the help of the same cotton ball, she follows the king and finds the six boys. The girl is out at the moment, but the boys, seeing in the distance someone coming, think it is their father and run joyfully to meet him, and she throws the shirts over them, and immediately they are changed into swans and fly away over the forest.

The next day the king comes to visit the children and asks the girl where her brothers are. She tells her father how she saw them being changed into swans. The king, fearing that the girl might also be bewitched, wants to take her home. But since the girl is afraid of her stepmother, she asks to be allowed to spend one more night in the castle. Then she goes to seek her brothers. After a long journey through the wood, she finds a small, miserable hut in which are six little beds. She creeps under one, and just as the sun is setting, the six white swans come in at the window and begin blowing on one another until their swans' down is stripped off like a shirt, and brothers and sister meet each other joyfully. But the brothers tell her that it is a robbers' hiding place and that, if the robbers return and find her, they will murder her. The boys explain that they themselves can only lay aside their swans' feathers for a quarter of an hour each evening. The sister asks how she can redeem them, and they tell her that for the next six years she must neither speak nor laugh. And during that time she must sew six little shirts made from star flowers, then throw them over the swans.

So the girl resolves to rescue her brothers. She leaves the cottage and, penetrating further into the woods, collects star flowers and then goes and sits up in a tree and begins to make shirts. After she has passed some time there, a king when hunting one day finds her and asks her who she is. She does not reply, but first throws down her gold necklace, and then her girdle, and afterward her rich dress in an effort to make him desist. But she is so beautiful that the king's heart is touched, and he falls so much in love with her that he takes her home and marries her.

Then comes the classical motif, for the young king has a wicked mother, now the girl's mother-in-law. When the queen gives birth to a child, the mother-in-law hides it and accuses the queen of having murdered it. This happens three times. The third time the king is obliged to let his wife be tried, and she is condemned to be burned as a witch. But just when the sentence is to be carried out, the time has elapsed, and the six swans fly over. The girl quickly throws the shirts she has brought with her over the birds, and the brothers stand up alive and well. But one shirt she has not had time to finish, so that the youngest brother keeps a swan's wing instead of his left arm. The queen can now tell what happened, the wicked stepmother is condemned to be burned on the scaffold, and the three children who had been hidden away are returned to the court.

Synopsis of "The Seven Ravens"[25]

A man had seven sons, and when at last a daughter was born, she was so weak and small that he decided to baptize her at once, as otherwise she would not go to heaven if she died. The father sent one of his sons hastily to a spring to fetch water for the baptism, but the boys all ran together, and because each strove to be the first to fill the pitcher, between them it got broken. The father first became impatient, saying that the boys were good-for-nothing youths and had forgotten all about the water while playing games. Then he became anxious lest the child should die unbaptized and, in his haste, said, "I would they were all changed into ravens!" He had scarcely finished speaking when he heard a whirring over his head, and looking up, he saw seven coal-black ravens flying over the house.

The parents, who could not revoke the curse, grieved very much for their lost sons, but comforted themselves in some measure with their little daughter, who grew strong and more beautiful every day. The girl, however, overheard people saying that she was certainly very beautiful but that the guilt of her seven brothers rested on her head. This made her very sad, and she went to her parents and learned what had happened. Then she set out on a long journey to the world's end to redeem the boys. All she took with her was a ring belonging to her parents, for a remembrance, a loaf of bread to satisfy her hunger, a bottle of water to drink, and a little stool for moments of weariness. First on her journey she came to the sun, but it was hot and fearful and burned up little children. Then she ran to the moon, but that was cold and wicked-looking and said, "I smell—I smell man's flesh." So she ran away quickly and came to the stars, which were friendly and kind to her and allowed her to stop and rest. Each star was sitting upon its own little seat, except the morning star (Venus), who was standing up and gave her a crooked bone and said, "If you have not this bone, you cannot unlock the glass castle where your brothers are." The girl wrapped up the bone in her handkerchief and went on, but when she arrived at the glass castle she discovered, to her horror, that she had lost the crooked bone, so she cut off her little finger and used that to unlock the door.

A dwarf came to the door, and she told him that she was seeking her seven brothers. He replied that they were not at home, but that she should come in and sit down and wait. He then carried in the food for the seven ravens upon seven dishes and in seven cups. The girl ate a little bit off each dish and drank a little out of each cup, but into the last cup she dropped the ring she had brought with her.

The ravens came in and prepared to eat and drink and noticed that a human had been there, for someone had eaten out of their dishes and drunk out of their cups. But when the seventh came to the bottom of his cup, the little ring rolled out, which he recognized as his parents' and he said, "God grant that our sister is here! Then we are saved."

When the maiden, who stood behind the door, heard these words, she came out, and immediately all the ravens received their human form again and embraced and kissed their sister, and they all went happily home together.

First there is an interesting little variation as far as the number symbolism is concerned—there are six swans and seven ravens; but if we look at the end of the story, we find that in both cases there are eight people: in one story there are the king and the queen and the six redeemed swans, and in the other the sister does not marry, so there are again eight. Thus, however it starts, at the end there are eight, which we can say in both cases has to do with the famous

problem of the relationship of seven to eight: it is the variation of
the three-to-four problem, which plays such an important role in
number symbolism. From Jung's commentary on dreams in the first
part of *Psychology and Alchemy*,[26] we know that the step from three
to four, the assimilation of the fourth function, is a very difficult
stage in psychological evolution. The seventh to the eighth would
be a differentiation of the same problem, because the dangerous
step from three to four can be divided into seven to eight, and then
only half a step must be made. By taking it in two parts, it is a little
bit easier. So the numbers seven and eight show a more differentiated approach to the problem of evil and the inferior function. In
number symbolism seven is usually regarded as the number of an
evolutionary process, as for instance in the case of the seven planets
of classical astrology. One could say that the seven planets were the
basic elements of the horoscope, and therefore the archetypal basic
elements on which every human personality is built. Everybody has
Saturn, Mars, the Moon, etc., but in a different configuration.
Everybody has at some time in life to realize these basic elements,
though according to the pattern of the horoscope the way this
happens is always different, which led to the idea that the seven
planets had to do with the evolution of the personality. There are
also seven days of the week and the seven notes of the octave.
Sometimes seven is the complete number, and sometimes eight, as
the return to the first on the higher level, as it would be in the
musical octave. The number seven contains a certain amount of
inner tension because it is subdivided into three and four. Jakob
Boehme, the mystic who went into a great deal of number symbolism, says that seven is the tension between the spiritual Holy
Trinity above and the four elements on earth below; the eighth is
the lightning which suddenly connects the two, the seven calling
for the eighth. Saint Augustine also speaks of the symbolism of the
seven. He says the six days of the week correspond to the work of
the Creation in Genesis, and on the seventh day God rested, that
is, the day of the Lord. Then you think it stops with the seven, but
he adds that these seven days are still in Time, and there is an
eighth which is Eternity. So we must count the eighth element,
and that would be a "not in Time" element; so eight carries, like

four, the meaning of the Self, the totality aspect; it steps out of the process of evolution into an eternal static state.

In the story of the six swans, the king gets lost in the wood and has to buy his way out by promising to marry the wicked old woman's daughter. The king in general represents the dominating principle of collective consciousness, and in fairy tales he very often is ill or in a difficult situation. The story, therefore, shows the classical situation when the principle of collective consciousness is stuck and lost, and no longer in a leading position and so cannot function appropriately any longer; it is lost in the wood, in the thick of the unconscious. The king cannot find his way out. One could say that there was black magic at the bottom of it, because the nodding old woman turns up who had probably bewitched him into getting lost in the first place. She turns out to be an evil form of the Great Mother, for she is the instigating figure in the cursing of the swans. Mechanical nodding is often attributed to demonic figures. There are other fairy stories where the heroine goes into the forbidden chamber and finds in it an evil, nodding skeleton.[27] In a parallel version she found in the forbidden chamber the figure of the Great Mother, called Maria the Cursed One. She is sitting on a fiery swing, so either nodding or swinging on a fiery swing is a similar motif. It is a basic archetypal idea that demons have a mechanical swinging movement, expressing a state of nonredemption. Many descriptions of the Greek underworld contain the same image: for instance, Sisyphus who has eternally to roll the rock uphill; the Danaides, who had to pour water through a sieve; or Tantalus with the ever-receding water and fruit which he could never reach to drink or eat. There is a meaningless eternal rhythm which nearly leads to the goal, but never quite, and that is the essence of torture, the eternal roundabout of meaninglessness; thus, such mechanical, eternally repeating movements are in mythology attributed to demons or cursed beings.

Psychologically, the motif occurs in psychotic material and expresses something torturing even to the onlooker: there are recurring better phases in which constructive fantasy material appears, the patient seems to improve, and one feels that a positive life movement is building up. But it all crumbles, for just at the decisive moment there is no ego to assimilate the unconscious material; so the ebb and flow—the building up and decomposing—follow in rhythmical procession. But eventually even such movements die down and people petrify and become dumb and stupid, and no inner process seems to go on—it does not seem to reach the surface anymore. This state is mythologically attributed to the effect of the dark side of the Godhead. In Christianity it is the punishment in hell which God imposes and where the weak and lost souls go. The mother goddess also is said to have this dark aspect, which manifests in this meaningless movement, and it is that which gives the old woman in our story the demonic aspect.

Witches frequently have daughters who are beautiful but who, in their character otherwise, are exactly like their mothers. The king marries the witch's daughter, and then his children are tortured by her. But he still has a little sense and smells a rat and tries to save the children, which is quite unusual, for generally he is caught in the witch marriage, and then the children are persecuted by the stepmother. Here the king removes the children and gets to them by the magic cotton ball, a sort of Ariadne thread, but that does not help. If the dominant principle of collective consciousness is worn out, then the children would represent the promise of the new spirit, the new principle, and this is now removed into the wood by the king himself—but in order to preserve it. The principle of consciousness in a single human being tends to become worn out. Then there is need for renewal, and this is always a dangerous moment; one fears the breakdown which is absolutely necessary for renewal; one fears to give up and to be for a short time faced with nothing. Therefore cowardice or ambition in the conscious ego tends to cling to the old ways and to prevent the renewal, and so evil gets in. Here this does not happen directly, because the children are removed. What would that represent?

It often happens to individuals, when they have reached this dangerous point, that they build up a double life; that is, one does not consciously repress the new side, but allows for it in a hidden corner of one's life. For instance, a middle-aged, overworked businessman who has the manager's disease tries to evade a breakdown, becoming more and more neurotic by conducting a hidden affair in a rational way, and allowing for it in a safe little corner where he can live his foolish feelings and the inferior function. He wants to have his cake and eat it too, and to organize things so as to avoid a clash. So on Saturday he goes to his girlfriend, and on Sunday he goes to church, hoping in that way to escape the conflict. Such people begin to get sentimental at the end of the week, but are still reckless sharks the other five days—they do something for their other side, but it must be done in the right way, for otherwise it won't work, if what was intended by the unconscious was a breakdown, a complete change of attitude and not a compromise. The stepmother gets at the children just as though the king had not tried to save them.

In a collective conscious situation, this would be a situation where the feminine principle has disappeared in its positive form and has turned evil. The feminine aspect in the whole story is negative—the only woman, except the heroine, is a negative mother figure. The principle of feeling and of nature is no longer recognized. Consciousness is too masculine and too rational, so that the underworld reacts in this negative form. The negative mother principle transforms the king's boys into swans.

Before looking at the symbolism of the swan, I want first to discuss the beginning of "The Seven Ravens." The raven and the swan are both birds of Apollo and in many ways very similar. In "The Seven Ravens," the father himself in a moment of rage pronounces the curse of his sons, and not the stepmother. It is not the father's conscious ego which acts but his uncontrolled affect, that is, his negative anima. So it turns out to be the same thing as in the first story—the negative femininity—for he does not mean what he says. The father, if he is not a king, represents the habitual conscious attitude of the people. He has the uncontrolled affect which brings about the destruction of his sons.

The second story is connected with the Christian problem of baptizing the girl as quickly as possible, for the boys drop the jug when they go to fetch the baptismal water. So the father, in a so-called holy rage, curses his children, for his intention to save the girl's soul does not come out right. Baptism, according to Christian teaching, guarantees the child an immortal soul and, in the Catholic Church, the *visio beatifica*. If the child is sickly, there can be an emergency baptism (instead of having it on about the third day as usual). If we understand this symbolically as representing the girl's fate, one could say that this girl is likely to have difficulty in getting into the Christian tradition. She is in danger of getting lost, from the standpoint of Christian consciousness. The father tries to force on her the old habit, and in so doing the accident happens. In a way there is a psychological parallel in the beginning of the first story, for the clinging of consciousness to the old principles and ways starts up the evil principle, and suddenly out comes the dark side of the father, whose uncalled-for affect falls upon the boys.

The boys in one case are turned into swans and in the other into ravens. The swan is mythologically rich in meaning. The *Handwörterbuch des deutschen Aberglaubens* (Pocket Dictionary of German Superstitions)[28] says that the word *swan* has the same root as the Latin word *sonare*, meaning "sounding" or "sound" and referring to the singing swan. The swan is supposed to sing very musically before its death, although this has been denied by most natural scientists. But Brehm points out that when swans become old, they get too weak to dive quickly for their food; thus they eat less and starve and are often caught in the ice, not having the strength to go to milder districts. Once caught, they are either eaten by other animals or die slowly from starvation. They seem, right to the very end, to complain bitterly, giving out a high-pitched cry. This strange cry made by the old swans when dying on the ice is probably the hook for the projection of the swan song. The swan is said to know of its approaching death ahead of time and is supposed—like many other birds—to be able to foretell the future and the weather. There is a German expression, *mir schwant*, meaning, "I have a vague hunch, or inspiration, or idea as to the future."

Because the swan is the bird that knows the future, it is holy to Apollo in Greek mythology and to Njödr in Nordic mythology and also plays a role in the famous mythological swan-maiden motif. There are many stories of hunters who find a swan who is really a beautiful woman. For instance, a hunter finds three beautiful women bathing, their feather garments cast aside, and he takes away one of the garments so that one woman cannot regain bird form. He then carries her off, but some catastrophe happens, and either she flies off and disappears forever or he can find her only after a long journey. That is the usual swan-maiden motif, in which the anima appears first as a white bird, generally as a swan. If, while wandering alone in the woods, you meet something odd and are not sure whether it is hallucination or a real human being, mythology says to look at the feet; for demonic beings have swan's or duck's or goose's feet, indicating not a human being but a ghost. In Old England vows were taken in the name of the swan, so there again the swan was endowed with a holy quality. The swan can be said to represent a spiritual aspect of the unconscious psyche. Like all birds, it represents intuitions and hunches, sudden ideas and feelings which come seemingly from nowhere and fly off again.

In the swan-maiden motif we have a hunter who is told of a beautiful woman who first appears as a swan. It is a question of how a man can get hold of his anima: he has to notice moods and half-unconscious thoughts which appear in the background of his consciousness, and hold on to them so that they cannot just disappear again. By writing down the mood or thought, he takes its volatility away and gives it a human quality.

But doing it once is not enough. Even a man who has realized what the anima is can let her slip back into her feather garment and fly out of the window. The same is true for a woman. If we do not watch the animus every day, it returns again to its old bird form. Constant, conscious effort is required to keep these inner entities in their connection with human consciousness, because their natural tendency is to escape; the swan brides will always tend to resume their feather garment and fly away, sometimes with and sometimes without the child. Therefore, negatively, the swan represents the flighty, inhuman quality of the anima. But in human form, she is greater awareness of the unconscious and the possibility of a greater inner realization of eros.

If we look at the swan-maiden story historically, it would refer to the pre-Christian stage. Martin Ninck's book, *Wodan und germanischer Schicksalsglaube*,[29] speaks of the swan as the natural companion of Wotan. If something which has already been in human consciousness is forced into a swan garment, this means a regression. Contents of the unconscious once integrated to a certain extent can, due to a deterioration of the conscious attitude, be repressed once more.

In the twelfth and thirteenth centuries of the Middle Ages, a beginning of the culture of eros was expressed among the Germanic peoples by the Christian knights serving their ladies and wearing arms in their honor, with which went a whole cult of relatedness between man and woman, and of eros in general. At the same time alchemy flourished and, not by chance, there was a connection of alchemy with the *Minnedienst*, where probably under Arabic influence the feminine principle had been recognized and attended to. With this went a certain recognition of nature and the body and the problem of matter. On account of the Reformation and the demonic extraversion of the Renaissance, however, this very hopeful beginning and the recognition of the feminine principle again disappeared and rationality stiffened. Even Meister Eckehart was forgotten. Alchemical symbolism lived a bit longer, but the *Minnedienst* disappeared completely. Thus a most promising psychological attitude, and a very important beginning, suddenly was repressed through the stiffening of the Christian collective conscious attitude, partly due to the split of the Reformation and the Counter-Reformation, but also to the technical rational development which began during the Renaissance. There was, of course, also a positive aspect in the historical progression. But for the development of the anima, it was a regression. We could say the anima was forced back into her swan garment.

In our two stories it is, however, a question not of the anima but of the animus appearing in a swan or raven form. In spite of their seeming difference, swan and raven have much in common. Not only in the Germanic but also in North American Indian and Eskimo mythology, the raven was originally a white bird. In the North American Indian and the circumpolar mythologies it is the great light bringer, a Promethean figure and creator god. When bringing down light and fire to mankind, he got so burned as to become black. In Germanic and especially in Greek mythology, there are legends which say that ravens were first white, but committed some sin and were cursed by Apollo and so became black. It happened also to the crow, looked upon as the raven's wife, who was Coronis, the mother of Asklepios. In the Bible the raven is an ambiguous bird, for when Noah sent it out from the ark, according to legend, it found land but fed on the corpses and did not return. Noah waited in vain and then sent the dove, which brought back the olive leaf. So the raven from then on got a bad mark in the Bible. In an article by Father Hugo Rahner on the heavenly and the earthly spirit, the heavenly spirit is represented by the dove, and the spirit of the devil and the witches by the raven.[30] But since opposites always contain the seed of their own opposite, ravens were also called very pious birds, for they had fed Elijah and also Saint John at Patmos. There is always a strange kind of double thinking about the symbolism of black and white. The French word for white, *blanc,* and the German word, *blank,* have the same root, which means "shining," "clear," and could apply to a shining black or a shining white surface. Psychologically this is not difficult to understand as the secret identity of extreme opposites. As soon as an opposite reaches its extreme form, it turns into its own contrast. From that angle you could say that the raven represents dark thoughts and also a sudden illumination in your mind. The bird in general symbolizes the involuntary concepts and ideas that suddenly possess us. We think *we* have them, but really they alight on our heads. It is not my thought because I have not yet thought it over. It just came to me. It is preconscious awareness of something. To catch it would consist of a critical assimilation of the thought.

In dreams ravens generally appear as thoughts with a melancholy tinge—sad thoughts. You have probably seen pictures, painted by depressed people, that show a dark wood, a desert, a stormy sea, or black birds everywhere, and which refer to the sad, depressing thoughts one has in such a condition: I am nobody and will never get better, never get anywhere, etc. The raven is therefore a destructive bird; but it is also God's messenger, because there is such a thing as a creative depression. If you admit those black thoughts—if you say, "Yes, perhaps I am nobody, but in what sense?"—you can dialogue with the unconscious. A depression is best overcome by going into it, not fighting it—the radio and the *Reader's Digest* only make it worse! It is much better to let such black thoughts come up and to dialogue with them. Then very often they become the bread bringers and connect us with God. A depression is really meant to reconnect one with the divine principle. The hermits went voluntarily into a depression and introverted with it, which meant not knowing anything anymore and being quite stranded. In such a condition the depressing thoughts bring the divine bread, which explains why the raven has a strange double aspect in mythology. Rational consciousness needs to be dimmed by a depression in order that the new light may be found, with new creative possibilities.

Taking up a connection with a swan maiden would mean a possibility for a man to develop his eros. In our two stories, however, it is a woman who takes up contact with her swan and raven brothers. Seen from a feminine angle, this would mean that the heroine takes up a connection with officially rejected thoughts. A woman's mind is usually closer to nature in its negative and positive forms. In the average world of the press and science, what is generally rejected in official thought and scientific and religious subjects is often picked up by women. Since they take matters of the mind less seriously, they have the great advantage of being freer and more flexible, because if a thing is not so important, then why not look at it in a detached way?

The following instance has always struck me as a classical example of the difference in the working of a woman's and a man's mind. I once told a professor of electronics about a parapsychological phenomenon in which three times a glass broke by itself before somebody died. The professor went up in the air and said that that was just chance. I held to my point, and he suddenly looked at me and said that if I was right, then he would shoot himself! I said that that was very narrow-minded, and why should we not investigate the question? He did not have to accept it. But he said that he had taught so many generations that the thing was such-and-such, and that everything else was unscientific nonsense, that he could not survive any change. That was an honorable reaction. The man stood for what he taught, and that is the best kind of scientist and teacher. He has substance, and for him what is true and what is not true stands. In a woman, it would have meant a silly animus stiffening. A woman's ultimate convictions are in the realm of love and its problems. In science she is freer. Change in her scientific ideas is not a question of life or death, she can say, "Let's look at the thing and check up on it and see if it works, and if so we can accept it," which explains why when new movements come up women are often the first to join them. Men take longer to turn to new contents and ideas, but women are more relaxed about them and can have a very positive effect upon the man by bringing him to a more flexible attitude. They act as *femmes inspiratrices* and have a fertilizing effect upon him through their free and creative play-attitude. In many civilizations there is the priestess, generally a mediumistic seeress, the woman who can sniff the wind and know what the weather will be.

In our story the heroine has to bring back into the human community something which had been in it, that is, her bewitched brothers, and that task has to be fulfilled by neither talking nor laughing for six years and by sewing star shirts. The star shirts against the witch's shirt is the recipe by which the girl can redeem her brothers. Enchantment and disenchantment are often achieved in fairy tales by covering with a garment or an animal skin—the wolfskin, etc. There are also many fairy tales where the witch garment or animal skin has to be quickly removed. A skin, or garment, indicates the modus, or the way, in which one appears, or it can be the mask, or the persona—a skin or garment under which you hide. I can appear as I am, or differently from what I am, in which case the garment begins to be a mask, the persona I want to show the world. The "naked truth" is the idea at the bottom of many mystical ceremonies in which the participants appear naked. On the other hand, a garment can also be the true expression of what one is, the way one manifests to human view. Probably most people feel sometimes that they are some vague mass of thoughts and actions, and it is a difficult task to express and make it recognizable to others. If you have for instance, an affect, you have to express it, although there are certain introverts who think the other person should be clever enough to guess. Such people live beneath an animal skin, they have no modus by which they can express what they fear or like or think of the other being. When you cannot express yourself, you drop back into the animal skin. When wrapped up in an affect, sometimes you cannot present its inner core. It must first be differentiated and integrated before you can express its basic content.

There are many ways of taking away the animal skin and bringing the human being back to human shape. Suppose it is vitally important that someone should express an affect, or resistance to another person—children must express resistances against parents, and analysands against the analyst—the whole question is whether it can be brought out in a human form, in which case it loses its wickedness, its sting, and its poison. If in a human way someone can say he does not like this or that, if it can be expressed decently, only an inhuman person would not accept it. But often one is caught in the affect, and then aggressiveness comes in. Sometimes analysands are so afraid of their aggressiveness in expressing a resistance that they write it down; but that does not help, because though they read it very nicely and humanly, the voice drops, or something, and one knows that the aggressive affect is still there. The feeling below has not been dealt with, so that the analyst feels inhumanly attacked; the affect has not been overcome, when only the surface is humanized. The difficult thing is that one's resistance should be humanized right down to the physical vibration, not only veiled in a polite form. One can pretend that one was quite polite and not aggressive, but the affect makes the atmosphere bad, for both persons can feel it and the other gets the physical impact. The humanization of such an archetypal dynamism is an aspect of individuation, for it means its integration, becoming conscious of it, which is awfully difficult. Mythologically expressed, it is the great task of getting a bewitched person back into human shape, a redemption motif which you find in all mythologies.

Sewing the star shirts, therefore, would mean working for many years in the deepest introversion and concentration, in order to find the human way to let these irrational unconscious contents— swans—reappear in human life in a way which does not shock or disintegrate the conscious world. It is a creative task. From a negative affect, what remains afterward is a reasonable statement of a difference. Sometimes animus possession can be recognized, but sometimes at the bottom of one's criticism or resistance is a true statement of oneself, when one can just agree to differ from the other person. Separation from the collective affect and its contagious effect is an aspect of individuation.

It is also possible, however, to cheat oneself when one humanizes a resistance. I have seen analysands again and again cheat themselves in this way. They fight with animus and anima, abreact the emotion, then think they do not need to talk about it. But this is an illusion! One should say, "Last week I had a hell of a resistance, and in the end I saw that it was my own animus, or anima." One should mention it. If you are in touch with somebody and hate that person for weeks and then get over it, why not mention it? It is inhuman not to do so. In a resistance there is generally a great deal of projection, but the analyst has done something to earn it, and it is important that he should know what started the drama. If the analysand speaks in the past tense, then the analyst can apologize, because, although it is the analysand's problem and now overcome, it is important to know what happened. Humanizing an animal or even bestial affect, or the civilized expression of negative opinions, is therefore an enormous task; it is the essence of culture.

9

Before the heroine's brothers became birds in our two stories, they were adolescents. In the context of feminine psychology a boy represents the honest enterprise and an impulse toward active life, also straightforward, naive ideas. Through the activity of the witch, the negative mother, this part of the young woman has been reduced to swans and ravens, that is, to otherworldly or melancholy fantasies. They need a star flower garment in order to return to the human realm. They could also be contents of a more spiritual nature, emotional, unconscious thoughts which need to be expressed in a humanly adequate manner. It is generally both, for emotion usually also contains a symbolic idea; and, vice versa, a thought which comes from the unconscious generally contains a tremendous amount of emotion. The material for the shirts is made from star flowers. In the woods there grows, on a leafless stem, a very simple little starlike flower called a *Sternblume*, a star flower. I do not know the botanical name. Such flowers are usually to be found in the moss under a tree where the sun shines. They are something like anemones, but rather more green, and suggest a star fallen into the green moss of the woods, a star growing from below instead of falling from above.

The motif of the star coming from below is archetypal and was of great importance in alchemical thinking. Paracelsus, the Swiss doctor and great alchemist, and one of his pupils, Gerhard Dorneus, or Dorn, whom Jung frequently quotes in his works on alchemy, expressed the idea that stars and herbs correspond astrologically. This thought has its origin in the Aristotelian-Arabic tradition of the Middle Ages, namely that every flower or herb has an astrological correspondent and is the earthly image of an astrological constellation; there is the whole concept of the *signatura rerum* behind it. In connection with this, Dorneus evolved an alchemical piece of active imagination, obtained not by painting or writing but by mixing substances. He says that at a certain stage of the work, it is essential to "shape the heavens below."[31] For this he recommends taking the dregs of old wine, the tartar (the deposit or the hard crust formed on the side of the cask), and distilling it until it obtains a liquid of blue color; then the heavens below will have been prepared. Into this, certain stars must be introduced, which is done by putting in yellow flowers, the Cheyri, and others, and thus the heavens below are established. This must be cooked, and the result represents the last stage in making the philosopher's stone, namely the ultimate union with the whole cosmic nature. When the heavens below have been produced, the alchemist is united with the *unus mundus*, cosmic divine nature.

The idea, as far as we can understand Dorneus, is the following. Before God created the world, He conceived it in his mind. A plan exists in the architect's mind before building, so God, as a good architect, conceived a mental image of the world and of everything in it, from which later developed the multiple realizations in matter. This sum of detailed models, all still one in the mind of God, is identified in scholastic teaching with the feminine archetypal figure of the Wisdom of God, and was called the sum of the *typi,* or archetypal ideas. Dorneus calls this potential divine world the *unus mundus,* the one cosmos that is still an undivided whole. By *unus mundus* is expressed the idea that a multiplicity of objects only comes into existence by the realization of this plan. Before this model plan of the world was materialized, there were no single objects; they were like germs united in a liquid, or something similar, rather than an immense sum of material objects as the material world really is. The oneness of the Godhead in matter was thus expressed. This one world that is hidden behind our real world is the dimension with which the alchemist unites himself and becomes one, but not in a pantheistic form. Pantheism is the idea of becoming one with the actual physical world, but Dorneus' idea is to unite with what is behind, the germ of oneness behind the multiplicity of actual existence.

The Chinese Taoist philosophy contains a similar idea: the enlightened man, the Taoist master, becomes one with the Tao; he lives with the *germs* of reality, but not reality itself. In the *I Ching,* hexagram 16 says in the second place: "Firm as a rock." The philosopher's stone, the wise man (the superior man) "knows the germs and acts at once."[32] By "knowing the germs," the *I Ching* means, for instance, the following facts. Let us assume that there is something like archetypal evil in the air; later it realizes itself by becoming an evil deed, or somebody's thought. Now it exists, and you cannot turn the wheel back as you could have done in its germlike state; when it was unconsciously constellated, but not yet realized, something could have been done about it. At that stage you can do something about fate, if you understand and can realize what is going on. The wise man, therefore, knows the germs and is capable of realizing what is going on behind the screen and can act upon these things and give them a better turn, or a creative expression. He is in connection with the world behind the world and recognizes the germs and acts at once. There is the same idea in the alchemist becoming one with the *unus mundus,* with the totality of the archetypal constellations behind reality. He knows and is in immediate connection with them, and that is the source of his creativity and also gives him some possibility of having a creative influence on what is going on. That is becoming one with the *unus mundus,* as Dorneus conceived it, behind his strange idea of establishing the heavens below and becoming one with them. The stars, as we know, symbolize archetypal constellations, the same thing as what the Taoist philosophy calls the germs, that thing which is not yet anything, which could mean a lot of different things, but is also not yet something definite.

The word *constellation* comes from *stella,* star. It is a very vague concept, because when we experience some exciting news, we say, "Now the problem has become constellated," and then feel that we have said something. We have a hunch of what we mean by that, but really we know absolutely nothing of what we mean, only that an aspect of the unconscious has been stirred. It comes up in the form of synchronistic events on the outside. Suppose a patient has an unusual dream of being threatened by, say, the waves of the sea, or a lion, but on the outside only complains about the boringness of life and having a headache. You can say that the unconscious has announced an archetypal emotional constellation, an X, but one could not yet say that it has been constellated on the outside. You make a mental note and the analysis goes on for three-quarters of a year, but all the time you have the feeling that that tremendous drive, the libido of the lion, has not yet been constellated in outer life. Then one day a charming man turns up and asks the woman to go out and have an aperitif with him; the husband makes no objection and they have a very nice time. The headache gets better, the husband dreams about a traffic accident, she dreams of burglars, and now the thing is constellated!

One always knew she was looking out the window for an adventure, something wanted to create heat, a conflict and adventure and life. I would say that the problem of the lion, or of the waves of the sea, hitherto latent, becomes constellated. To understand the dream six months beforehand would be to know the germs. A bit of the biography of the woman is now constellated. When she had the dream, it was ahead of her and far away, but when the earthquake comes it is actually constellated. That is how we usually use the word. There is already a certain order in such a constellation—an archetype implies order, and arrangement; there is a pattern, and you see what the thing is driving at, more or less. As you know, the symbolism of the lion has an infinite multiplicity of meanings and can take different forms. After three months it might be the just-so story of a love affair, or a divorce, or a psychotic upset, or a suicidal attempt, or a tremendous outbreak of emotion and its suffering and the enlargement of consciousness—you cannot predict which. The one thing you may be sure of is that life will not go on smoothly for the next ten years!

Historically, the word *constellation* comes from astrology. As Jung says, astrology is a medieval, scientific attempt to describe synchronicity with the help of, or by watching, synchronistic events in the sky. The star map is a beautiful mixture of order and disorder; there are regular and irregular events, like meteors. Behind the word *constellation* there is a whole mystery; one knows, more or less, what one means by it, but it points to a mystery.

To make a shirt with star flowers would mean something paradoxical. She sews the shirts with the purpose of redeeming birds from their animal shape, giving them a human way of expression, but she uses an archetypal constellation, a star, which seems most *inhuman*. The shirts are a paradox—by the use of an archetypal constellation, you help these contents to be humanly expressed! But consider what we do when we interpret a dream or a myth properly, we amplify the material with other archetypal motifs, we use archetypal motifs, as a garment for the dream by which its content can be integrated. That is how we interpret unconscious material, and we only learn mythology in order to have enough knowledge of archetypal constellations with which to sew shirts for our own and our patients' unconscious contents!

Flowers, in general, also have to do with feeling. We use them to express feeling, for instance, at births, marriages, funerals, and so on. That the rose symbolizes love, eros, is well known. Instead of using up the stars from heaven, the girl could have done something with stones, or she could have used flowers. That she used star flowers points to the feminine need of a feeling realization of archetypal constellations; for in a woman realization takes place via feeling, enlightenment usually comes to her in that realm.

She makes the shirts while sitting in a tree, a refuge probably from wild animals. One would still take refuge there in an African jungle, where it is advisable to fasten yourself in a tree for the night. Our cousins, the apes, spend the night in trees for the sake of safety. So trees have the basic idea of being above the ground and relatively safe from most types of snakes and other dangerous animals. In comparative religion, the tree, and the climbing of a tree, often has the meaning of approaching heaven, like going to the top of a mountain to converse with the gods and the ghosts who are supposed to be in the sky. Mircea Eliade describes in his book *Shamanism* how the Siberian shaman at the time of initiation climbs a birch tree and there speaks with the spirits. [33] In an ecstatic state the novices make connection with the other world and come down as initiated and enlightened people. The shaman instructor climbs a higher birch tree and the initiate a lower one nearby, and a rope is stretched from one tree to the other, down which the instructor sends all the objects the new initiate will require for his duties: the drum, the girdle, etc., down along the rope. The heavenly powers give the initiate what he will need afterward in his work as a shaman. Only the shaman and such people are connected with the other world, and the magical connection is made via the rope, which the new shaman gets when sitting in a tree during his initiation. When he comes down from the tree, there is a great celebration. He was in a state of ecstasy and in connection with the other world, which means being in connection with and tied to one's own process of individuation and inner psychological growth.

I have heard a story which shows how the archetypal symbol of the tree can still break through. A boy in the United States at the age of about sixteen or seventeen got into a state very near schizophrenia. His parents were frightened that he might become insane and sent him to an uncle, a farmer in the Midwest, hoping that hard work might help. The boy arrived but instead of doing the hard work climbed a tree, where he made a nest and took up a lot of food. The farmer, instead of calling a psychiatrist or insisting on the hard work, said, "To hell with him. If he wants to sit in a tree, let him," and he left him alone, and nobody bothered him except to give him food. He remained in the tree for three weeks or a month, just sitting in his nest, and then came down, completely reasonable. The upset was over and he was okay. That was a narrow and lucky escape. The boy saved himself by following the archetypal impulse and had the luck not to be prevented by his friends. You could say he went through a shamanic initiation. He probably had visions from the collective unconscious in the tree; it was probably quite a remarkable experience. Had he been prevented, he might have had to be hospitalized. So this archetype is still very much alive, as evidenced by this story of a boy who had just enough instinct to cure himself and keep himself from madness. Sitting in a tree, therefore, means retreat from reality and retiring into the realm of the spirits. It is as though, instead of avoiding the thing which threatened, one retired into it. The danger is a complete loss of connection with reality, and the advantage is that the threatening unconscious becomes a second womb, out of which rebirth can take place. The tree has therefore also a maternal quality, something from which one can fall like a fruit; it represents a process of spiritual rebirth. In many countries there is a superstition that children come from trees. Climbing up a tree and climbing down again is a process of psychological rebirth. So people in a difficult situation sometimes live "in a tree" for a while, or normal children build a nest and play at living in a tree; it is the fantasy and magical world. In the United States one says, "Go climb a tree" to someone in a bad temper, or you can "drive someone up a tree," or "up the pole," away from human contact.

During the time the heroine of the fairy tale is up the tree, she must not speak or laugh, which is often the rule during a state of incubation. In primitive incubation rites, boys are often shut up in a hut, or in a sweat lodge, and have to be silent. The words *mysticism* and *mystic* come from *myo,* keeping one's mouth shut. To put one's finger over one's mouth implies a secret about which one should keep silent. So mystical silence is the conscious variation of something that is less positive when it happens to one unconsciously. When an overwhelming and emotionally latent content of the unconscious constellates, it makes the human being dumb; it cannot be expressed. You probably know of states of emotion in which you cannot speak. If an analysand touches an emotional complex and cannot speak anymore, that is not due to lack of goodwill, for it cannot be talked about, so that possibly the most essential things do not come out for five or six years. The analysand gets near the content but cannot talk—the emotion becomes too great. The catatonic state is the extreme expression of such a condition. On the other hand, when one decides not to talk about something in order to keep it inside and allow it to grow, neither spoiled nor contaminated by the vulgar thought of collective consciousness, then silence becomes the quality of consciously and silently covering up a mystery, in order that it may become a religious experience. Silence protects the content of the unconscious against collective misunderstanding externally and in oneself as well. We all have the banal interpretation in us, the "nothing but" reaction, by which we can harm important inner contents.

Everyone who has done creative work knows that *in statu nascendi* the creative idea should not be talked about. A writer should not show or discuss what he is writing with too many people. He usually knows when the work is in the delicate state of growth. Someone may say, "Yes . . . very good," but just that little hesitation after the "yes" can rob him of his courage to go on—it is as delicate as that before it is finished. A hesitation in the response or a silly question may lame him. One may criticize it oneself once the "child" has been born and there is a certain distance; but when it is half formed, one cannot talk about it.

While in this state of silence, the heroine is discovered by the king, who takes her home and marries her. But even when she has children, she remains silent. Though she becomes the queen and goes back into human life, she yet goes on working on the redemption of her brothers, and in keeping to that process in silence, she really leads a double life. She is the queen but secretly has this second occupation, about which nobody knows, and this double life involves her in misunderstandings and misinterpretations. The wicked mother-in-law takes her children away and accuses her of having murdered them. This motif often comes up in the legends since the middle of the thirteenth century. It is archetypal and is built into many fairy tale variations, and appears in many different countries and stories, so it must be very essential and typical. However, it is not a situation produced by one cause or constellation only. It can be brought about through the negative mother or the negative father complex; it can have different archetypal reasons, though the solution is very similar. The double-life problem of the queen is, in one way, connected with the king, the dominant of collective consciousness, for he listens to his wicked mother, who persecutes the new queen.

Although the latter is productive and has fulfilled her normal feminine life, yet there is something going on behind the screen, a second process, which leads to misunderstandings. Sometimes the stepmother, or the mother-in-law, can alienate the king from his wife. Then she is slowly driven into complete isolation, and her heroic deed consists in keeping silent; the pressure in the situation does not succeed in forcing her to disclose her secret, in spite of the threat to her life. She endures the misunderstanding of those around her, and her highest endeavor is applied to keeping the religious secret. Her plight could be likened to that of Job, who, at the time of his deepest depression and difficulty, was surrounded by loving friends with their collective misinterpretations. In such a situation nowadays people tell you that you are clinging to a neurotic idea. To you, it is religious loyalty to God, that is what it feels like inwardly. But since others talk like that, perhaps it is just an animus idea or possession; for there is something in you that puts the same question. To have that innermost instinctive assuredness that tells you what is what is extremely difficult when one is torn by doubts and really does not know whether one's animus or one's real nature is speaking. For example, a woman may love a man who disappoints her in some matter of relationship, and something within her says that she is a damn fool and that it is not a proper relationship for her. But another voice tells her that that is her animus and that she should hold on even though the situation looks bad. Then again, a voice says that she is tying herself to the wrong problem. Generally, a woman's individuation process has to pass through such phases, and who can say what is the right thing? Dreams may be a great help, but even they are not always clear; so one may be left alone, like Job sitting among the ashes and covered with boils. But this is the moment in which a human being can discover his immediate and personal connection with the Godhead.

Keeping the discussion within, and not allowing disruptive forces to bring it into the open, is one of the ultimate vital battles in the process of individuation. Here it goes so far that the woman is condemned to be burned at the stake as a witch, but even so she remains loyal to her inner task. The solution comes in the classical way—by chance—or, as we would prefer to say, synchronistically. The six years are over and the swans come and she throws the shirts over them, redeems them, and is liberated from the stake. But one sleeve she had not finished, and the youngest brother has a swan's wing instead of his left arm. One could say with Goethe: *"Uns bleibt ein Erdenrest, zu tragen peinlich"* (in Sir Theodore Martin's translation: "Alas! still with earthly taint is he encumbered"); though here one could also say: *"Uns bleibt ein Himmelsrest, zu tragen peinlich"* (Something of the heavens remains with us, awkward to carry).

In India the Atman, the divine spirit, especially in the form which rather keeps out of creation, in contrast to Brahman—though they are the same—is often symbolized by the swan and is said to be like a swan hovering over the sea with one leg in and one leg out of the water. If he should pull out the second leg, the world would cease to exist. Maya, the illusion of the world, goes on because Atman does not pull out his second leg. In this fairy tale you could say that three-quarters, or five-sixths, of the Atman is in the world, but one wing is in the other. Had the left wing been finished and become an arm, there would be no problems and no questions left over. It is like a religious and spiritual question mark which can never be integrated and perhaps should not be, for then everything would be too clear and too settled. One would know all about it, and that would be death. When interpreting unconscious material, one has a kind of conscience about it. If one interprets it too superficially, one feels that one has not got to the depth or essence; but if one interprets it thoroughly, one comes to the point where it seems enough, though the fullest explanation has still not been given. Even the best is never the whole, and is only relatively satisfactory. The archetypal basis must remain a mystery, which the best interpretation cannot solve; it has its wing in the other world and can never be quite pulled over into this one. The Catholic teaching is that every dogma has a clear, comprehensible part which the Church Fathers can discuss, but that there is also a mystery about which one can never be enlightened. It is that spiritual question mark which remains, even if a satisfactory and full attempt has been made to bring into consciousness the secret content of the symbol. If, in a banal way, we took the swans as the woman's animus, it would mean that the animus always also contains the element of being a mystery, something inexplicable which is the secret of both its beauty and its awkwardness. This last boy is a cripple, with a silly swan's wing and only one hand with which to act; it is something unsettled which belongs to the element of being human.

The brothers and sister kiss each other, the persecution by the mother-in-law is shown up, and she is burned as a witch. She is the evil manifestation of the negative mother, the toad at the bottom of the well, which is now removed, and the others, the six brothers and the king and queen, live together and make eight, the symbol of totality.

In the story of the ravens, there are several differences, for instead of climbing a tree the girl goes on a long journey. She goes to the sun and moon and stars and gets help from the morning star; this is a variation of the archetypal motif called the "heavenly journey." It is also to be found with the shamans and in antiquity, as well as in the Book of Enoch in the Jewish tradition. Initiation takes place through a long journey and the final return to earth, when one is a prophet and a shaman, knowing about the things of the other world. The alchemists tell of their alchemical journey when an angel took them to the firmament and star powers initiated them into the knowledge of alchemy. In fairy tales on feminine psychology, when the heroine makes the quest by such a heavenly journey, there is very often a reversal of values, in which the sun is the most evil power, the moon rather evil, and the night with its teeming stars beneficial, in contrast to the usual interpretation by which the sun is the source of enlightenment and the night the darkening power to be avoided. This motif is to be found in most mystery journeys concerned with the problem of eros, of love, whereas when it is a question of going into the Beyond to find spiritual and mental illumination, the sun is of the higher value. In the Persian Mithraic mysteries, for instance, in the time of Christ, the novice goes through the stages of the raven, the lion, the sun runner, and the fathers before becoming one with the sun god. The sun, for a man, is a symbol of the Godhead and of the Self, the goal of initiation and the most positive symbol of the mystery. But here, and in many other initiations, there is the same thing reversed, even down to the symbolism of Mozart's *Magic Flute*, where the prince says to his bride, "Do not trust too much the sun or the moon; come down with me into the darkness of the night." The darkness is the goal and the sun is a destructive burning power.

You remember the motif we discussed briefly in *The Girl without*

Hands in which the king had to put the napkin over his face. There we saw that consciousness is destructive to certain processes in the psyche. The most beneficent power for the girl on this journey is the morning star—that is, Venus, the principle of love and all its symbolism. Venus, the principle of eros par excellence, helps her. There are problems which cannot be solved by pulling them into consciousness, but only by following one's own feeling, and that is very often essential in a woman's process of individuation. Venus gives the girl the crooked bone with which to unlock the glass castle where the seven ravens are imprisoned. This is an important symbol. It is the wishbone in the chicken with which, as with the double cherries, the one who gets the bigger end has his wish, which must not be disclosed. There are all sorts of superstitions connected with the crooked bone, and one common to the whole of Europe is its use in love charms. In the Middle Ages, a frog's leg was put in an anthill, and when the ants had eaten away all the flesh, it was used for love charms. With the crooked bone, a love charm could be made. Probably the crooked bone that Venus gives the girl has some similar meaning. We might ask ourselves, what has a crooked bone to do with a love charm? It probably has to do with hooking! That is an old association, but we also speak of a hook for projection. It is probably the archetypal fantasy that you need such crooked bones in the hope that your positive projection will not fall off, but will hold on to the other. The girl puts the crooked bone given her by Venus in her handkerchief, but loses it, and then, after a little hesitation, she cuts off her little finger and uses that as a key for the glass castle.

The cutting off of the little finger suggests a painful sacrifice, giving a bit of one's own flesh; the sacrifice would have been too easy if Venus' crooked bone had been used: seemingly, love magic alone no longer works; a woman has to suffer and contribute to the problem if she wants to develop and redeem her own personality. We can also say that we can use all our fingers as hooks, in order to grab something, and if we cut off one, we lose a hook. It is a sacrifice of ego wishes. A woman in love involuntarily has also an intrigue or plot: "I want," "I wish," "He must," etc. There is always the intrigue and the plot, beginning with walking past the place where one hopes to meet "him" and then looking surprised, though in the morning it had all been planned. That is hooking with the ego. Cutting off the finger would mean cutting off the egotistical planning and plotting and the intentional attempts at hooking in. There is always the crucial problem as to whether or not the fulfillment of love is meant by the Self; if not, then it must be sacrificed.

In chiromancy each finger is attributed to a planet, and Mercury rules over the little finger, so its sacrifice would be the cutting off of mercurial planning or plotting, the ego use of it—using the cleverness of the witch for ego purposes. The woman thinks she hooks the beloved, but she gets caught herself. She becomes the victim of her planning and so loses her freedom, from which arise the innumerable tragic cases one so often comes up against. A woman sometimes comes into analysis with an ego purpose: she is interested in a particular man, whom she has tried unsuccessfully to hook—she was too neurotic—but the devil says that if she were all right herself, then she could do it! So she comes with a clever mercurial plan so that she may be able to hook more efficiently. And if the plan fails, she walks out of analysis and throws the whole thing over and thus confesses that her ego plot has failed. That is one of the various dangerous corners of feminine psychology in the process of individuation. We need to sever the little finger, to sacrifice the ego plans and hand the whole thing over to the Self. To love someone is quite legitimate, but one should add *Deo concedente* (God willing). Similarly, when a man begins to work with the unconscious in analysis, the anima will impose upon him concepts and a *Weltanschauung* which will disgust him. Even though he knows that the knowledge he will acquire is essential to him, there is the question as to whether he really is willing to risk his career. But with a woman it is the sacrifice of the ego planning in love that is the important step, and the story shows how the girl sacrifices that by cutting off her finger to open the glass castle.

Glass illustrates a condition of being partially cut off. In a wooden or stone castle, you are completely imprisoned in every way. In a glass one, however, you are mentally free, but emotionally cut off. Glass is a nonconductor, which is why it is used for windows.

Neither heat nor cold pass through it; it is an isolator, although you can at least see through it. People say in analysis, "I see the problem quite clearly, but I do not feel it." They are behind a glass wall. That is being partly cut off, not intellectually, but emotionally; one is imprisoned by the glass wall. The spirit can also be a negative imprisonment, if an emotional experience is intended by the Self. Let us take it practically: a man, an intellectual introvert, falls in love with a woman; his anima is projected onto her. The unconscious gives him this experience because it wants to get him into a feeling experience and into life. But at that moment the man says, "But Jungian psychology says that such a thing is only anima projection, so I will go home and do some active imagination about her." What he says is quite all right. It is in accordance with Jungian psychology and sometimes of the highest value, but it is not meant to be applied at this moment. Thus, what would have been the spirit becomes imprisonment and a hindrance. It is paradoxical: the spirit redeems one if one is too emotionally involved, and imprisons one if one does not live enough.

A glass castle does not show you how to get into action. You see the situation but cannot do more, for you do not know how. In analysis you talk the thing over and agree with the analyst and see the situation, but what can you do about it? Sometimes the analyst sees a way out and how to break the glass by making an emotional attack himself, but very often one has no such inspiration and must leave it to fate. Here breaking through the glass is done by the sacrifice. Nothing cuts a woman off more from inner and outer life than ego plots, for in them is a kind of mechanism which arrests life and stops the process. A woman who goes into analysis in order to become more attractive and be able to hook the man is calculatedly misusing the spirit and shutting the door against anything spontaneous. Her calculation precludes the irrational events of life and imprisons everything.

In the house the girl finds the seven ravens and a dwarf attending them. He is a kind of servant, but also the owner of the castle where they live. The dwarf is a symbol of the creative power of the unconscious. In German and Grecian mythology he is the great craftsman. A certain class of Greek dwarfs were called the dactyls (fingers). Dwarfs are miners, smiths, jewelers, sculptors, musicians, and so on. They generally belong to the surroundings of the Great Mother and personify creative impulses. That which is plotting, when connected with the ego, turns, when cut off, into creativity. Creativity is the alternative for intriguing and plotting, and women who indulge themselves in this way do not want to cut off the finger of plotting for the creative dwarf. And this gives us the tip as to where the ravens went! They went to a secret, earthly creative power, which means that all that energy, all that mental vitality which this girl had missed—her brothers—is living in the unconscious with the creative dwarf and must be redeemed. By the symbol of the ring the ravens become connected with her again and turn into human beings and return home joyfully with her.

Of the two stories, this one is the less satisfactory. The girl just goes home with her parents; it is a restitution of the former infantile situation, and the dwarf is left behind. In "The Six Swans" the infantile mark remains only as the left wing of the youngest brother. Even in life, however, the process of individuation does not always go on. Sometimes it is only a "cure," though at other times there may be a much greater development. Where the process of individuation halts is a just-so story.

10

For our last story, I would like to return to the problem of the negative mother complex on a deeper level. It is the problem of relating to a feminine aspect of the Godhead in its numinous and sometimes dangerous side. The positive half of the antique Great Mother has been partly integrated into the figure of the Virgin Mary. Many other aspects of the Great Mother have been lost, but they reappear in certain fairy tales.

Vasilisa the Beautiful[34]

Synopsis of the Tale

In an empire in a faraway country there once lived a merchant and his wife and their one beautiful daughter called Vasilisa. When the child was eight years old, the wife suddenly became very ill. She called Vasilisa to her deathbed, gave her a doll, and said, "Listen, my dear child, these are my last words and don't forget them. I am dying and leave you my blessing and this doll. Keep it always with you, show it to nobody, and whenever you are in any trouble, ask it for advice." Then she kissed her daughter for the last time and died.

The merchant mourned his wife for a long time, but then decided to marry again and chose a widow with two daughters. But for his daughter Vasilisa, the marriage was a disappointment, for the new wife was a real stepmother who gave her all the hard work to do, hoping that the sun and wind would spoil her beauty and that she would begin to look like a peasant girl. But Vasilisa bore everything without grumbling and became more beautiful every day, while her stepsisters got thinner and thinner and uglier all the time, because of their envy, although they sat still with their hands in their laps all day. The doll, however, always comforted Vasilisa and did a lot of the work for her.

A year passed in this way, but Vasilisa, though much sought after, was forbidden to marry before her stepsisters, whom nobody looked at. Then the merchant had to go away to another country. In his absence the stepmother moved to a house at the edge of a great forest. In this same forest there was a little house in a clearing in which the Baba Yaga lived. The Baba Yaga permitted nobody to approach, and anyone who did she ate up. The stepmother, for whose plans the new house stood in exactly the right place, always sent Vasilisa into the wood, but she always returned safely, thanks to the doll.

One autumn evening the stepmother gave the three girls work to do. One had to knit and the other to embroider, but Vasilisa had to spin. The stepmother then put out the fire, left a small light burning so that the girls could see to work, and went off to bed. The candle burned down, and the stepsister took her knitting needle to clean the wick, and in so doing deliberately put it out. But one daughter said she didn't need any light, her knitting needles gave enough, and the other said that her embroidery needle gave her enough light too, but that Vasilisa must go to the Baba Yaga and fetch fire; and they pushed her out of the room. The latter went to her room and fed her doll as usual and told her about going to the wood. The doll told her not to be afraid, but to take her along and nothing bad would happen.

Although terrified, Vasilisa put the doll in her pocket, crossed herself, and went into the wood. Suddenly a man in white rode by on a white horse, and day came. Farther on, a man in red rode by on a red horse, and the sun rose. All through the night and the next day, Vasilisa walked through the wood and in the evening came to a hut surrounded by a hedge made of human

bones with skulls stuck on the posts. The doors were made of
bones, the bolt to the door of a human arm, and in place of the
lock there was a mouth with grinning teeth. Vasilisa was almost
senseless with horror and stood rooted to the spot. Then suddenly another rider came by, this time all in black and sitting
on a black horse. He jumped off and opened the door and
disappeared as though swallowed up by the ground, and it was
black as night. But soon all the eyes in the skulls that made the
hedge began to twinkle, and it was as light as day in the
clearing. Vasilisa trembled with fear, but didn't know where to
go and stood still.

Then the trees began to rustle, and the Baba Yaga appeared
sitting in a mortar, steering with a pestle, and wiping out her
tracks with a broom. When she reached the door, she sniffed
and cried out that it smelled like Russians and asked who was
there.

"I am, Grandmother. My stepsisters sent me to you to fetch
the fire."

"Good," said the Baba Yaga. "I know you. Stay with me for a
bit, and then you shall have the fire."

So they went in together, and the Baba Yaga lay down and
told Vasilisa to bring her everything that was in the oven to eat.
There was enough there for ten, but the Baba Yaga ate everything up and left only a crust of bread and a little soup for
Vasilisa. Then she said, "Tomorrow, when I go out, you must
sweep up the yard, sweep out the hut, cook the midday meal, do
the washing, then go to the cornshed and sort out all the
mildewed corn from the good seed. Everything must be done by
the time I get home, for otherwise I shall eat you."

When the Baba Yaga began snoring in bed, Vasilisa gave the
doll the food she had and told her of the hard work she had to
do. But the doll said she should eat the food herself and not be
afraid, yet say her prayers and go to bed, for the morning was
cleverer than the evening.

In the morning when Vasilisa woke up, the eyes in the skulls
were just shutting, the white rider ran by, and the day came.
The Baba Yaga whistled, and the pestle and mortar and broom

appeared; the red rider rode by, and the sun came up. When
the Baba Yaga had gone, Vasilisa was left quite alone and
troubled as to which work she should begin, but it was all done,
and the doll was just removing the last seeds of the mildewed
corn. Vasilisa called the doll her savior, saying it had saved her
from great misfortune, and the doll told her that now she only
had to cook the dinner.

When evening came, Vasilisa laid the table and waited, and
when the Baba Yaga came, she asked if everything was done.
"Look yourself, Grandmother," said Vasilisa.

The Baba Yaga looked at everything and was furious not to be
able to find any fault, but she only said, "Yes, it's all right," and
then called on her faithful servants to grind her corn. Thereupon three pairs of hands appeared and began to sort out the
grain. The Baba Yaga ate just as much as the evening before and
then told Vasilisa she should do the same work the next day, but
in addition, she should sort the poppy seeds in the granary and
clean the dirt away.

Again Vasilisa asked the doll, who told her to do the same as
the evening before, and next day the doll did everything Vasilisa
was supposed to do. When the old woman came home, she
looked everything over and then again called to her faithful
servants. The three pairs of hands came and removed the poppy
seeds and pressed out the oil.

While the Baba Yaga was eating her meal, Vasilisa stood
silently beside her. "What are you staring at without speaking a
word?" asked the Baba Yaga. "Are you dumb?"

"If you will allow me to do so, I would like to ask some
questions," said Vasilisa.

"Ask," said the Baba Yaga, "but remember that not all questions are wise; much knowledge makes one old."

Vasilisa said she would only like to ask about the riders. The
Baba Yaga told her that the first was her day, the red her sun,
and the black her night. Then Vasilisa thought of the three
pairs of hands, but didn't dare to ask and kept silent.

"Why don't you ask more?" said the Baba Yaga.

"That's enough," said Vasilisa. "You said yourself, Grandmother, that too much knowledge made people old."

The Baba Yaga then said that she was wise only to ask about what she saw outside the hut, but that now she would like to ask *her* questions, and she asked how Vasilisa had managed all the work.

Vasilisa said that her mother's blessing helped her. "Is that so?" said the Baba Yaga. "Then get out of here. I don't want any blessing in my house." And she pushed Vasilisa out of the room and out of the door and took a skull from the hedge with the burning eyes in it and put it on a pole and gave it to Vasilisa, saying, "Here is your fire for your stepsisters. Take it home with you."

So Vasilisa hurried away and by the evening of the next day arrived home and thought she would throw the skull away, but a voice came from it saying she should not do so but should take it to her stepmother. And because Vasilisa saw no light in the house, she did just that.

For the first time the stepmother and her stepsisters came to meet her in a friendly way and told her they had had no fire since she left, that they had not been able to light any fire and what they fetched from the neighbor was extinguished as soon as it got to their room. "Perhaps your fire won't go out," said the stepmother. She took the skull into the living room, but the glowing eyes stared unceasingly into hers and her daughters' eyes, right down into their souls. They tried to hide, but the eyes followed them everywhere, and by the morning they were burnt to ashes.

When day came, Vasilisa buried the skull, shut up the house, went into the town, and asked a lonely old woman to let her stay with her until her father came home, and so she waited. One day she told the woman that she was bored, with nothing to do, and that she should buy her some thread and she would spin. But the thread which Vasilisa spun was so even, and was so thin and fine as silk hair, that there was no machine fine enough to weave it, so Vasilisa asked the doll for advice. In one night the doll got a beautiful machine, and in the spring when the cloth

was finished, Vasilisa gave it to the old woman and told her to
sell it and keep the money. The old woman took it to the royal
castle, where the king noticed it and asked how much she
wanted for it. She said nobody could pay for that work and that
she had brought it as a present.

The king thanked her, gave her presents, and sent her away.
But no tailor could be found to make the stuff into shirts, for it
was too fine. So the king called the old woman and said that
since she had spun and woven the cloth, she should be able to
make the shirts. Then she told him a young and beautiful girl
had made it. The king said the girl should make the shirts, so
Vasilisa made a dozen of the finest shirts, and the old woman
brought them to the king. Meanwhile Vasilisa washed herself
and combed her hair and put on her best clothes and waited at
the window.

Presently a servant came from the court and said that His
Majesty wanted to see the artist who had made the shirts, so
that he could reward her with his own hands. Vasilisa followed
the servant to the palace and appeared before the king. When
he saw the beautiful Vasilisa, he fell in love with her and said
he would not be separated from her. She should be his wife.

He took her hands and put her on the throne, and they were
married the same day. Soon Vasilisa's father came back from his
travels, rejoiced over her good fortune, and from then on stayed
with his daughter. Vasilisa also brought the old woman to the
palace. And the doll she kept with her to the end of her life.

This story is much richer than the German and other Cinderella
versions.[35] The *dramatis personae* are the merchant, his wife, and
their only daughter. The wife dies when the daughter is eight years
old. In fairy tales the age of fourteen or fifteen is often an important
age for a girl since it is a transition stage and the end of early
childhood. But here the fatal change takes place when the mother
is replaced by a stepmother. In general, ruling persons in fairy
tales represent dominants of collective consciousness, and the
heroes are often princes or poor peasant people. But this time there
is a kind of average bourgeois milieu, so we can take this father

figure as a symbol of the average collective spirit. The father does not play a great role; he is neither good nor bad and appears only at the beginning and at the end, where the problem does not seem to be very concentrated. The whole drama takes place in the feminine realm. The merchant's wife dies suddenly. As shown by the fact that she has no name or title, she would represent the average feminine type in life, the habitual type repeated over and over again in a country. There are always women who live the average life in various forms. But here there is suddenly an accident, and the life which collapses and cannot function anymore is replaced by something magical—that is, the mother's blessing and the helpful doll.

In the German version of Cinderella, the mother dies and is buried. On her grave grows a tree on which there is a bird, or from which there comes a voice which helps the girl, so she gets all she requires from the tree. In an Irish version, she finds a tortoiseshell cat that gives her everything she needs. The general motif is that after the death of the positive mother figure, something supernatural and numinous survives; that is, the ghost of the mother enters into an animal or an object and is incorporated there. In primitive countries, ancestral ghosts are often incorporated in fetishes and so carry on with their helpful functions.

What does it mean when a human being is replaced by a cat, tree, or doll? Archetypal contents sometimes appear in human and sometimes in other shapes. Only if they approach consciousness, then they come in human form. Human personification of a content of the unconscious shows that it can be integrated on the human level. One has a kind of feeling or vague idea as to what it could be. When an animus figure appears as a human being in a dream, you know that it can be dealt with, more or less, and you can usually make the working hypothesis that the dreamer has a general idea as to what it could be. But if there is a destructive voice coming from a grave, which would also be a personification of the animus, you would say that she could not deal with that, for it is removed and relatively autonomous and is therefore more powerful and has not yet entered the field of consciousness.

The death of an archetypal figure is its transformation, for archetypes in themselves cannot die. They are eternal, instinctive inherited dispositions; however, they can change one form of symbolic appearance for another. If they lose their human shape, it means they do not function anymore in a form which can easily be integrated into human life. Here the positive mother archetype of the little girl dies, but there remains with her the doll, representing the deepest essence of the mother figure, though not the human side. Most daughters have a certain archaic identity with their mother if they have a positive relationship with her, especially in childhood when the child talks to her doll as the mother talks to her, even repeating the mother's voice and words. Many women with a positive mother complex arrange the linen, cook for the family, and decorate the Christmas tree "as mother did," even educating the children in the same way. That creates a continuity of the same form of life, with the idea that everything goes smoothly and life goes on. But it has the disadvantage of preventing the individuation of the daughter, who continues the positive feminine figure as a type, not as an individual, and cannot realize her specific difference from her mother.

If the mother dies, that means, symbolically, a realization that the daughter can no longer be identical with her, though the essential positive relationship remains. Therefore the mother's death is the beginning of the daughter's process of individuation; the daughter is confronted with the task of finding her own femininity in her own form, which entails going through all the difficulties of finding it. The archaic mother-daughter identity is broken off, and Vasilisa realizes her weakness. Again and again it is the great problem in feminine psychology. Women, even more than men, tend to identify with their own sex, and to remain in this archaic identity. In a girls' school, for instance, one girl copies the other's new hairstyle or way of talking. They are like a flock of sheep, all of the same type. As far as I know from what I have read, the same thing seems to be true in primitive villages. The archaic *participation mystique* has a great impact on women, who in general are more interested in eros, in relationship, and are identical with each other and swim along together. The fact that they have trouble in disidentifying accounts, perhaps, for a certain "bitchiness" among women. Because they are so apt to identify, they malign each other behind their backs. Being unconscious of their own unique personality, they indulge in all such tricks in order to make a separation.

In the Swiss mountains there exists a relationship between doll and ghost in the spook known as the Doggeli or Toggeli (little doll). The lonely man in the mountains who lives with no woman around is oppressed by the Toggeli, which comes in by the keyhole and sits on his chest and suffocates him, and he wakes up with a nightmare and aroused sexual feelings.[36] The doll here personifies a primitive anima with sexual desires and fantasies. The same Toggeli sometimes comes as the haunting spook; it also comes through the keyhole and makes little rapping noises. There you have the same relationship between doll and ghost as in this Russian story. The basic archetypal idea is the same as that of the fetish, which you meet up with all over the world.

Usually the doll is regarded as the projection of the child's fantasy of having children. If you watch little girls playing, they imitate the whole mother-child relationship. But this seems not to be the only aspect of the doll, for in an earlier stage of childhood it is more an object which contains the divinity. Many little children between two and four cannot sleep without perhaps the washcloth near their pillow, or a little teddy bear, or some kind of fetish, which has to be in a certain place, for otherwise the child cannot sleep and is exposed to the dangers of the night. It is not yet the child's child, like the doll, but is the child's god; it is like the soul stones of the Stone Age men. In those days people made so-called *caches*, some of which have been found in Switzerland. A hole was made in the ground, stones of a special shape were collected, and a nest was made in which they were kept. The place was kept secret and was a symbol of the person's individual secret power. Australian aborigines still have such caches.

In the Easter Islands, Thor Heyerdahl,[37] after slowly becoming intimate with the population, discovered that some families had a key hidden under a stone that opened a door down into the earth. But only one member of the family knew of this hole in the earth, or cache, in which were stone carvings of the most different types, some of them recent and not particularly artistic, but others of beautiful old imported Indian sculptures, as well as stones of different regions and a number of animal sculptures. Lobster fishers had a beautiful stone lobster, which, if rightly kept, provided the lobsters, a kind of hunting magic. Formerly such stones used to be washed and brushed four times a year. The owners waited until nobody was around, then took the stones out and cleaned them, spread them on the sands to dry, and then hid them away again. When the man who had the secret died, another member of the family was always initiated, though not necessarily the eldest son, perhaps even a nephew. There you see the original meaning of the magic object which has the divine power and guarantees the survival of the clan. These stones are a symbol of the Self; they represent the secret of eternity and uniqueness, and the secret of the essence of the life of the human being.

The early relationship of the child with the doll or with the washcloth carries the earliest projections of the Self. It is the magic object on which the life of the child depends and by which it keeps its own essence, and therefore it is an awful tragedy if it is lost. Later on it turns more into the parent-child play. The archaic identity between mother and daughter is the unconscious foundation from which the individuation of both begins. This is at the bottom of a major problem which I have met with in several cases in my practice. I have had to analyze mothers who could not get away from their daughters and daughters who could not get away from their mothers. They could not detach, and there were constant quarrels. The daughter's marriage made no difference, and that the daughter had left home was no help—the problem could go on to any age.

In the second half of life the mother usually cannot get to her own work and creativity and does not know why; the daugher is out of the house, and she has the time, but somewhere there is sand in the machinery. One of the mothers in such a case had the following dream: She saw a big potato and a smaller one attached to it, just as in oranges there is sometimes a small orange inside, which can happen in any fruit. Out of the potato, at the joint between the two, came a pole with a crucified snake around it. This winged snake had a crown on its head with light coming from it. It was a kind of tree-of-life symbol and very impressive, but at the bottom were these two potatoes in the earth. The mother was tortured over the problem of her daughter, who seemed to be going the wrong way in life. She tried constantly to have it out with her. The two would talk and cry together, but to no effect. According to the dream, something is not right; the potatoes are in the earth and still attached to each other, yet the tree of life is growing. The process of individuation is developing in a bad spot, in a place of evil where something is tied and the borders are not clear. There is such a basic archaic identity of mother and daughter that a superhuman effort has to be made for them to get away from each other, and only then can each one become completely conscious of her own personality. Both must take back all their projections and become individual themselves, and that is very difficult for all women. You hear of mothers eating their sons, but in many cases they are in a worse way tied up with their daughters. It is a natural phenomenon, and a typically feminine problem. In such cases one always finds that the mother has projected a symbol of the Self onto her daughter and, since the daughter represents the Self for her, she cannot get out of the projection. In a woman's psychology, the Self is represented by an older or a younger woman, just as for men there is the older man or younger man, the *senex* and *puer,* the God-Father and God-Son, the father and the boy, the oldest and the youngest. The image of the eternally old or the eternally young woman probably has to do with the timelessness of the Self. If the Self appears as a young person in a woman's unconscious productions, it means the newly and consciously discovered Self. Then the Self is my daughter. But insofar as the Self was also always within me, the Self is my mother and existed long before my ego consciousness. Feminine ego consciousness rests on the foundation of the Self, which has always existed and is the eternal mother. Insofar as I discover the Self within and let it enter completely naturally into my life, it is my daughter. That is why the Self, like the father and son in male psychology, is represented by mother and daughter in feminine psychology.

In the moment when Vasilisa receives this magic doll from her dying mother, instead of being identical with the mother, she begins to realize a germ of her own personality, the first hunch of the Self, which one perhaps does get at about the age of eight. It is the first initial realization of being a personality, though one cannot yet guess how it will take shape in one's own later life.

The merchant then marries the witch with the two daughters, three jealous bitches who persecute the girl. This is an archetypal motif: where the pearl is, there is also the dragon, and vice versa. They are never separate. Frequently, just after the first intuitive realization of the Self, the powers of desolation and darkness break in. A terrible slaughtering always takes place at the time of the birth of the hero, as for instance the killing of the innocents at Bethlehem when Christ was born. Some persecuting power starts at once to blot out the inner germ. Outwardly, it is often that the innermost kernel of the human being has an actually irritating effect upon outer surroundings. Realization of the Self when *in statu nascendi,* when only a hunch, makes a person unadapted and difficult for those around, for it disturbs the unconscious instinctive order. Jung often said that it is as if a flock of sheep resented it bitterly that one sheep wanted to walk by itself.

In Germany, group psychology experiments have been made with hens and other birds. Hens and crows, for instance, observe a certain pecking order. There is the rooster, and his first wife, who has first rights. The others have special rank in the order in which they may eat and build their nests. Most animals, and also apes, have an order which one calls the alpha, beta, gamma order. Some psychologists say that in a human group, or in a crowd, people also try to peck each other. The alpha hen is generally the most disgusting and pushy person, and the best in I.Q. are the gamma and delta hens. Clearly, wherever people form a group, there is this interplay of unconscious balance; however, if any one person gets just an idea of the Self, he falls out of the group, and the balance has to be reestablished. Now that one factor is out, the others feel the gap and are naturally angry and try to force the miscreant to the former unconscious level. If you analyze one member of the family, usually the whole family begins to wobble and gets upset. Insofar as we are herd animals, we have within ourselves that essential conflict between the inertia which wants to remain in the flock, and the disturbing factor, the possibility of individuation. A woman who gets the first hunch of the Self is immediately attacked, not only by the stepmother outside, but from within, by the inner stepmother, that is, the inertia of the old collective pattern of femininity, that regressive inertia which always pulls one back to do the thing in the least painful way. As in many other Cinderella stories, the stepsisters are characterized as lazy, and the heroine has to do tremendously hard work, such as separating grains, which entails a superhuman effort. There is the conflict between that which calls upon you to make the superhuman effort and the desire to follow the old pattern.

As soon as the merchant leaves the country, the stepmother and her family move near the woods; that is, the stepmother regresses from the human way of functioning to the borders of vegetative unconsciousness. Women, much more than men, especially if they do not have a strong animus, vegetate in an amazing way. They can live ten or twenty years like plants, without either a positive or a negative drama in their lives. They just exist. This is a typical form of feminine unconsciousness and means sinking into inertia, into doing things the easy way and just following the daily plan. That is known as the conservatism of woman; there is no conflict but also no life. The stepmother here has a wish to push out Vasilisa, but she just goes to live near the woods and hopes the thing will happen. She has a plot and wants Vasilisa to be eaten by the Baba Yaga. That is *the* name for the archetypal witch in all Russian fairy tales. She is a great magician who can turn herself into a well or a paradisiacal garden in which the hero is torn to pieces "to the size of poppy seeds," or she turns into a gigantic sow that kills the hero. In our story she is not completely evil, though when she hears that the girl is a "blessed daughter" she tells her she does not want her in her house. In a hidden way, she is not thoroughly evil, and sometimes even helpful; she wonderfully portrays the Great Mother in her double aspect.

There is a Russian story of the Maiden Tsar, in which the Baba Yaga lives in a rotating little round house standing on chicken feet, and you have to say a magic word before you can enter.[38] The Tsar's son goes in and finds her scratching among the ashes with her long nose. She combs her hair with her claws and watches the geese with her eyes, and she asks the hero, "My dear little child, are you here by your own free will or by compulsion?"

One of the great tricks of the mother complex in a man is always to implant doubt in his mind, suggesting that it might be better to do the other thing; and then the man is lamed. But the hero in the story says, "Grandmother, you should not ask such questions of a hero! Give me something to eat, and if you don't . . . !" Whereupon the Baba Yaga goes and cooks him a marvelous dinner and gives him good advice, and it works! So it depends on the hero's attitude. She tries to make him infantile, but when she sees he is up to her, she helps him.

So the Baba Yaga can be good or bad. Just as the male image of the Godhead has usually a dark side, like the devil, so the image of the feminine Godhead, which in female psychology would be the image of the Self, has both a light and dark side. Usually in Catholic countries the light side is personified in the Virgin Mary. She represents the light side of the Great Mother, of the man's anima, and of the woman's Self but lacks the shadow. The Baba Yaga would represent a more archaic similar figure in which the positive and negative are mixed. She is full of the powers of destruction, of desolation, and of chaos, but at the same time is a helpful figure. Viewed historically, she probably represents the surviving image of the late antique Greek Hekate, the queen of the underworld. In Hellenistic times this goddess of Hades became more and more identified with the Neoplatonic world soul, and as such she became the feminine spirit of the universe, a goddess of nature and of life as well as death, who was even praised as Soteira, the feminine savior. Her daughter was Persephone, with whom she was secretly identical. This throws a light on the heroine of our story, who is called Vasilisa. This is identical with the Greek Bassilissa, which means queen and which was one of the titles of Persephone.[39] Russian fairy tales have been deeply influenced from the south by the late Greek civilization, and thus we have in Baba Yaga and Vasilisa really a survival of the great cosmic goddesses Hekate and Persephone. The divine rank of the Baba Yaga is clearly proved by the fact that she has three riders at her disposition—"my day," "my night," and "my sun." So she is a cosmic Godhead. There are also the three pairs of hands which sort out the grain— that unspeakable, horrible secret no one ought to ask about. The three hands are probably the secret of complete destruction or death. The Baba Yaga sits in a mortar, steers with a pestle, and with a broom blurs or extinguishes all her traces. Human witches like to do the same thing with the famous "Hush, hush" technique—"For God's sake, do not mention me!" Mother Nature likes to hide herself, it is said in Greek philosophy.

The mortar and pestle are important symbols in this story. The mortar as a vessel, naturally, is a feminine symbol. The Virgin Mary is called the vessel of grace, and "the Holy Grail" has also been applied to the Virgin Mary. The Baba Yaga, too, has a round vessel in which substances are ground to powder. She sits in a vessel that serves to pulverize matter. In alchemical literature the basic fantasy of the alchemist was that at bottom there is one ultimate basic material of the universe on which all the rest is built up. This is still the working hypothesis for many physicists—the idea of a basic building material which would unify the whole of nature, and by means of which one could get to the root of the phenomena of the universe. This hunt for the basic material has always haunted the human mind and particularly the natural scientist's. It is, so to speak, God's own secret. It was the material with which he built up reality and, therefore is divine, or contains a divine secret. In former times, before the splitting of the atom, the way of getting such a basic material was to burn everything to ashes and call that the basic material, or to pulverize it to the finest dust in a mortar, and the idea was that that was the *prima materia*, the most elemental basic element of matter. The Latin verb *tero* means to grind, and from it is derived a very interesting word used in Christian theology, namely *contritio*, contrition. If you realize your sins, you feel remorse and penitent. If you get to the bottom and feel annihilated by your sins, then you are reduced to ashes and pulverized and are in a state of contrition, which would be the deepest kind of remorse, which has the highest merit; by contrition you can be healed of all your sins. It is a realization of the shadow, which goes so deep that one can say nothing more in one's own favor. As in all highly disagreeable situations, it has the advantage that you are at the bottom of the hole and cannot fall lower. Therefore, it is the turning point. The ego in its negative aspect has been pulverized, has reached the end of its selfish willfulness, and has to give in to greater powers.

The Baba Yaga has this instrument of contrition, the pestle and mortar; therefore, she symbolizes that life power which, with its ultimate truth, will bring the human being to his own ultimate truth. Hence her archaic connection with the principle of death. Many people keep a little bit above the truth and reach this stage of complete contrition only when they have to face death. We are like corks. When God does not depress us too much, we float on the surface, but when death approaches people suddenly shut up and sink down to something more substantial. On the deathbed their expression changes and for the first time you feel that they are quiet and really themselves and that all the fuss of the ego has come to an end. So the Baba Yaga is also the demon of death; she brings this ultimate contrition. She is the great alchemist who reduces everything superficial to its essence.

In our story the Baba Yaga goes to sleep, leaving the girl to select the good from the bad grain. This is a theme to be found in many Cinderella fairy tales and appears also in the ancient story of Amor and Psyche. It is a typical task in mythology for the heroine. Separating the good from the bad grains is a work of patience, which can neither be rushed into nor speeded up. The Greek word *krino* means to discriminate, to make a distinction between A and B; it is a work of careful, detailed feeling judgments, but not discrimination as done by the male logos. When the latter is confronted with chaos, he says, "Let's find a mathematical formula," and the like. That is the bird's-eye view of the logos principle; it does not look at details.

The feminine principle also has its way of seeing clearly, but it acquires it in a different psychological way, more by the selection of innumerable details, showing that this is this and that is that. For women it is important to go into things in detail, to see, for instance, how and where a misunderstanding began, for this is frequently caused by a lack of clarity. By working it out in detail, the grains are selected. In a problem of relationship, one has to do this all the time. Boring as it often is, and gossipy as it seems, a psychological problem cannot be worked out without all these little details. Some women like to be a little unclear, giving rise in that way to those marvelous witch muddles where nobody knows what is what anymore. That is the famous way by which women get into their shadow troubles. Jung always said that women love to be unclear even about a rendezvous, and to add something such as, "If I am not there, ring up So-and-So." They make a vague arrangement, then a big scene if the thing does not work. Men do it also, but women much more. The shadow cannot intervene if one is precise.

I can give you an example. A daughter has a pair of ski shoes she cannot wear anymore. The old mother thinks the other daughter should have them. Then the daughter-in-law comes in and tries them on, but says they are too big. The old mother suggests wearing socks inside, but they are still too big. The old thinks that the daughter-in-law has refused them and tells the other daughter to take them, but they cannot be found—the daughter-in-law has taken them with her! Then the son has to defend his wife, and there is a general family battle because all these ladies did not take the trouble to be clear as to what they meant! The daughter-in-law *seemed* to refuse them, but went off with them! At the back of such things there is a *participation mystique* among the women. So the process of becoming conscious for a woman is that, within herself, she has to become clear about her positive and negative reactions and know where they are, instead of making a lot of muddles and half muddles. That is a superficial aspect of a very deep problem. The old mother had not come to terms with the mother archetype. Promising the ski shoes first to one daughter and then to her daughter-in-law, and then leaving it all undecided, is just laziness in relationship. The insidious thing at the back of it is that, as a mother, she does not function rightly, and therefore creates muddles. If you go further into this, in itself a silly incident, you will see that there is a kind of uncertainty of instinct. She didn't know whom to mother, or whose needs to answer or not answer; and she wasn't clear about the feeling needs of the other women and the necessity of holding the family together. All that was, in the deepest sense, uncertain in her. Such a woman has sacrificed much too much of her private needs and life to her family, and consequently hates the family somewhere, which is often expressed in the form of symptoms. For example, one mother got diarrhea and had to go to a sanatorium, and her dreams quite clearly said that she was once again sick of the whole lot, but the only way she knew of pulling out was by retiring to the sanatorium. She always put on this unconsciously deliberate pretense at the worst possible moment; namely, just when the family needed her. That is a part of the devilish mechanism. Thus, behind that superficial vagueness, if one digs deep enough, one generally finds a very great problem constellated.

Therefore, when the witch gives Vasilisa this task of sorting grain, it is as though she makes a test saying that if the girl could make the right selection, she would not fall into the witch's power.

11

The motif of corn seeds is often connected with the underworld mother goddess, and among other things, seeds are a symbol of the souls of the dead and of the ancestral ghosts. In ancient Greece, near the hearth in the house, pots were placed in which were corn seeds made up into a kind of fig jelly with other ingredients. The pots symbolically represented the womb of the underworld, the womb of the earth, and the seeds were the dead who rest in the earth, like the corn that resurrects in spring. The dead, or the ghosts, were called Demetreioi, those who belong to Demeter and who rest, like corn, in the womb of that goddess. In a festival held at about the date of our All Souls' Day, the pots were uncovered, and it was believed that the underworld was thus opened. The Latin expression that Karl Kerényi often uses is *Mundus patet,* the cosmos is open. For three days the ghosts lived with the living. They came back and roamed about the house, and everything was full of spooks; they participated at the meals, where a portion was always put aside for them. Then, after three days, they were driven out of the house with olive twigs and holy water and told that now they had had enough and were to return to their own world and not spook about and disturb the living any longer, and the lids were replaced on the pots.

Poppy seeds also point to the world of the dead and the ghosts. They are nourishing and also have a soporific effect similar to hashish and all those remedies which, according to primitive belief, are a means for contacting the Beyond, such as chewing ivy leaves and other poisonous substances. So poppy seeds have to do with the mystery of sinking into the Beyond, the underworld, and getting into touch with its secrets. Thus, in its deepest meaning, grains have something to do with the mystery of life and death and of transformation; this metaphor appears in the Bible, where Jesus speaks of the grain of wheat falling into the ground and there dying and then bringing forth much fruit (John 12:24). The analogy in alchemical writings is referred to as the problem of *multiplicatio.* They say that at a certain moment when the philosopher's stone is made, the vessel is opened and the stone begins to emanate a transforming activity, and every metal touched by it is transformed into gold. The analogy is that the philosopher's stone is made inside a vessel, where it goes through dissolution in the darkness and then resurrects. The vessel is opened and the stone develops into an activity which was called the process of multiplication. The psychological analogy seems to have to do with the fact that when one succeeds consciously and positively to relate to an archetypal constellation, there is a widespread effect. If the rainmaker, or the medicine man, gets in touch in the right way with the powers of the Beyond, rain falls over the whole country. Confucius said that if the noble man sits in his room and has the right thoughts and writes down the right things, he is heard a thousand miles around. The Taoist philosopher Chuang-tzu always comments on the point that as long as the ruler of the country tries to do the right thing, actively making good or bad laws, the empire will get worse and worse. If, on the contrary, he retires and gets right inwardly, then the problems of the empire are solved by themselves too. Another variation is the story of the ruler of the Yellow Earth who went to the Original Mist, the primeval mist, saying he wanted to do the right thing and be inwardly right, so that people did not cheat in his empire and everyone had enough to eat. Original Mist simply said, "I have no idea how you can do that." So the ruler of the Yellow Earth left his empire and for three months sat on straw in a hut, and then returned to Original Mist and said, "Could I humbly ask you how I could bring myself into order?" Original Mist replied that he should not think of putting things right, but should stay in reality and not bother about outer things, stay where he was, and so on. Then the ruler asked, "And what about nature?" To which Original Mist replied, "You always think nature comes to an end, but she is only at the beginning; you always think nature knows her aims, but it goes much further. You always think nature has now given everything, but nature has still more in store." But then he added, "I don't want to talk to mortal beings; the people are fading away, they are dying. I am alone; I am eternal." And he turned away from the ruler of the Yellow Earth.[40]

All these stories refer to the secret that ultimately we can touch something which is the universality or oneness of nature, which generally manifests itself in synchronistic events. If one succeeds in getting oneself right about a problem, miracles begin to happen, and the outside falls into place too, as though one had had an effect which, rationally, one could not possibly have had. One probably should not think of cause and effect in this connection, for we have not *caused* things to get right; they get right, synchronistically. I have quoted earlier the Chinese saying in the *I Ching* that "the superior man knows the germs and acts at once" and so brings things into order. One could compare the corn and poppy seeds to these germs, for they are germs of situations which one has to clarify in the moment when they are still germs. And if, patiently, one succeeds in doing so, then one can disentangle, or give a possible turn to, impossible situations.

How deep these things go one cannot say, but I think that has very much to do with feminine godhead and her uncanny powers. Women to a great extent—and the less they know about it, the worse it is—rule even life and death in their surroundings. If the husband dies, or the children die, very often the women in that family had something to do with it. But it would be inflation, and it is absolutely destructive, if a woman *thinks* she is responsible, for then she identifies with the Great Mother goddess. As an ego, the woman is responsible only for her conscious deeds and no more. I have seen many prepsychotic borderline cases who became psychotic by thinking that they were responsible to a greater extent than they were.

I remember the case of a mother through whose mind the thought flashed, when saying goodbye to her son, when he went to war, that she wouldn't much mind if he didn't come back—and he didn't! And then she was convinced that she was responsible for his death. That is plain inflation! It is quite natural that people who live together should at times wish each other dead. I have never analyzed any human being, man or woman, where I couldn't see that they had such wishes against others, half consciously and half not. That is nature, and it is better to admit it. Neither have I analyzed a mother who, from time to time, hasn't wished all her children at the bottom of the sea—not literally, but, "For God's sake, let's get rid of the whole lot!" If the ego identifies with that in the wrong way, the devil is loose. But all the same, though the ego is only responsible for what it does, there is underneath this tremendous nature in woman which wishes for life or death for those around her. I would say that the dark side of the Self in every woman has that capacity of wishing for life or death. If it is not misused in white or black magic, if the ego remains with its own task, this has a tremendous effect. People blossom in the surroundings of a woman who is in the right relationship with herself, because then she is rather like the positive mother goddess who makes corn grow. But if the relationship with her own inner self is wrong, she is more likely to emanate the effects of the death goddess Hecate and put a blight of death over those around. Children sometimes look marvelous and blossom in a house where the mother may shout that she wishes they were all in hell! Why? Because, in her own way, she is right with Tao. Her positive instinct supports the children with a positive vital something which gives them security, even though she may tell them they are the devil's spawn and horrible brats.

The Cinderella task would be *the* task of the woman, to penetrate into the depths of her secret, small effects and to bring consciousness and selective discrimination into that hidden nature of hers, which operates in her background. If she can penetrate that realm and there separate bad from good, she does something which corresponds to the hero's deeds of slaying the dragon, or building the new town, or freeing the people from terror.

In analysis one often has to sort out such seeds with the analysand. For instance, once a woman from South Africa went on a trip with her husband and their two boys to fish in a river, and the boat overturned. The two boys could not swim, and the father carried both ashore but then collapsed with a heart attack and died on the spot. The woman couldn't drive the car, or was too much shaken to do so, and the three sat there for a day and a half until someone came by and found them and brought them back with the husband's dead body. Later the younger son began to behave in a completely psychotic way. For two months he did no work at school and then didn't go at all, but climbed onto the roofs of lower cottages and houses, and stood there absolutely raving and throwing knives at the passers-by. He never slept, but cried and raved the whole night through and looked absolutely mad and miserable. The mother went to doctors all over the world and everybody, including myself when she consulted me, thought that it had to do with that trauma, the horrible accident in which the father lost his life and their sitting out in the cold with his dead body.

I asked her about the boy's dreams, and, among others, she told me the following: he was shut in a room where there was a television—that was some years ago when in that country not everybody had a television, so it was rather a thrill. The door of the room was shut, and a voice said, "You must stay in here from now on, and your life is a failure." That dream had just knocked him out. Here is the plain statement of the beginning of the psychosis. He is shut up with the images of his own unconscious; he is cut off from life, and life is from now on a failure—at seven years old! And the outer picture said exactly the same thing. Diagnosis: hopeless!

But something in me revolted, and I couldn't accept that and thought that perhaps the dream could have a prospective meaning, for something in it did not seem to indicate a psychosis. The dream was plain, clear, and well constructed, which was healthy. In its wickedness the dream had a healthy smell—a smack in the face, but so well given that it didn't seem psychotic; it was too plainly wicked. So I wondered who would benefit from such a slap in the face, and thought that a madly, morbidly ambitious person might. For somebody crazily and psychotically ambitious, it might be a good thing to have to face the fact that one's life was a failure, that one just had to sit in one's room and everything was finished! I asked the mother whether the boy had always been ambitious and had tried to push himself in school. She said no, that he was quite an average boy and didn't care if the others were better than he; he wasn't ambitious. Then I wondered if it was the mother's ambition for the boy, so I made a shot in the dark and told her that the boy's trouble had nothing to do with the accident to her husband, but with her, and that she was exaggeratedly ambitious for the boy, which was what was ruining him. She broke down and howled and howled and howled—tons of sea water—and admitted it! Apparently she had always spun hero fantasies onto her husband, who was a rather miserable, delicate, introverted, helpless little man, and had always been disappointed. Directly after his death, the weight of her ambitious demands fell upon the son, and as she preferred the youngest boy, it fell upon him. After the accident she had read some psychological books about what happened to a fatherless child, about the Oedipus complex, and decided that her son should not become a mamma's boy, so began to be absolutely hard with him, planning to make him into a hero.

Imagine the situation of a small boy who had lost his father with such a horrible shock, and whose mother, instead of comforting him, dropped him like a hot potato! That was enough to make a boy go up on the roof and throw knives at people—anybody else would have done the same, looked at from the boy's standpoint. Well, she was a tough woman, tremendously vital and quite intelligent, so I told her what I thought of her. The next day when she came, she said the boy had slept eight hours completely normally and in the morning had gotten up and gone to school. The real trouble had been her dream of the hero, and the boy had to be the hero. She had the hero archetype in her unconscious, but was too lazy to live up to her own capacities—so she thought that her men should do it, if not her husband, then her boy. To live a heroic life herself would be too much trouble. The hero fantasy was the seed, the germ, that constellated the archetypal layers of the unconscious. If she had sorted those seeds, known what was in them, she would (a) not have put her hero fantasy onto her husband or son, and (b) probably have discovered that she had to do something herself. It was the tremendous greater potential within her that had such destructive effects, something positive at the bottom of her soul that had negative effects, since she had never sorted it out within herself. Naturally, she alone was not responsible for the husband's death and the boy's behavior, because another person might not have emanated any negative effects. People always try to project their fantasies onto others, but a fairly healthy person shakes them off, unconsciously and instinctively. If I had had to analyze her husband, I would not have spoken of the wife as the guilty person, but looked to see what was wrong in him, and that woman shouldn't now say that *she* was responsible for the two events; that is only true *cum grano salis*. The extent of her guilt lay only in not having sorted the seeds.

If a woman has a powerful animus, she just has it; it cannot be gotten rid of. One can only make the best of it, and our experience is that one is less possessed if one makes some use of it. All that business of burying the husband and then quickly reading up what Freud had written and then determining to make the boy a hero—that is animus! She was already in the thrall of the animus. But usually, if a woman does something about a powerful animus, it wears off a little, and the needle swings back to the feminine side. If you have worked like a man, then you are apt to feel that it would be nicer to be a woman and not work so hard.

The question of guilt is terribly delicate, one simply does not know where to put the exact borderline. To some people one has to say, "For God's sake, do not have such a silly inflation as to think you are the mother goddess of nature and that you govern the life and death of those around you." But to those who have the illusion that they always do the right thing, one has to say, "Well, I do think it is a little strange that two of your husbands died!" It is a question of a millimeter, one thing to one person and the opposite to another. Some people exaggerate their guilt, and the dreams show that they have an inflation. Then one must say, "Nonsense, you are not powerful enough to kill all those men! You would just like to feel like the mother goddess who is responsible for everything, and that is a silly inflation. Nature killed your husband. He died of cancer, or a heart attack, and not because of you!"

One can just as well say that the suicidal man chose her because he wanted a rock against which to wreck his ship, and therefore he is guilty, not she. It is a question which can only be decided individually with oneself and with the others involved. One must try to make a balance from the dreams, find a middle attitude without an inch too much or too little guilt. That is exactly the work of the sorting of the seeds, trying to become conscious down to the very bottom of the situation and then to know what's what, and what has what effect, and to be as humbly conscientious about it as possible, but without inflation or making sweeping statements. Quite practically, sorting the seeds would require an enormous amount of careful self-discipline and great conscientiousness, and to do it for a long time would be the woman's heroic deed. Such work strengthens consciousness and the feeling of responsibility, because, as I have said, the devil tells you all the time that one more or less doesn't matter, or that there are no more black seeds in that—and there you are!

Now comes the problem of the three pairs of hands, about which the heroine prefers not to ask any questions. As we cannot understand this motif from that one fairy tale, I would like to amplify it, for it is an archetypal motif that has many variations which are very revealing. There is a Grimm's fairy tale called "Mrs. Trude" ("Frau Trude").[41] A little girl who is very obstinate and never obeys her parents lives near the woods and is told by her parents not to go into the woods or to Mrs. Trude's hut, or that will be the end of her. Naturally, she slips out of the house at the first chance and goes there. At the door of the hut a black man meets her, on the stairs a man in green, and at the top, a man in red clothes. They just quickly walk past her, and she enters Frau Trude's room. There the old witch with the big nose sits by the fireplace. The child, shivering slightly, says, "Frau Trude, who was that black man?" And the witch says, "Oh, that was only the chimney sweep." "And who was the green man?" she asks. Frau Trude answers, "Oh, that was the huntsman." Then she asks who the red man was and is told that that was the butcher. And then the little girl says, "I looked through the window, and I didn't see you, but the devil with a fiery head." "Oh," says Frau Trude, "so you saw the witch in her right form. I have long waited and longed for you, and you shall give me a good light," and she takes the little girl and turns her into a piece of wood and throws her into the fire. When the wood is glowing hot, she sits beside it and warms herself and says, "That gives a good, bright light!"

In the Vasilisa tale the men were white, black, and red, and here they are red, green, and black. Obviously the black man is the devil, who also very often appears in fairy tales as the green huntsman, and the red man is another form of the devil. So, actually, those are three of Frau Trude's familiars, namely three aspects of the devil. Frau Trude, or the Great Mother goddess, generally lives in close association with the dark underworld God-head, the devil, and there is very often this triadic structure. In our civilization, this lower triad is a compensation for the upper trinity. Just as the Virgin Mary would be the female figure in the upper trinity—God the Father, God the Son, and the Holy Ghost— with the Virgin Mary a little outside, so there is a quaternity below with Frau Trude and three aspects of the devil, the divine under-world totality against the spiritual and positive divine totality. The three pairs of cut-off hands, therefore, probably refer to the same kind of secret, namely that of a close association of the mother goddess with the last ultimate principle of evil and destructiveness, which is at the bottom of the abyss of every human being.

As we cannot take this figure of the Baba Yaga as a personal content of the unconscious, but rather as a personification of what one could call nature itself, as a nature goddess, we can say that the pairs of hands refer to the unthinkable cruelty and murderous-ness of nature itself. Nobody who has normal human feeling can avoid being shocked by this incredible cruelty at some time in life. One sees how animals eat each other, and we can thank God when it is possible not to have to look at it. In fact, we blind ourselves; we look and turn away. We have probably all had the mortal shock of discovering how nature deals with her children, of seeing a human being slowly and cruelly eaten up by cancer or some such disease which just slowly consumes the person. The worst sadistic torturer, a psychotic torturer, could not have as cruel fantasies about how to torture people to death as nature has. Sometimes, for instance, in the woods, or on the mountains, you see a roebuck trying to crawl over the ice with a cancerous growth hanging from it—the other roebuck kick it aside, and it sinks, then struggles up and walks a few steps farther, dragging itself along for weeks with the cancer, until one day, thank God, it does not get up anymore. Or a fox will partially eat a swan frozen on the ice and leave it to struggle for hours and hours with a wing eaten away—unless a human being chances to come by and give it the *coup de grâce*. Who is responsible? Those are the horrors of nature which nobody can swallow; it is something one cannot even talk about. And this fairy tale says that it shows a certain kind of healthy reaction, or wisdom, not to poke into these things too much and not to ask too many questions. How would a question help? There is no answer! We can shake our fists at the goddess, but that doesn't help, and we shall never figure out why this is so—it is just so. This is the abysmal shadow of Baba Yaga, an abyss into which one can only look with horror and turn away. Nature has that secret of killing in the most cruel way, and also giving birth in the most beautiful way to the most beautiful things.

Another German fairy tale in the collection *Deutsche Märchen seit Grimm* (German Fairy Tales Since Grimm), called "Waldminchen," contains the same motif as "Frau Trude," but in a milder form.[42] The parents of an obstinate little girl tell her that if she is not obedient, the Waldminchen will come and fetch her. The child also has the habit of teasing the other children a bit cruelly at school. One day a green-looking old woman comes out of the wood, grabs her, and carries her away into the woods to a lot of very nice children who are picking daisies and amusing themselves. Waldminchen tells her that she must behave nicely with the children and play with them, that she wants to educate her and will stay with her. The child is rather frightened, but behaves and plays with the children and has a very nice day. They get good food, and the Waldminchen looks after them, but the next morning the little girl starts her old tricks again, and the children complain. "All right," says Waldminchen, and she seizes the little girl and puts her through one of the three water mills in the woods. There are three men standing around—the male consorts of the great goddess—and they throw her into the mill, and she is ground to bits and comes out the other end as a very hunchbacked old woman. Waldminchen says, "What is old should become young and what is young should become old." When the child sees herself in the mirror, she is very downcast and absolutely in despair. But she has to stay like that for some time. When she has learned her lesson, Waldminchen puts her again through the mill, but in reverse, and she is young again. Then the father appears. His sorrow over his lost child has turned him into an old man, so he is put into the rejuvenating mill, after which the two walk home, and the girl behaves and becomes a good woman.

The nature goddess has a mill, which grinds people instead of corn, the mill of youth and old age, a milder form of life and death. Here the goddess is timeless, and is the great magician who bestows youth or old age upon people. If you compare what happens to the three girls (Vasilisa, the girl in "Frau Trude," and the girl in "Waldminchen"), you will see that the facets shown by this nature goddess depend on the attitude of the visitor. In "Frau Trude" the girl was a silly, infantile, wicked little creature and got destroyed. In "Waldminchen" she only got punished. Vasilisa, who behaved correctly, was helped. So Mother Nature's attitude depends on the human being. It is interesting to see that infantile curiosity is looked on as something extremely destructive. Curious inquisitiveness, as far as I have seen, is not so often punished in myths about heroes, though it often attracts destruction to the heroine. The fact that Vasilisa does not ask about the hands saves her life, but the "Frau Trude" child pokes into secrets which should be respected.

When women have an undeveloped animus, when they have not worked on the animus, their mental functions often remain fixed on gossip and thinking about their neighbors. They get interested in a divorce in the neighborhood and want to know how it came about. They talk in a half-psychological way. It is more than just interest in the divorce, it is a kind of germlike psychological interest. For instance, there is the thought, "Why do men and women quarrel?" But it never gets farther; it remains on the level of curiosity, and they never get to the bottom of anything. If such a woman could say, "What does this have to do with me? I am not interested in a personal way, but am fascinated by the question as to why men and women do not get on with each other," she might get somewhere. But instead it remains stuck in a kind of half-developed mental operation, neither disinterested nor objective, which, I think, is typical for an undeveloped animus. That has to do with destructive inquisitiveness, and there the devil has his hand in it.

The problem of the divine function of evil is something one cannot really touch on openly because people always blow up about it. It is so ambiguous that one can really only do what Vasilisa does, yet, in some mysterious way, evil in its worst destructiveness is connected with the laws of life. For instance, one could say that Bergen-Belsen and Auschwitz had a positive side, for they shocked European civilization into realizing their shadow. But we cannot say that! We have to stay on the human side and say that that was simply plain murder and that no devious excuse about a secret positive effect can be made. Otherwise, we become demonic, the very thing we have looked at. It happens that natural scientists get into that demonism of thinking like nature. A famous man, named Nikolai, wrote *The Biology of War,* in which he absolutely coldly, and from a natural scientific standpoint, investigated the question as to war's being a good or a bad thing from the standpoint of the biology of the race. He asked whether it destroyed the good or the bad elements, and so on. To study that needs a demonic mind. Our human nature revolts at looking at things in such a way—but go to a university, go to people who discuss the atomic question. They are in that spirit of nature! They speak of mass destruction and how to deal with it; they are possessed by the evil hands.

On the other hand, perhaps it is sometimes a man's fate that he has to expand into such thoughts. Physicians, for instance, must acquire some of that demonic mind, because they deal too much with nature and its cruelty. In the first semester, when corpses are dissected, either the student walks out and says he cannot become a doctor, or he has to acquire something of the demonic coldness of nature and say that there are always thousands of people who die, and one must be able to look—for that is reality, But if one doesn't *know* what one does, one becomes completely devilish oneself. A doctor, for instance, may impersonally watch a horrible disease in a patient, who for him is number so-and-so in bed so-and-so, suffering from a disease which takes such-and-such a form; but one day his wife or little daughter gets the same disease, and he gets the shock of his life. Then usually there is the awful conflict between the cold medical man who simply sees the illness as a process of natural science—how it will proceed and end—and the human being to whom that is now a unique event and a feeling catastrophe. It is the clash of the two attitudes.

In our tale it is not evident whom the hands belong to. That gives a hint that one should not ask what is behind. I think, to a certain extent, it is a woman's task to hold on to the personal side against the cold spirit of natural science. A doctor has to expose himself and say that he cannot be sentimental but has to face such things and be detached. A surgeon cannot operate if he is sentimental about the person on whom he is operating. But the woman has to put the emphasis upon and hold to the human side, where things and diseases are unique, and the feeling reaction remains unique, where one does not in a cold, statistical way write off the other human being. If a woman starts to think like that, it is always from the animus, and it has a very destructive effect. She should preserve the personal atmosphere between human beings. To create the human atmosphere of eros is one of her tasks, and to that belongs the necessity of not investigating too deeply into those shadowy things, into the impersonal, cold cruelty of nature.

Vasilisa has to sort out the grain, and then those mysterious hands take the sorted grains and we do not know what they do with them. Why could Baba Yaga, the great magician, not sort them out herself? We do not know, but it seems possible that she could not do so; that ethical discrimination is something specifically human which transcends the otherwise known Nature. That is what Jung thought: that man transcends the Godhead a very minimal bit, because of being a little more conscious. In this, man has to help the Godhead and serve Him or Her, but naturally that does not mean that we can eliminate evil either from God or from Nature.

We can work on the unconscious, but we cannot eliminate evil from nature or prevent millions of creatures dying a cruel or dreadful death every second on this planet. We shall never be able to remove sickness and death out of the world. There are limits to what humans can do and a place where Nature takes over. She will never stop those mills.

The Far East civilizations try to cope with this problem in a different way: by seeing the relativity of good and evil and then detaching from the problem. Lately I have just reread a little in Chuang-tzu, and it struck me that sometimes he says that the wise or great man just looks at Nature and becomes like her. There is a certain reckless cruelty in that. The Taoist wise man, as Chuang-tzu represents it, should not mourn too much if his greatest friend or his wife dies and if his head pupil or his master dies. He performs the mourning ceremony, but no more, and for our christian tradition this is rather shocking. But then, and that comforted me a lot, there is another place where Chuang-tzu says the really enlightened Taoist master does not *strive* to be good, but is just like nature; he lets things be. He neither strives to save nor to do anything good, and if the other is ill he would not go and nurse him. That looks like nature taking its course—the other is ill, so that's that. But then he adds that he loves everybody from the overflow of his natural goodness. There is natural feeling sympathy for the other person, and that is allowed, but to strive out of moral, ethical principles is against nature and therefore dubious; it has a secret countereffect. But if, out of an overflow of natural goodness, I go and nurse my friend when he is ill, carried by a natural élan, then I am not doing evil. That is permitted, because there will be no comeback in the way of feeling demands, or wanting the other to show gratitude. It's the most subtle way of transcending the ethical and getting into something which is perhaps the nearest to being absolutely good, but it is so subtle that one can only describe it in paradoxes. In the West it is much more difficult because we have done much more on the side of striving for the absolute good and have accumulated such an abyss of horror on the other side that our problem has become insoluble.

There is another type of story concerning the dark mother figure in which the heroine intrudes into the secret of the Terrible Great Mother and then denies having done so. There is, for instance, an Austrian story called "The Black Woman," in which the black woman is the owner of a castle.[43] She hires a poor farmer's girl to do the cleaning work, and she is not supposed to go into one particular room, but does so, and finds that the black woman is slowly being turned white by her work. The girl quickly withdraws, but thereafter is continually persecuted by the black woman as to whether she has been in the room or not. She simply lies and says she has not, with the result that at the crucial moment when she is on the point of being burned as a witch, the black woman, who is now white, announces, "Had you once said that you had been in the room, I would have reduced you to dust and ashes, but now you have liberated me and you will be rewarded." She was rewarded for lying!

In another German variation the girl pokes into the horrible secret of the mother goddess, who says afterward to her, "My child, did you see me in my suffering?" and the girl denies it, saying she had noticed nothing. She, too, is rewarded for her lies. So not poking into Mother Nature's secrets, or lying about it if one has done so, pretending one has not seen anything even though one did, is a great deed and the right thing to do, according to the story. If the mother goddess were a human being we could understand it; she does not want her shadow, her deficiencies, or her suffering to be seen. Though she pretends to be the great goddess, she is really a very needy, suffering, unhappy creature, and that is what she does not want the human being to see. But this is something we meet with every day! If you try to touch an analysand's shadow, they simply explode and go for you. An analysand may have a horrible shadow, which you may see in the first hour, and sometimes they say, "You always talk about other people, but what is *my* shadow?" You can just say that you have noticed nothing, that you do not know the analysand very well yet. You have to lie, because if you touch that box of dynamite, the whole thing will just blow up and all the relationship with it.

Probably there is an analogy to this human situation, but here it is the goddess who wants to be tactfully protected, and that has to do with a deep-rooted, primitive, religious attitude. Such an archaic attitude can still be found among men in the Alps. Above Seelisberg, there is a beautiful path with a view of the whole of the Vierwaldstättersee, the Lake of the Four Cantons; but when you

round the corner, suddenly you see the lake from a completely
different angle. If the sun in shining, the lake, instead of being
green, is light, and there is a wide, open landscape and the vista of
the whole of the Alps. If you can be impressed by the beauty of
nature, you will experience a moment when you catch your breath.
Even Swiss cowherds, who are rather tough people, are apparently
impressed by that, for they say that at this corner very often the
cows suddenly disappear. At this moment, they say, you must be
very careful and not panic or look for the cows, or some accident
might happen, one of the cows might fall into the abyss or you
might fall over the edge. They say you must crack your whip and
go on calling to the cows as though they were there, and pretend
that nothing has happened, and after a few minutes they will once
more be walking along in front of you! That is a religious gesture!
When I am overwhelmed I am likely to have an animal-like panic
reaction, which would immediately react on the cows, which are
extremely sensitive to the state of the cowherd, and if he is in a
panic, they too are lost, or might do anything. But if one is in a
panic, it is no good preaching to oneself, so the cowherd just
assumes that the cows are gone and pretends at the same time not
to have noticed it. He lies to himself and so saves his own skin and
the whole situation.

The same thing happens when people have a very severe shock—
there is a delayed reaction. If you tell them that a near relative is
dead, they perhaps just thank you for telling them and go on with
what they were doing—that is, they just block off the shock by
pretending nothing has happened, until the worst is over, and then
they generally break down and cry and have a normal reaction. To
very sensitive people who could collapse through a shock, this
helpful delay in nature occurs, and the pretense of not having
noticed is a deep saving instinct in man and the basis of many
religious rituals. I think it should be recognized positively as a
healthy reaction in certain situations. But why does Mother Nature
want that? That it is good for us, and was good for Vasilisa, is clear;
but why does Mother Nature herself not want to be seen in her
evil aspect? Naturally, we do not know what she is, in herself. But
I am speaking figuratively and asking, why does the archetypal

figure which seems to represent something like the power of nature want to hide its horrible aspect? We have to think naively! It looks as though she were ashamed of herself. She behaves exactly like a human being who is ashamed. There seems to be a tendency in nature which longs for the greater consciousness of man—that makes for a strange theology! We cannot say whether this is absolutely true, but the documents of the unconscious say so. And if that *were* true, we would have a fair chance that, in spite of the catastrophic developments with which we are now confronted, nature intends to save man and to go on with the experiment "Man," which we are.

We cannot assert in a metaphysical way that nature in itself really does that, and it is the same when talking about the figure of God. Jung always insists that he is not saying metaphysically that God is so, but that the *image of God* is so in man, and the unconscious psyche manifests in such and such a way. I would not call that *only* a projection. The unconscious is nature in man, so one must say that nature, the psychic nature in man, describes nature as wanting to become more human and less cruel. That it is absolutely so is beyond the possibility of scientific investigation. We can only state that the unconscious psyche of man mirrors nature as having such a tendency, and it seems both healthy and helpful for us to believe it. Whether it is *an und für sich* (in itself) or not is something one can never say in psychology, for we do not know what nature *an und für sich* really is. We can only say that nature mirrors itself in our unconscious as something infinitely horrible and cruel, but that it has a secret longing to get out of that. So this is the source of a certain optimism in the Jungian approach. Why should we work with people if they were only devils?

If one looks at evil things too closely, and not in a mature way but naively, one gets cynical. If you walk through the museum which now exists about Auschwitz, what is your conclusion? Schopenhauer said that another man is to a human being just good enough to grease his boots with his fat. If you embrace that philosophy, the next consequence is that you say, "I am going to take a Luger, or a Colt, and I intend to survive and to hell with the others! They are murderers anyhow. They all want to kill me, so I am going to shoot first." That's the consequence! If I cannot do the human thing of turning away, then by looking at it, I act out myself the cruelty of nature. That's why in the reverence of the chthonic god in antiquity, people turned away and covered their faces, and when they prayed to Hecate, they put on a black veil over their heads, so as *not* to see her—in order not to become like her.

12

According to different myths, there are many different reasons for the dark side of nature. In the Christian myth it is the result of the Fall of Adam and Eve; in other myths a split occurs in the divine realm; in still others it is the disappointment of the goddess of nature. An Eskimo version, with different variations, is to be found in many circumpolar tribes.[44] Sedna, their mother goddess, or goddess of nature, lives under the sea and produces the whales, seals, fish, and so on, and the Eskimos, who live on these animals, pray to her for luck in hunting. Some versions say that Sedna was a strange woman who did not want to marry an ordinary man. A suitor from far away came one day, either in human form or as a seagull, and she followed him. But when she arrived at his home, she was deeply disappointed, for there was no food, he did not look after her and neglected her completely.

So Sedna sent a message to her father to fetch her home again. The father came and, in some versions, killed the unsatisfactory lover or husband. In revenge, the seagulls, or the ghost of the dead husband, caused a storm to overtake them on their way back in the boat. In order to save his own life, the father threw his daughter into the sea. She held on to the side of the boat, but he took a knife and cut off her fingers, so that she fell into the sea. Afterward, in revenge, either by magic or through talking to them, she got dogs to attack her father, and they ate his nose, or hands and feet, or both.

The father and daughter, who had crippled each other, lived together under the sea. Sedna then became the great goddess of nature and was benevolent to human beings and was also the mistress of death. She was the hidden goddess of nature, having the stores of life and death. The souls of the dead Eskimos went to live with her at the bottom of the sea. If they had behaved well, they had a relatively good life, but if not, they were tortured by her animals. Sedna and her crippled father stayed in a hut under the sea, and from time to time she accumulated a lot of lice on her head. A shaman had to dive down and rid her of them, and then fertility returned to the land of the living. So every time when it happened that the whales or the seal did not come at the right time, then the medicine man had to see to her head. Her evil side was due to her disappointment in love. Her father and her husband both let her down, so that she never attained a positive connection with the male principle.

There is a similar doctrine in the Kabbalah which teaches that the unsatisfactory aspect of reality exists because the Shekhinah is separated from God, and that if this feminine principle were reunited with God, the world order would be restored. So ethical people who strive toward higher consciousness try to restore the hierosgamos, working toward a reunion of the male and female divine principle. So if we look at different myths, evil is not always due to man's transgression, but to all sorts of different metaphysical causes. It is a very frequent motif that the myths recommend that man should be very tactful in dealing with the evil side of the divine principle. This is what the Old Testament also recommends, namely, the fear of God. If I allow myself to criticize God, it is a kind of inflation—as though God were my brother, or Mother Nature my sister, and I intended to put my finger on their sore spots, as I could with a fellow being. But the Divinity is not a fellow being whom I can criticize. My neighbor I can criticize if I want. But to criticize God shows a lack of realization of the difference of level, and thus in the Bible God advises man to fear him, that is, to keep within certain limits and know that God is not to be judged on a human level, and that we must be fully aware that our human standards do not apply to the Divinity. Job held to the fact that God did him an injustice, but he stood by his human standards and did not give in to those friends who tried to convince him that God was right and that he must have been wrong. He was respectful enough to realize that he could not presume to accuse God of injustice. He said it once and then, "I lay my hand on my mouth. I have spoken once, and I will not answer; twice, but I will proceed no further" (Job 40:4–5). And by that he adhered to his human standards, knowing that he was a creature with human limitations, with an anthropomorphic view of reality. The Godhead has always been experienced as transcending the human, both in light and in darkness, so that not to dig into the dark side would mean recognition of the fact that that is something which one cannot presume to do. That would be a gesture of utter humility; man cannot make himself the judge of the whole of reality. We are a part of it, and have certain standards of value and instinct by which we live, but we cannot be and are not the final judges, and this we should realize in all modesty and self-limitation.

Vasilisa has that modest attitude, and additionally she has the protection of her doll. The latter we have interpreted as a magical object, so that one can say that she protects herself with a religious ritual in a way which could be compared to that of the Christian who wears a crucifix for protection. By such a gesture we express that we need divine protection and that we cannot cope with evil with our intellect alone.

I think this is a very practical problem in psychotherapy and also, naturally, in general contact with other human beings. If, for instance, you have ever analyzed another person, or even if you have had a nonanalytical but deep *Auseinandersetzung* with someone (an encounter in which you sort out your differences without aggression), you know that sometimes you come up against a state of opposition where it is impossible to go any further. In a quarrel, you may have to realize that the other person is absolutely and utterly possessed and incapable of discussing things on a reasonable or human level, that as soon as you touch the subject, the other goes off on a tangent into an utterly possessed state, and you are up against something you cannot deal with, namely a dark archetypal situation. Naturally that happens quite often to an analyst, for if you touch a deep problem of the analysand, you may reach a place where you feel you cannot go further. The contact is com-

pletely blocked, and the analysand is no longer willing to listen or
to accept any of your arguments.

If over a long period such a constellation persists, then many
people make the mistake of retiring from it with a flow of talk,
instead of giving it complete respect and silence. The practical
indication is to drop the treatment, but one should not say that the
other person is hopelessly animus- or anima-possessed, or possessed
by evil, or by this or that and that therefore one must drop the
therapy. That is what our ordinary affective human ego would say.
The more one wastes affect and words, the worse one gets entangled in the wrong way. One should realize that even if one considers
the analysand to be completely wrong and possessed by evil,
possessed by a blindness of some kind, it is not deliberate on his
part. It is not his evil will; nobody is possessed voluntarily. It is a
tragic fate which should be respected in silence. So it is better to
say that the treatment cannot go on since we are blocked. Obviously, if I cannot help the analysand anymore, I am wasting my
time, and the analysand is wasting time and money, so it would be
better to separate in peace.

One should respect the evil constellation through silence and not
dig into it and talk about it emotionally. But women, in particular,
being more interested in relationship than men, again and again
commit the mistake of continuing to talk about such emotional
constellations and make them much worse in that way. My own
bad experiences have taught me that it is much better to have the
attitude which people had in antiquity—namely, of covering one's
head and walking away and letting things take their own course,
but silently, for even if all one has to say is true, and one could say
a great deal that was true, one is digging up more and more
darkness and improving nothing. One is not up against human evil,
but the evil of nature in the psyche of the other person.

So it is eminently practical—and really what Christ meant when
he said it—that we should not resist evil. He warned against the all
too human tendency, the inflation actually, to pursue shadow
problems which are not one's own. One should say, "I have done
my human best and have not succeeded, but have been shown my
own limitations." It is even better not to name the other person's

evil. In the ancient Greek civilization and in our Middle Ages, people avoided naming evil powers. Also in most primitive societies it is taboo to talk of ghosts and dark spirits by name. We also say that one should not invoke the devil, because if you do, he is there. The mention of the name constellates the object right away; not to mention it would be the religious attitude of respect. One retires respectfully to one's own estates, one's human limitations. Most religious systems where evil is still recognized as an entity commend such an attitude. Jung showed that the great danger of the Christian teaching, of the *privatio boni,* of the nonexistence of evil, is that it causes an inflated identification with the good, a wrong kind of inflated optimism.[45] The idea that we can clear up the dark corners of nature and the Godhead has given the white civilization an enormous drive and optimistic élan, but also an inflation. It is a very subtle problem, because if one did not believe in the possibility of cleaning out dark and dusty corners in the human soul, and thus improving the situation of the human being, one could not be an analyst. But when that optimism goes an inch too far, one is inflated.

Saint Thomas died when writing an article on penitence, which, naturally, is also the problem of evil; so it is a pretty dangerous thing to touch, if done with the naive optimism with which Christianity has inculcated us, and which Christ himself did not teach. This light, rational attitude is really an inheritance from the Platonic, Neoplatonic, and Stoic philosophies and not an influx from genuine Christian teaching.

Toward the darknesses of nature, a fearful and respectful attitude, and full awareness of one's own limitations, is the right religious attitude. Vasilisa provides us with a model when she asks about certain things in Baba Yaga's hut, but when it comes to the dark hands, she does not inquire, and Baba Yaga compliments her for it, saying that too much knowledge makes you old. One could take that quite literally. When one is young, one pokes into everything out of sheer juvenile optimism and gets some good bangs on the head. Slowly, as one becomes older, one retires more into oneself. That also can go too far, for, as you know, old people can overdo it by damping young people's ardor over every enterprise, discouraging them by saying it won't work, and one shouldn't try. Such skeptical conservatism goes too far; there should be a balance. But if Vasilisa had inquired about those hands, she might have had some horrible experience and lost her élan for life, and that is something to remember. How much evil can one afford to see without losing one's appetite for life? If one has to, if one's destiny forces one into it, one has to take it, but to load the boat with evil which is not in one's own fate and has been picked up out of sheer curiosity is not recommended.

That's why, for instance, most of the really good primitive medicine men do not advertise their activity. They have no therapeutic enthusiasm and do not poke into evil, or go about telling people they should go into treatment. They prefer to confine themselves to the evil with which they are actually faced. Only if somebody persecuted by evil comes and asks for help do they unwillingly consent, which shows that they are much more aware of the dangerous living reality of evil and that one should not take on oneself more than is absolutely necessary. It may be, if one likes someone, that one has to share in that person's fate and meet that evil, but otherwise it is better to let sleeping dogs lie, for the dog might turn out to be a sleeping devil much better left to sleep.

When Vasilisa leaves the hut, she takes with her the skull with the burning eyes. On arriving home she thinks she will throw it away, but the skull says she should take it to her stepmother, so though she does not know what it has in mind to do, she does so, and then the skull's glowing eyes stare unceasingly at stepmother and stepsisters until they are burned to ashes.

Being stared at all the time would be equivalent to having a bad conscience. One has the constant disagreeable feeling that one cannot hide. There is a beautiful poem by Victor Hugo about Cain, who, after he had killed Abel, had the hallucination that an eye looked at him all the time. He ran to the end of the world trying everywhere to escape, but the eye of God always followed him. In the end he entered a tomb, pulled the stone lid over, and sat there in the dark, but then he lifted his eyes and saw that God's eye was even in the grave and still watched him. That would be the tortures of a bad conscience. You could say that the absolute knowledge in the human soul knows of good and evil and that one cannot escape. Conscience is not without reason related to the word *consciousness*. Conscience is a form of ethical consciousness which one cannot escape, even if the police do not catch one.

After Vasilisa has gone into evil, she constellates this conscience for her enemies. After she has been with Baba Yaga and has herself looked into the depths of evil, she constellates this protection for herself, this positive fruit of the very disagreeable job of looking at her own shadow. In general, looking at one's own shadow is purely disagreeable, it is no fun, and the results also are not very amusing, but it has one great advantage: the more one knows about one's own wickedness, the more one is able to protect oneself against that of other people. The evil within oneself recognizes evil within the other. If I am naive about my own evil intentions, then I shall fall victim to those of others. Everybody can lie to me and I shall believe them, or they will play tricks on me, and I shall fall for it every time and be the poor babe in the wood, the fool who had such good intentions, but whom the evil world has treated badly. That does happen, especially to young people, and generally to naive people—they are really harmed by evil people. But indirectly, they themselves are guilty, for they haven't sufficiently realized the evil within themselves. If they knew more about that, they would acquire a kind of extrasensory perception for the evil of others. If, as a woman, you know about your own jealousy, you can look at another woman and catch the flicker of jealousy in her eye, and then know that you have to be careful with that woman, that it would be wiser to keep out of her way. But if you do not know what jealousy is, and have never seen your own jealous side, you cannot protect yourself and may do something silly where the other can take advantage of you. It is the same with men. The more one has looked in the mirror and watched one's own face for hate, jealousy, dissatisfaction, etc., the better one can read the other person's face and be wise enough to keep out of the way. One can thus avoid evil, but only by knowing how evil one is oneself, for only then has one an immediate, instinctive awareness and recognition. The idealistic fool who gets cheated by everybody and always has bad tricks played on him cannot be helped by pity, but only by being led to his own shadow. Awareness of his own evil will enable him to defend himself better.

If you want to become an analyst, naturally one of the most important things is to be able to protect yourself against destructive influences to which you are particularly exposed—as much as a doctor working in a hospital for infectious diseases. Those who have integrated much of their own darkness have a kind of invisible authority, as though they had gained weight and authority, and people do not seem to dare to attack them, instinctively feeling that they would get a slap in return. There are schoolteachers who have no need to assert themselves by thumping on the table and giving punishments all the time. The children fear them instinctively, because they feel the crocodile—or whatever stands behind that man—and they realize that impertinence could lead to trouble. The master can therefore teach undisturbed, in contrast to some young teacher who is full of enthusiasm and naive and innocent. When analyzing schoolteachers, I have often seen that the more they have obtained insight into their own shadows, the more they have gained some adult quality through which the whole problem of authority fades away. The more one realizes of one's own shadow, the more one gets condensed and thus unapproachable—knowledge of one's dark side serves as a protection.

The girl does not burn her stepmother and stepsisters out of revenge, which would only have involved her in her own shadow. That would have been the natural reaction—a tremendous resentment because she had been tortured, but then evil would have spread like wildfire. She has the skull, the destructive thing with her, but it is not her ego who uses it. The skull acts on its own; the revenge takes its natural course, as it were, without her taking part in it. In practical language, that is what is meant by giving somebody who has evil intentions a rope with which to hang himself. For instance, you may have a position which someone else, tremendously ambitious, wants. If you fight the other, it is just a question of ambition against ambition, but if you give up your own ambition and retire and let the other have the post, or defend the position only passively, the other is punished in getting the fruit of his own ambition and being eaten up by it. When you give the other enough rope—perhaps power—he has the worst possible punishment; he gets eaten up by his own evil. People are driven by their successes—but one can walk away; one is not one's brother's keeper. For a friend you must make some effort to discourage him or her, but otherwise do nothing. In the course of nature, evil always burns itself up in the end, and that is letting nature take its course. A human being's shadow generally has to do with greed of some kind—either sex or power or something else. Such greedy libido is fire which burns itself up—people are burnt up by their own greed, and it is wise not to interfere with this.

In the case of Vasilisa, the stepmother and her daughters wanted to destroy her and so sent her to the Baba Yaga, but it is they who are burned up with what they intended for her. So the skull does not represent Vasilisa's shadow, but the stepmother's and the stepdaughters', which now comes back on them, leaving Vasilisa unharmed. Once at a Fastnacht, Jung made up a wonderful verse about the poisonous dragon, to the effect that if a poisonous dragon appeared, one should not get upset, for the dragon had only forgotten his own fate: that he had to eat himself—the uroboros!

So you must just remind the dragon of his duty, and he will say, "Oh, yes," and will eat himself up! But you have to remind him, that is, bring a little bit of consciousness into the situation. It doesn't mean letting things go, but putting a little drop of consciousness in and then retiring. Nature will take its own course and ultimately destroy the evil. The positive seed of life within darkness is stronger than the whole darkness, as Saint John said when he spoke of the darkness longing for the light. Realization of evil can also have a positive aspect and reinforce one's wish to live. Many people suffer from a kind of apathy. A lack of desire to live can be genuine, coming at the beginning of the fading of vitality or the onset of old age or as the result of some kind of illness or even an objective necessity to retire from life. But this lack of desire may also be seen in people who are merely not connected to, or are unaware of, the depths of darkness. They are, as it were, too good and have illusions about their own goodness. If one penetrates the horror of the destructive darkness of one's own nature and one's wish for death, then normally there comes the counterreaction and a desire to live. This positive instinct springs from the realization of opposites. Living means murdering from morning to evening; we eat plants and animals. We buy the meat, but do not see the slaughtering of the animals; yet, as a matter of fact, we thus take a part in the whole of nature. An Indian botanist, Sir Chandra Bose, has discovered that even plants suffer pain and even get slight temperatures when wounded. If you cut off a leaf, the plant's temperature will increase for at least two days. So vegetarians cannot have the illusion that they do not share in the wheel of destruction. We are murderers and cannot live without murdering. The whole of natural life is based on murder. That is a terrible thing to realize, but, at the same time, if one is not very morbid by nature, such a realization brings acceptance and, strangely, the wish to live and the desire to accept one's guilt individually, for that is the guilt of living and living is guilt, in a certain sense. The realization of destruction and the wish to live are very closely connected.

A patient's dream might illustrate what I have in mind. The dreamer had a much too high-up religious, idealistic attitude and therefore a split-off shadow, which manifested in sudden outbursts of affect, but mostly in paranoic ideas: everything everywhere was evil, everybody had some *arrière pensée,* and generally these accusations were not true. Naturally, the patient herself was a dreadful liar. She dreamed that she made a religious pilgrimage and suddenly, on the left, in a house, saw a decrepit old woman with a sick cat and a voice said: "This is existential fear" (*Seinsangst*). The woman was terrified by this and asked a mature female figure, "Is it true that particularly people who suffer from existential fear and nervousness love cats?" The elderly woman, a symbol of the wisdom of nature, said, "Yes." Then the dreamer quarreled over fifteen centimes with a very emotional shadow figure. The latter got into a rage, and the dreamer was absolutely terrified and did not know what to do. Then they both went to the mature woman, who turned to one and then the other and told both that they were right: that is, the emotional shadow figure and the frightened dreamer too.

At the back of her too high-up attitude, this dreamer suffered from existential fear, which is perhaps one of the most basic problems in cases where a child has not received enough maternal love. It is a deep, nervous feeling of insecurity about everything, and, in one way, the cat would be compensatory, for it is, in a natural way, egotistical. One has only to think of the symbolism of the Egyptian cat goddess Bastet to see that, mythologically, the cat is a symbol for the enjoyment of life and gaiety, and therefore the exact opposite of existential fear. A cat walks into the room when hungry and meows and gets milk. The dog reacts more as we do and shows gratitude, but the cat is a princess. She behaves as though she were conferring an honor on you, giving you the privilege of serving her and giving her milk. Then she rubs herself against your leg and affords you the privilege of stroking her! That is so suggestive that naturally you bend down and humbly do so and feel very honored! When the cat has had enough, she walks out! She neither thanks you nor attaches herself to you. It does not matter who strokes the cat—what is important is that she gets attention. The cat is therefore something absolutely divine and the right compensation for people who have existential fear. People who suffer from such fear should cultivate the idea that they are conferring an honor on others by coming into a room and "letting themselves be stroked." They should take this as a symbol, and then they would feel secure and would learn what everyone who has a negative mother complex must learn: to look after themselves with the recklessness of nature. The animal does not deplore things in an infantile way but just takes things in the way which suits it. It uses man and animals and everything else for its own purposes, and that is *the* solution for that fear. In this woman's dream she is under the spell of her fear, and therefore she should love cats and meditate on what they mean.

If people are too sensitive, too easily frightened, and say things like, "If anybody shouts at me, I can't stand it," then you may be quite sure that they themselves are tremendously aggressive in their shadow side. And, vice versa, the people who explode in aggression all the time are simply cowards. They constantly explode because they are afraid. If you are aggressive, and check up on yourself, you will discover this—even animals attack when they are frightened. One should never touch a dog suddenly, for if frightened it might bite, whereas approached quietly it will not. Keepers in the zoo who have to look after dangerous animals know that the art lies in not frightening the animal. We react in the same way. Naturally, someone who suffers from existential fear will be dangerous, aggressive, and emotional, and that is at the root of all paranoic states and aggressiveness.

The mature woman in the dream who says that both sides are right indicates the solution. She would represent the Self who brings the opposites together so that fear and aggression are in the right proportion. It also shows that the problem cannot be solved by understanding, only by outgrowing it. It is one of those problems which one can only slowly and emotionally outgrow and not just conquer intellectually. It requires long practice in being less frightened on the one side and less aggressive on the other, watching one's fear while trying to give oneself security, putting a break on one's own aggressiveness until one can slowly bring those two natural elements into the right balance, and thus outgrow this fatal constellation. In women the negative mother complex often engenders a lack of basic vital security. It is at the root of all kinds of destructiveness and inability to meet life. If one can integrate that problem emotionally, one acquires authority.

There is a lot of amplificatory material on the subject of integrated aggression in Eliade's book on shamanism. In one chapter he speaks of the shamans as the "hot ones." Blacksmiths all over the world are looked on as the original medicine men and magicians, because they rule the fire, and the medicine man is the man who has integrated his own devilish, dangerous element, which is the secret of his authority. Integrated evil has given him authority over his tribe.

Ultimately the whole problem boils down to a fact beautifully illustrated in an Irish fairy tale on masculine psychology, but the point applies also to feminine psychology.[46] A hero goes into the land of the other world where a king kills all his daughter's suitors by means of a magic competition. He says to the hero, "You have to hide three times and I must find you, and then I hide three times and you have to try to find me. The one who finds the other three times can behead him." So, inevitably, this king's daughter remains unmarried for a long time. Our hero comes to this country. He owns a little talking horse, which tells him to go in for the competition and that it will help him. The king consults his black magician, who tells him to hide once in a fish in a pool and once in a ring on his daughter's finger, and so on, but the little talking horse always tells the hero where the king is to be found. But the king says that he will now find the hero three times and that he should go and hide. On the advice of the talking horse, the hero hides once in the horse's broken tooth and once under the hair in the horse's tail and once in the horse's hoof. The king asks the black magician for help, and the latter consults all his books, trying to find the hero, but there is nothing in the books about that; he can do nothing. So the hero is allowed to behead the king and marry the princess.

The decisive factor in this story is that the animal is stronger than either black magic or book knowledge. The magician has supernatural knowledge, but it is out of a book and is codified, while the hero benefits by his horse's living wisdom. That is the only difference between the two competing powers, so it is the animal instinct which decides. Jung once went so far as to say that goodness which is beyond instinctiveness is no longer good, and wickedness which is anti-instinctual cannot succeed either. If I try to be better than my instincts permit, I cease to do good. If I want to do evil in order to survive, this is only possible as long as my instinct goes with it. If I do more evil than my instinct allows, then I destroy myself. Instinct, or the animal, is the final judge, for that is what gives my good or evil intentions the right measure.

Chuang-tzu gives a famous simile called "Breaking Boxes Open." It says that in order to protect oneself against boxes being opened—that is, jewel cases, trunks of silken clothes, and treasures—putting cords around them and a lot of locks on them is what the world calls intelligent. But if a strong thief comes, he will take the whole box on his shoulder and will hope to goodness that the locks and the cords hold, so that the contents will not spill out. Chuang-tzu then tells of a peaceful country in Tzu where the peasants were very moral and everything was orderly. (Cords and locks stand for morality, for good behavior.) So the land prospered. A robber took possession of that country and was then very insistent that good behavior should continue. Everybody must continue to work and behave properly, and it was now the robber who enforced this because he wanted the country to go on prospering. Neighbors, whether big or small, did not dare criticize or kill him, and for twelve generations the country remained in his and his descendants' possession. Therefore, as you can see, robbers and thieves are very much interested in good behavior!

Another story goes even further. Someone asked Chuang-tzu whether robbers have moral attitudes. He said, "Of course, for otherwise they could not be robbers. A robber must know intuitively where the treasures are to be found, and that is his greatness; he must be the first to go in, and that shows his courage; he must know whether a coup is possible, or not, and that is his wisdom; he must afterwards make a just distribution among other gangsters, and that shows his goodness. It is absolutely impossible, therefore, for a robber to be a robber without having great moral qualities. So you can see that as human beings need ethics in order to survive, so do robbers in order that they may be good robbers. Now there are few good and many bad people in the world, therefore obviously morality teachers do not help the world but rather cause damage."[47]

What he is really driving at is that goodness which requires an artificial effort is not goodness. It can just as well serve the purpose of the robber, and, on the other hand, if a robber is a naturally good-natured man, he is not a bad sort of fellow. The important thing is to be true and natural and genuine in one's own nature; that is more important than to be artificially ethical or unethical. I do more damage if I am artificial in either way than if I am just myself, instinctively and healthily. In the latter case I also do a certain amount of damage, but—since to live is to murder—the damage I cause is relatively small, which is why Chuang-tzu always speaks against teachers of morality, showing up their secret destructiveness in estranging man from his natural goodness, which is just to be and to survive and to cause the minimum of damage necessary for survival.

Now, the doll in our story is such a symbol of instinctiveness, but in this case it is more a fetish which has supernatural powers.

Other fairy tales give parallel symbols of the helpful instinct. There is one which Barbara Hannah has also mentioned in her course on animals. It is an Austrian fairy tale called "The Little White Cats."[48] In it a girl falls into the evil hands of her stepmother, a destructive witch who has also bewitched the ruling king of the country and turned him into a black raven which is imprisoned in a mountain beyond a frozen lake. The girl saves four little cats from drowning and cares for them, and one day they appear with a golden carriage and carry the girl across the frozen lake to the raven, which she kisses and redeems, and then becomes queen. In this case the helpful factor is not a doll, but a golden carriage drawn by four little white cats, which is otherwise a complete parallel to the doll. It is the helpful symbol which carries the heroine to her goal and brings her to her right life and makes her a queen. There we can see how much the right attitude has to do with instinct, with the instinctive totality, and how even the cat, which we consider an unethical creature, is there represented as the absolutely positive and redeeming thing. The carriage would symbolize the fourfold structure of consciousness: the instinctiveness of which one is conscious, in contrast to that instinctiveness by which one is unconsciously driven, and that would establish the correct balanced attitude.

To return to the story of Vasilisa: After the stepmother and stepsisters have been burned up, Vasilisa goes to town and finds a lonely old woman with whom she decides to live. While with her, she spins such beautiful cloth that it attracts the king's attention. Through the intermediary of the lonely old woman, he asks her to make the shirts for him, and then falls in love with her and she becomes queen. Afterward she calls the lonely old woman and her father to the court so that the four live together: the father, the lonely old woman (who is obviously a positive mother and replaces her dead positive mother at the beginning of the story), the king, and herself, the queen. So it ends with a typical quaternity, the fourfold symbol of totality. It is one of the most complete stories in this sense. The story switches back and forth several times: the heroine first has a positive mother, who dies; then she falls into the hands of a stepmother who is completely destructive; then she goes to the Baba Yaga who is destructive—but not to her—so there in the archetype there is already more or less a balance of black and white. The Baba Yaga is only destructive to the bad side and not to the good, and she respects Vasilisa. Afterward the story switches again to a positive mother figure—the lonely old woman in the town, who from that time on becomes her positive mother. Nothing else is said about this lonely woman, but she is obviously positive. It is a complete fourfoldness of the mother aspect which is described, and what distinguishes this last mother figure is her complete humanity. There is nothing else interesting about her; she has not even a magic doll as did the first mother, who could not have been completely normal since she could give a magic doll to her daughter. The stepmother is completely human but destructive, Baba Yaga is a goddess, and now we return to what one would call plain humanness, as the ultimate stage of transformation.

We saw before that the woman who was left alone, like Sedna in the Eskimo story, is generally evil. The Arabs still say, "Never go near a woman who lives alone near the borders of the desert because such women are possessed by jinns." And it is very true that if women live alone for a long time without being in touch with men, they generally fall into the hands of the animus. It is very difficult to stand loneliness without getting overwhelmed by the unconscious, and in a woman's case naturally by the animus. So if this woman can live alone without falling into the devil, she must, though it is so little explained in the story, be of high quality, somebody who has reached a very high level of consciousness and humanness.

The need for relatedness is of the highest value and the essence of feminine nature, but a bit too much of it makes it negative because it makes that dependent clinging which men fear so much in women, and which is altogether a great evil by which women who establish relatedness so easily destroy all the good they do. If their eros—which means genuine interest in the other person and in establishing relationship, being there for the other person—gets the least bit too dependent, clinging to and needing the other, it is already on the downward grade into the devouring aspect of the female. If one is attentive to one's relationships, it is infinitely difficult to find the right balance. Say someone you like is ill; the natural movement is to ring up and inquire, but if you do too much of this, the other feels that you want to mother and make him dependent. If you do nothing, you are not related, and if you do it, the other feels as if you had made a claim on him. Great tact is needed so that the other has no feeling of being devoured, nor is there a cold unrelatedness, and that makes the difference between positive loneliness, which means independence, and the devouring mother, the devouring female. The lonely woman, therefore, since the context shows her as a positive figure, probably here represents the ultimate capacity for independence, a feminine quality very difficult for women to acquire. It entails constant watching of one's own shadow drive and the symbol of this independence is that lonely woman who now in complete selflessness becomes the intermediary between Vasilisa and the king. She makes the king aware of the girl who spins such wonderful material.

The very beautiful silk shirts which attract the king have a certain parallel with the shirts in the story "The Six Swans," where the heroine had to make star flower shirts to redeem her brothers. This time, however, the king has not to be redeemed, but the heroine gets in contact via the shirts and so wins his love. He wanted the woman who could make such beautiful shirts. It is said of her spinning, weaving, and sewing that the thread is so wonderfully fine and the material so delicate that the shirts are accordingly delicate and beautiful.

We say in German, "My shirt is closer to me than my coat"; it would imply an inner subtlety in understanding life. Such a king would not rule by regulations, or make crude speeches prepared for him by his prime minister, but would be able to penetrate the actual quality of a situation in a very subtle way. That is what the differentiated anima bestows on a man and what higher consciousness gives to a woman—the capacity for living the "just-so-ness" of life in the right way, something very mysterious and very subtle. It gives the intimate attitude which can take things just as they are instead of making sweeping judgments, and it gives the subtlety of the feeling touch. Here the positive functioning of the feminine principle is not to become outwardly dominant, but to give the ruling principle the necessary subtlety. That is what a woman can achieve. She does not need to push herself into the foreground and wear beautiful clothes. She makes them for the king, and if he wears such shirts he will be a good king. Taken symbolically, he will be a king who can adapt to the situation, see it intimately, and have a feeling about it beyond the general coarseness of the collective reaction.

If we take Vasilisa as the symbol of a woman, it would mean that she bestows subtlety on her animus. Jung said that the animus is always a bit off the point, which is because it lacks subtlety. It is just this being off the point which is so irritating, as when one says something which is generally true but does not fit the actual situation. Suppose a woman's husband flirts with another woman. The wife can say that they are modern people and her husband should be free, so she will shut her eyes to what is going on. She might be completely wrong. Perhaps—and I have seen such cases— he hopes she *will* put her foot down, and if she does not, he feels she does not love him, does not care much. Or her animus may tell her that she *must* put her foot down, that a woman must defend her rights, express her feeling, and that he would only think she does not love him if she does not make a scene—so she does this and is completely wrong, for she suffocates something in her husband's anima development which should have been allowed to live. Therefore, if one follows either recipe, one is sure to be wrong, because in all such situations there are always two possibilities, and both are half true. As long as one clings to rules one will do the wrong thing and, naturally, being driven by one's own shadow serves that animus argument for what one wants to do anyhow. The jealous woman who is simply driven by her jealousy will insist that a woman must defend her rights and so on—actually she is simply jealous—and the other will be driven in the opposite way. To give the animus subtlety, or the right shirt, would mean finding the attitude which suits the situation, knowing instinctively what is right *in this special case,* knowing how to act in each individual case, and for that, much subtlety and individual feeling into the situation are required. On such things the woman's animus goes off the deep end, for there is, of course, the famous partnership between shadow and animus. The shadow wants to do something in a driven way and the animus provides the right collective justification, and then the whole situation is wrong! But to be married to the king who has these beautiful shirts would mean that one had a superior way of judging the situation. That would be the symbol of such shirts, and that is one of the highest achievements of the feminine process of individuation—the attainment of that subtle rightness which makes Vasilisa a queen. The latter symbolizes a model of femininity for the new age to come.

Notes

1. See Marie-Louise von Franz, *An Introduction to the Interpretation of Fairy Tales* (Dallas: Spring Publications, 1978).
2. See Marie-Louise von Franz, *The Golden Ass of Apuleius: The Liberation of the Feminine in Man* (Boston: Shambhala Publications, 1992).
3. C. G. Jung and Carl Kerényi, *Essays on a Science of Mythology* (New York: Pantheon Books, Bollingen Series XII, 1949), pp. 139ff.
4. *The Complete Grimm's Fairy Tales* (New York: Pantheon Books, 1972), pp. 237ff.
5. Cf. J. Bolte and G. Polivka, *Anmerkungen zu den Kinder- und Hausmärchen der Brüder Grimm*, 5 vols. (Leipzig, 1913–1927), vol. 1, p. 434.
6. Max Lüthi, *Volksmärchen und Volkssage*, 2nd ed. (Bern & Munich: Francke Verlag, 1966).
7. Michael Fordham, *Children as Individuals* (New York: G. P. Putnam's Sons/C. G. Jung Foundation for Analytical Psychology, 1969).
8. Erich Neumann, *The Origins and History of Consciousness*, trans. R. F. C. Hull (New York: Pantheon Books, Bollingen Series XLII, 1954).
9. Virgil, *The Aeneid*, trans. W. F. Jackson Knight (Penguin Books, 1966), chaps. 1 and 6.
10. John Erskine, *The Lonely Venus*.
11. C. G. Jung, *The Archetypes and the Collective Unconscious*, vol. 9/i of *The Collected Works of C. G. Jung* [CW] (New York: Pantheon Books, Bollingen Foundation, 1959), p. 75.
12. Cf. Aniela Jaffé, "Bilder und Symbole aus E. T. A. Hoffmanns Märchen 'Der goldene Topf,' " in *C. G. Jung: Gestaltungen aus dem Unbewussten* (Zurich, 1950).

13. Konrad Lorenz, *Antriebe tierischen und menschlichen Verhaltens:* Gesammelte Abhandlungen (Munich: Piper, 1968), pp. 21ff.
14. *The Complete Grimm's Fairy Tales*, p. 664.
15. C. G. Jung, *The Practice of Psychotherapy*, CW 16 (1954), pp. 203ff.
16. *The Complete Grimm's Fairy Tales*, p. 160.
17. Jung, *The Archetypes and the Collective Unconscious*, CW 9/i (1959), p. 99, para. 185.
18. See C. G. Jung, "Rex and Regina," in *Mysterium Coniunctionis: An Inquiry into the Separation and Synthesis of Psychic Opposites in Alchemy*, CW 14 (1963), para. 349.
19. Translated from Knud Rasmussen, *Die Gabe des Adlers* (Frankfurt am Main: Societäts-Verlag, 1937), p. 121.
20. *The Complete Grimm's Fairy Tales*, p. 399.
21. Mircea Eliade, *Shamanism*, trans. Willard R. Trask (Princeton: Princeton University Press, Bollingen Series LXXVI, 1974), pp. 50, 484f., 111f.
22. C. G. Jung, *Kindertraum-Seminare* (Seminar on Children's Dreams) (Olten: Walter Verlag, 1987), p. 345f.
23. *Indianermärchen aus Nordamerika*, in the "Märchen der Weltliteratur" series (Jena: Diederichs Verlag, 1924), p. 155.
24. *The Complete Grimm's Fairy Tales*, p. 232. For the variations, see Bolte and Polivka, *Anmerkungen*, vol. 1, p. 427.
25. *The Complete Grimm's Fairy Tales*, p. 137. For the variations see Bolte and Polivka, *Anmerkungen*, vol. 1, p. 227.
26. C. G. Jung, *Psychology and Alchemy*, CW 12 (1953), pp. 63, 151f, 155ff.
27. Marie-Louise von Franz, "Bei der schwarzen Frau," in *Studien zur analytischen Psychologie*, vol. 2 (Zurich: Rascher Verlag, 1955), p. 1.
28. See the entry "Schwan" in Hoffman-Krayer, *Handwörterbuch des deutschen Aberglaubens* (Berlin & Leipzig: Walter de Gruyter & Co., 1927).
29. Martin Ninck, *Wodan und germanischer Schicksalsglaube* (Darmstadt: Wissenschaftliche Buchgesellschaft, 1967), pp. 69, 167, 178, 224, 229, 234, 254f., 278, 327.
30. Hugo Rahner, *Greek Myths and Christian Mystery*, trans. B. Battershaw (New York & London, 1963).
31. Jung, *Mysterium Coniunctionis*, CW 14, para. 663f.
32. *The I Ching*, Richard Wilhelm translation rendered into English by Cary F. Baynes (Princeton University Press, Bollingen Series XIX, 1967), hexagram 16, line 2.

33. Eliade, *Shamanism*, pp. 123ff.
34. *Russian Fairy Tales* (New York: Pantheon Books, 1973), p. 439.
35. Cf. Bolte and Polivka, *Anmerkungen*, vol. 1, pp. 165ff.
36. Gotthilf Isler, *Die Sennenpuppe* (Basel: Krebs, 1971), pp. 136, 140.
37. Thor Heyerdahl, *Aku-Aku: The Secrets of Easter Island* (Penguin Books, 1958).
38. *Russian Fairy Tales*, p. 229.
39. Cf. Sarah Iles Johnson, *Hekate Soteira* (Atlanta, Ga.: Scholars Press, 1990).
40. Cf. Dschuang-Dsi [Chuang-tzu], *Das wahre Buch vom südlichen Blütenland*, trans. Richard Wilhelm (Jena: Diederichs Verlag, 1923).
41. *The Complete Grimm's Fairy Tales*, p. 208.
42. "Waldminchen," *Deutsche Märchen seit Grimm* (Jena: Diederichs, 1922), p. 231.
43. Von Franz, "Bei der schwarzen Frau."
44. *Indianermärchen aus Nordamerika*, pp. 367, 368.
45. Cf. C. G. Jung, *Aion: Researches into the Phenomenology of the Self*, CW 9/ii (1959), paras. 75–114.
46. "Der Königssohn und der Vogel mit dem lieblichen Gesang," *Irische Volks-Märchen* (Jena: Diederichs, 1923), p. 224.
47. My translation of Richard Wilhelm's German translation. Cf. book 10 in B. Watson, *Complete Edition of Chuang-Tsi* (New York: Columbia University Press, 1968), or the versions by H. A. Giles (Allen and Unwin, repr. 1961) and J. Legge (Oxford, 1891).
48. "Die Weissen Katzerln," *Märchen aus dem Donaulande* (Jena: Diederichs, 1926).

Index

Aeneas and Dido, 24–25
Aetnae (Aeschylus), 11
affects, 145, 148, 206–207
Agamemnon, 28–29
aggression, 65, 206–207
alchemy, 77–78, 139, 145–147, 155, 179
"Amor and Psyche" (Apuleius), 2, 24–25, 114
angel, 99
anger, *See* rage
anima, 2, 16, 100–101, 107, 117–119, 138; negative, 136; problem, 43–44; women, 2
animals, 166, 208; bridegroom, 114
animus, 39–40, 51, 65, 77, 100–101, 107, 117–119, 138, 166, 211, 213; attacks, 31; attitude, stiff, 41–42; beard, 76; destructive, 71–73, 90; irritated, 66–67; possession, 31–32, 94, 116–117, 143–144, 153; powerful, 184; reaction, 40–41; undeveloped, 188–189
anthropos, 22
apathy, 204–205
Apollo, 136
apples, symbol, 91, 93
archetypes, 1, 4–9, 15–16, 18–19, 70, 91, 102, 133, 143, 146,

150, 183, 198–199; forgotten god, goddess, 28–29; god, goddess, 29–30; mother figure, 24; resentment, 31
astrology, 29, 133, 145–147
Augustine, Saint, 133

Baba Yaga, 172, 173–174, 175, 186, 200–201, 211
Baumann, Carol, 45
bear, 61–62, 63–65, 66, 68, 77–80
beard: symbol, 74–76; entanglement image and, 79–80
berserk, 63–65
birth: miraculous, 16; supernatural, 26–27
Boehme, Jakob, 133
"Breaking Boxes Open," 208–209

caches, 168
castration, 75
catatonia, 151
Catholicism, 1, 33
cat, symbol, 205–206
chastity, 33
child, children, 29, 95–97, 135
Chinese philosophy, 147, 179
Christ, 65, 179, 199
Christianity, 1, 3–4, 8–10, 42–43, 136–137, 139, 197–200

Chuang-tzu, 208–209
collective consciousness, 36, 42–
    43, 61, 87–88, 91, 103, 139;
    fairy tales and, 4–8
collective neuroses, 34–35
collective spirit, 166
collective standards, 95–97
collective unconscious, 25, 118
colors, meaning of, 186
complexes, 29–30, 92
conflict, 135–136
conscience, bad, 201–202
consciousness, 93–94
conservatism of women, 172
constellation, 147–149; of uncon-
    scious contents, 87–88, 92
cord, 123–124
corn seeds, 178, 180
creativity, 7, 17, 118, 159; depres-
    sion and, 27
crow, 139–140

dactyls, 158–159
daughters, fathers and, 3
death, 166–167, 186–187; dreams,
    42, 78; wish for, 204–205
Demeter, 12, 24
dependence, 211–212
depression, 91–92; creativity and,
    27, 140–141
differentiation, 2
dissociation, 42
divorce, 17–18
Doggeli and Toggeli, 168
doll, symbol, 168
dragon, 204
dreams, 16–17, 91, 119–120, 124–
    126, 177, 182, 185; death,
    42–43, 78; of dwarfs, 67; Jack
    Frost, 126; of moon god, 122;
    positive, 78; of potato, 169–
    170; of pregnant women, 45–

46; of prison, 127–128; of rav-
    ens, 140; religious pilgrimage,
    205–206; of threats, 148;
    women's, 53
dwarf, 66, 67–68, 70–73, 77–80,
    158–159

egg, 21
ego, 16, 158, 170, 175; complexes,
    29; formation, 21–23; as hero/
    heroine, 18–20; infantile, 20;
    and self, 19–20
emotion. *See* affect
enantiodromia, 37
entanglement, 79–80
eros, 2, 26, 92, 95, 139, 141, 190,
    211–212
Eskimos, 120–121, 124, 139, 196–
    197
evil, 36–37, 86–87, 189, 191, 194,
    197, 200; knowledge of, 202–
    206; of nature, 199; women
    and, 53

fairy godmothers, 19, 28, 30–31,
    37–38
fairy tale titles: Amor and Psyche,
    70; The Black Woman, 191–
    192; Briar Rose, 5, 10–15, 24;
    Cinderella, *See* Vasilisa the
    Beautiful, 165, 166; The Girl
    without Hands, 80–85; The
    Little White Cats, 210;
    Maiden Tsar, 172–173; Mrs.
    Trude, 185–186; Oll Rink-
    rank, 74, 77; Rumpelstiltskin,
    67; The Seven Ravens, 131–
    132; The Singing Soaring
    Lion-Lark, 114; The Six
    Swans, 129–131; Sleeping
    Beauty, *See* Briar Rose; Snow
    White and Rose Red, 56–61,

77; Vasilisa the Beautiful, 160–165; Waldminchen, 187–188; the Woman Who Became a Spider, 107–113
father, 117; complex, 48, 90, 94–95, 95–97, 118, 152; daughters, 3
fear: existential, 205–206; of God, 197
feeling: aggression, 206–207; differentiation of, 2; inferiority, 54; oversensitive, 54–56, 206–207; personification of hurt, 31
feminine principle, 1
fertility, 121
finger, cutting off, 156–157
fishing line, 79–80
flax, symbol, 45
Fordham, Michael, 19–20
forest, 96–98
frog, symbol, 27–28, 37

Garden of Eden, 53, 93–94
germs, 147–148, 180
ghosts, 43, 168, 178
glass castle, 157–158
godmother. *See* fairy godmother
gods, goddesses, 25, 26, 29–30, 178, 180, 181; forgotten motif, 28–29; nature, 188; neglected, 29
The Golden Ass (Apuleius), 2, 70
Goldee Topf, Der (Hoffmann), 43
goodness, artificial, 209
guilt, 30, 94, 184–185

hair, symbol, 75
hand, 85, 99, 185, 190; silver, 96
"head" people, 116
heavenly journey motif, 155–156
Hecate, 181

hermaphroditism, 121
hermits, 98
hero, heroine: birth of, 16–17; as ego, 18–20; as mother's fantasy, 181–184
Holy Grail, 11, 93–94
hooking, 156–157
Hopi creation myth, 92

I Ching, 147, 180
individuation, 71–72, 78, 99, 102, 123–124, 143, 156, 157, 159, 167
infantility, 92–93, 125–126
inflation, 199–200
initiations, 61–62, 74, 75, 106–107
instincts, 207–208, 209–210
intellectualism, 88–89
introversion, 96–98, 142–143
intuition, 79, 137–138

jealousy, 202, 213
Jaffé, Aniela, 43
Jewish tradition, 2, 155; Kabbalah, 2, 39, 197
John (of the Cross), Saint, 140, 204
justice, 38–39

Kabbalah, 2, 39, 197
king, 36, 91, 101, 102–103, 134, 152, 207–208; as dominant collective spirit, 95–96
knitting, 46–47

laws, man-made, 38–39
laziness, 92
libido, 17
lies, 193
logos, 26, 39

loneliness, 97, 211
love charms, 156

The Magic Flute (Mozart), 155
magician, 208
male-female differences, 33–34
marriage, 79, 94, 113, 116, 118;
    cross-cousin, 77–78; neuroses
    and, 35
masculine, integration of, 66
mechanical nodding, 134–135
Mercury, 157
miller, 86–87
monogamy, 33
moon, 121
mother, 64–65, 69, 95–97, 136,
    152, 181–184; complex, 32–
    33, 45, 48–49, 51–53, 55,
    94–95, 173, 207; identity
    with daughter, 167, 169–170;
    death of, 166, 167, 170–171;
    fantasies of, 181–184; god-
    dess, 186; maternal pity and,
    70–73; unconscious of, 180–
    181
mutatis mutandis, 100
Mysterium Coniunctionis (Jung), 91
mysticism, 151

narrow-mindedness, 126–127
nastiness, 39–40
natural mind, 50
nature, 97–98, 189–190; cruelty
    of, 186–187; dark side of,
    196–198; oneness of, 180;
    principle, 122; punishment
    by, 39; unconscious and, 87,
    194
Neumann, Erich, 19–20
neuroses, 30, 31, 36–37, 43; col-
    lective, 34–35; nervous talk-
    ing, 75–76
number symbolism, 132–133, 186

objectifying experiences, 23–24
objectivity, 17–18
opposites, 42, 70, 140, 206–207;
    realization of, 205; union of,
    104
*The Origins and History of Con-
    sciousness* (Neumann), 19–20

pantheism, 146–147
participation mystique, 167–168,
    176
passivity, 26–27, 89, 94–95
pecking order, 171–172
persona, 142
pestle and mortar, 175
pity, 70–73
poppy seeds, 178–179, 180
possession, 124
potato, dreams of, 169–170
pots, 178
power complex, 54
The Practice of Psychotherapy
    (Jung), 77–78
primitives, psychology of, 80, 92–
    93, 105
prison, dreams of, 127–128
projection, 194
Promethean myth, 93
Psyche, 2, 21–22, 24
*Psychological Aspects of the Mother
    Archetype* (Jung), 32
Psychology and Alchemy (Jung), 133
psychosis, 35, 43, 124, 126–127,
    134–135, 182
puberty, 43
puer aeternus, 73, 170
punishment, 38–39

quarternity, 210
Quattrocento, 37–38, 39
queen, 152

rage, 64, 68–69
raven, 136, 139–140
realization, 22–23
rebirth, 151
redemption, 143
Reformation, 139
regression, 138–139
relatedness. *See* eros
religion, women's identity and, 1
religious attitude, 64, 197–198
religious collective experience, 25
representations collectives, 6–10
repression, 44, 139
resistance, 143, 144
revenge, 38–39, 203–204
rhythmic movements, 134–135
robber, 208–209
romanticism, 43–44
rose, 54–55

sacrifice, 156
Samson and Delilah, 75
schizophrenia, 6–8, 21–22, 114–
    115, 126, 150
secrets, 102, 104–105, 152–153,
    181
Sedna, 196–197
seduction, priests and, 53
seed: the dead and, 178–179; sort-
    ing of, 175–176, 190
Self, 20, 22–23, 91, 169, 170,
    171, 181–182, 207; knowl-
    edge, 202–206; symbols of,
    123
self-esteem, 32
senex, 170
sensitivity, 54–56, 206–207
sexuality, 32–33, 61–62, 117–118;
    awakening of, 29
shadow, 192; animus and, 17; com-
    plexes, 29; infantility of, 54

Shamanism (Eliade), 123–124,
    149–150, 207
shirts, 142–143, 212, 214
silence, 151–153
sins, 93–94
Sisyphus, 134
sleep, 44, 55–56
Sophia, 2
spider, 115, 127–128
spindle, 44–45, 49, 51
spinning, 45–49, 115
spontaneity: loss of, 95–97; regain-
    ing, 100
staring, 201–202
stars, 142, 145, 147, 149
stealing. *See* thief
stepmother, 56
sterility, 26–27
stinginess, 127
stones, 168–169
suffering, 102–103
suffragists, 67
suicidal man, 184
sun, 102
swan, 136–138
symbols: apples, 91, 93; beard, 74–
    76; cat, 205–206; doll, 168;
    flax, 45; frog, 27–28, 37; hair,
    75; numbers, 132–133, 186;
    spindle, 44–45; thorns, 54–
    55; of totality, 155
synchronicity, 148–149, 180

taboo, breaking of, 113–114
talking, nervous, 75–76
"Tante Einsprung," 65
Taoism, 147, 179
thief, 71–73, 91–92
Thomas, Saint, 200
thorns, symbol of, 54–55
Timaeus (Plato), 49

totality, symbols of, 155
touchiness, 54–56
transformation, 78, 179, 211
tree, 99; sitting in, 149–150

unconscious, 151–152; feminine, 172
uroboros, 204

veiling the face, 103–104
Venus, 24–25, 156
Virgin Mary, 1, 25

weaving. *See* spinning
wise old woman, 44–45
witches, 135, 171. *See also* Baba Yaga

Zeus, 11, 25